History of Ethics
Volume I

Date: 1/12/12

History of Ethics

Volume I

Graeco-Roman to Early Modern Ethics

Vernon J. Bourke

Axios Press
P.O. Box 118
Mount Jackson, VA 22842

888.542.9467   info@axiospress.com

Distributed by NATIONAL BOOK NETWORK.

Library of Congress Cataloging-in-Publication Data

Bourke, Vernon J. (Vernon Joseph), 1907–1998.
        History of ethics / Vernon J. Bourke.
            p.   cm.
        Includes bibliographical references and index.
        ISBN 978-0-9753662-3-3 (v. 1 : pbk. : alk. paper) —
        ISBN 978-0-9753662-5-7 (v. 2 : pbk. : alk. paper)

        1. Ethics—History. I. Title.

BJ71.B66 2008
170.9–dc22

                                                                2007051386

Contents

Part Three

Early Modern Ethics: 1450–1750

Introduction

THE PRESENT HISTORY attempts to provide an account of the ethical theories of Western philosophers from the beginnings, five hundred years before Christ, to the present. All the writers on ethics that I know to have any importance are included, with the exception of strictly contemporary ethicians. There are simply too many of them for one volume, so key members of different contemporary schools have been selected. Such broad scope means that lengthy expositions of the individual views of these thinkers cannot be given. However, I have tried to emphasize the key contributions of each thinker, in the field of ethics only. In cases where the ethical theory depends rather directly on a writer's epistemology, psychology, metaphysics, or other such position, this speculative background is sketched briefly.

This is not a "critical" history; that is to say, I have not attempted to offer my own evaluations of the theories covered. My intention has been to give an open and fairminded presentation to each type of ethics. There are some that I like better than others but my preferences are not permitted consciously to intrude. In teaching courses on all periods of the history of philosophy for almost forty years, first at the University of Toronto and later at St. Louis University, I have come to feel that the best criticism is found in philosophy's own story. Sometimes earlier thinkers are neglected, or unfairly appraised, in subsequent centuries, but good thoughts have a way of rising to the surface and eventually making themselves evident again.

Ancient and medieval ethical theory centers on the problem of how man in general is to achieve well-being. Before the Renaissance it was generally assumed that all men are by nature ordered toward the attainment of one ultimate end. In different writers this over-all goal is described diversely but the orientation of all premodern ethical thought is teleological. This means that the focal point of nearly all the ethics covered in the first two parts of this history is the question: How may man best live and act, so that he will reach his final objective as a man? On the other hand, modern and contemporary ethical theories focus on the problem of practical judgment: How can one explain and justify "oughtness" in human experience? This contrast between the older and the modern viewpoints is a matter of different emphases and not an absolute shift in the meaning of ethics. The ancient or medieval thinker was, of course, aware of the importance of moral obligation and judgment; he was certainly not unacquainted with the importance of the "ought-to-be-done." Similarly, although they do not stress ultimate ends and final causes, nearly all modern ethicians recognize that the results of human actions and attitudes are implied in the awareness of every ought.

Thus, from the time of the first Greek philosophers, ethics has had but one meaning: it is the reflective study of what is good or bad in that part of human conduct for which man has some personal responsibility. The variety of meanings given to "good or bad" (or other evaluative terms) in this moral context is what makes the diversities of position in the history of ethics. Religious moralities with no reflective or theoretical base are not included in this history, unless they have had some important influence on ethical thinking.

Always a problem in a work such as this is terminology. I have tried to avoid jargon peculiar to but one minor thinker or one narrow school but where specialized terms occur they are explained. Often it has been convenient to use the classifications developed by Thomas E. Hill in his excellent book *Contemporary Ethical Theories*. There, six self-explanatory categories are used: ethical theories may be skeptical, approbative, process, psychological value, metaphysical, or intuitive, in their types. These classifications cover most of the possibilities of variation in the field. Incidentally, English writers have not been able to agree on what to call a person who works at ethics: I usually write "ethician" but have no objection to "ethicist." "Moral philosopher" is an older term and I use it as equivalent to ethician. The name "moralist," however, has a different meaning: it suggests one who moralizes, rather than a person interested in the theory of ethics.

As far as geographical scope is concerned, no effort is made here to treat Oriental ethics; not that it is unimportant, but its study requires a background and linguistic equipment that are not mine. Most theories presented in this history have some direct relation to, or impact on, the cultural development of Western man. Perhaps they will not tell us clearly what is the best way to live, or even what is an unassailable ground for moral judgment, but they do provide a wide variety of important suggestions as to how we might think on these human problems.

Part One

Graeco-Roman
Theories

Chapter I
Early Greek Eudaimonism

THE FIRST GREEK philosophers were not primarily interested in ethics but in speculation concerning the constitution of the physical universe. However, some of the predecessors of Socrates made fragmentary contributions to moral theory. Among the first were the Pythagoreans, who were organized into a religious brotherhood during the sixth century B.C.E. and continued as a school of practical philosophy into the first centuries of the Christian era. Their founder was Pythagoras of Samos (fl. 530 B.C.E.), who remains an obscure figure, despite biographical sketches by Iamblichus, Porphyry, and Diogenes Laërtius. It is impossible to distinguish his

personal views from the ethical thinking of his immediate followers, because our only sources of information are fragmentary quotations and summaries found
in much later Greek writings.[1]

Mathematics and music were central studies in
Pythagorean schools. That numbers and harmonious
proportions constitute all reality was the basic conviction of the Pythagoreans. They saw the human soul
as the life spirit which endures after the death of its
first body and may take up its abode subsequently
in another human or animal body. This theory of
metempsychosis, or transmigration of souls, is ethically significant since it provides for the rewarding
of good action and the punishment of evil in these
subsequent reincarnations.[2] Possibly the most important Pythagorean contribution to ethics stemmed
from their study of mathematical means. Mathemati-
cally, the "mean" was a function midway between two
extremes, combining and harmonizing the best features
of each. In practice, the Pythagoreans used the idea
of the mean to locate good health as a medium condition between excess and defect in temperature, in the
amount of liquid in the body, in the taking of exercise, and so on. It was but logical for the Pythagoreans
to think of good moral behavior as a mean between
extremes. When Aristotle later developed his sophisticated theory of moral virtue as a golden mean between
extremes of vice, he gave full credit for the basic idea to
the Pythagoreans.[3]

The Pythagoreans also developed a theory of opposites in which the "limiting" and the "non-limiting" were the chief pair. They understood limit as a definite and measurable characteristic of anything, and the non-limited as that which defied attempts at definition and measurement. Their standard geometrical example of the latter was, of course, the diagonal of any rectangle: it is impossible to express its length simply in terms of the sides. The diagonal is then a surd, an irrational number. Falsehood and envy are thus identified by the Pythagoreans with the non-limited and irrational.[4] This is the beginning of one very important approach to ethical problems, the view that good means what is rational and intelligible. Thus, in the fourth century B.C.E., a later Pythagorean, Archytas of Tarentum, first enunciated the principle of "right reasoning" as the key to good behavior: "Right Reckoning, when discovered, checks civil strife and increases concord . . . (it is) the standard and deterrent of wrong doers."[5] It is quite possible that Aristotelian and medieval theories of right reason *(recta ratio)* as the norm of ethical judgment are directly indebted to Pythagorean intellectualism. The classic Greek respect for the life of reason *(logos)* is already evident in the early Pythagorean teachings.

Contemporary with the early Pythagoreans but not members of that school were certain individual philosophers who made minor contributions to moral theory: Heraclitus, Democritus, and Anaxagoras. The first of these, Heraclitus of Ephesus (fl. 500 B.C.E.) is best known for his cosmological teaching that all things are in constant flux or change. Actually, many Heraclitean fragments suggest that there is an ever present rational pattern *(logos)* in this process.[6] Heraclitus had the notion of "law" as a principle of regularity in natural processes but he was also well aware of the importance of law *(nomos)* in the political sense. Associated with his respect for law and order is Heraclitus' view that the strife between opposites (such as love and hate) is to be resolved according to a measure *(metron)*. The Heraclitean measure is close in meaning to the Pythagorean mean. Some recent studies of Heraclitus suggest that his moral views are of primary importance in his teaching.[7]

In Democritus of Abdera (fl. 420 B.C.E.) we have the first appearance of one of the key themes in Greek ethics: *eudaimonia* as the condition of man's "well-being." Democritus' ethical treatise *On Cheerfulness* has been lost but we have reports on it in Seneca and Plutarch.[8] Though usually classified as a materialistic atomist, Democritus in fact stressed the soul as the locus of human well-being. His concept of *eudaimonia* includes both the notion of "good existence" *(eu-esto)* and "good feeling" *(eu-thumiē)*. Indeed, his emphasis on serenity of spirit or undismay *(athambiē)* is now regarded as an anticipation of the Epicurean condition of *ataraxia,* the poised attitude of the moral sage. One fragment reads like a Stoic maxim: "Medical science heals diseases of the body but wisdom rids soul of passions."[10] Quite evident in Democritus is the recognition that virtue consists in moderation, or in measured activity.

The first philosopher to teach his subject in Athens was Anaxagoras of Clazomenae (500–428 B.C.E.). He had no formal ethical teaching but he did introduce the notion of Mind or Intelligence *(nous)* into Greek philosophical speculation. Anaxagoras suggested that "Mind is infinite and self-ruling, and is mixed with no thing, but is alone by itself."[11] Aristotle gave Anaxagoras credit for the soberness of his thought but criticized him for failing to use nous consistently in explaining cosmic events.[12] In any case, it was Anaxagoras who provided the Greeks with a term which enabled later thinkers to discuss the mental aspects of human conduct and world order.

From the fifth into the fourth century B.C.E., the Sophists constituted an ill-defined group of Greek teachers. The name meant "wise man" but Aristotle claimed that "the art of the Sophist is the semblance of wisdom without the reality, and the Sophist is one who makes money from an apparent but unreal wisdom."[13] Plato liked them no better, calling the Sophist "a paid hunter after wealth and youth."[14] Sophistry was not really a school of philosophy. The Sophists (1) taught for money, (2) taught mostly practical subjects, and (3) were inclined toward skepticism, subjectivism, and practical relativism.

The most important of the Sophists for the history of ethics was Protagoras of Abdera (fl. 440 B.C.E.). We know his views through the unfriendly reports of Plato, Aristotle, and later writers. Protagoras probably shared the general sophistic attitude of skepticism toward absolute judgments on truth and lightness. He was a religious agnostic in a period when most Greeks professed some sort of faith in the gods: "As to the gods, I have no means of knowing either that they exist or that they do not exist."[15] Protagoras took a relativistic position on ethical judgments. Plato's dialogue *Protagoras* depicts him, at the start, as defending against Socrates' professed skepticism the view that virtue can be taught. At the end of the dialogue, however, the disputants have reversed positions and Protagoras is denying that virtue is teachable.[16]

Protagoras' most famous teaching was that man is the measure of all things.[17] Whatever this means precisely, it is the first noteworthy assertion of the philosophy of humanism. Some interpreters think that Protagoras understood "man" in terms of the species and was simply saying that we are bound to view reality and action from the standpoint of humanity. Such an interpretation would closely align him with the common Greek respect for the judgment of rational beings. In fact, Protagoras did advocate the practical virtue of good judgment.[18] On the other hand, it is more probable that Protagoras meant that each *individual* man is the sole judge of what is true or right for himself. This is the interpretation suffered by Sextus Empiricus: "he posits only what appears to each individual, and thus he introduces relativity."[19] In the sphere of ethics this would imply that there are no fixed laws, rules, or judgments—and that in the final analysis all opinions are equally valid. As Aristotle says in discussing the teaching of Protagoras: "If, then, reality is such as the view in question supposes, all will be right in their beliefs."[20] This, of course, appears to Aristotle to offend the principle of non-contradiction and would be equivalent to the statement that there can be no scientific knowledge of ethics.

Of the other Sophists, Thrasymachus of Chalcedon (fifth century B.C.E.) is alleged to have taught that "might is right." In the first book of his *Republic* Plato introduces "Thrasymachus" as a character who claims that "just or right means nothing but what is to the interest of the stronger party."[21] Later, Plato (without mentioning Thrasymachus) suggests that this teaching is the conclusion of an attack on a natural-law approach to justice: the Sophists say "that the honourable is one thing by nature and another by law, and that the principles of justice have no existence at all in nature, but that mankind are always disputing about them and altering them. . . . They are told by them that the highest right is might. . . ."[22] Whether this sort of ethical positivism was actually taught by the original Thrasymachus is a matter of conjecture.

Callicles of Acharnae (late fifth century B.C.E.) is reported by Plato[23] as teaching another version of the "might is right" theory. Callicles' argument is that laws are made by the many weak men in order to control and restrain the few who are strong. The right and the just thus become mere conventions imposed by the popular majority. The early Greek poet Pindar is quoted as saying that according to "natural justice," unimpeded by the devices of popular legislation, might would be right, for the stronger would have their way without challenge. Hippias of Elis (fifth century B.C.E.) was still another Sophist who emphasized the conventional and artificial character of moral law and advocated self-satisfaction as the ethical ideal.[24]

Despite the fact that he left no written works and gave no formal teaching, Socrates can well be regarded as the founder of ethical studies. In Athens (470–399 B.C.E.) he engaged in informal discussions in public places and private homes. Sometimes he talked with Sophists and older scholars but his audience usually consisted of young men who were curious about Socrates' views and amused by his professed ignorance and his ability to reveal the pretensions of their teachers. His thought is now partly known through various reports in Xenophon, Aristophanes, and Plato. Later classic explanations of Socratic wisdom (from Aristotle down to writers in the early Christian period) are abundant and divergent. He was and is, however, the one man generally admitted to have best personified the life of the philosopher. Aristophanes presented him (in *The Clouds*) as a semiludicrous figure. Xenophon (in *Memorabilia*) recorded several Socratic discussions, admired his rugged personality, but possibly simplified his profound thoughts. Plato was the one witness who had the understanding and literary power to transmit Socrates' wisdom to us. The problem with the Platonic account is that it is too rich: Socrates is the chief speaker in most of Plato's dialogues. It is difficult to know where the real Socrates ends and the literary Plato begins to offer his own thoughts through the mouth of his spokesman, "Socrates." Plato's *Apology, Crito,* and *Phaedo* tell the touching story of Socrates' final days, of his trial on trumped-up charges and his death in prison.

There are books that present Socrates as an ethician with teachings on most of the key issues of traditional ethics. One of the best of these, by Miles Dawson, offers nineteen chapters on a broad variety of topics.[25] Its selections deal with the rational character of virtue, the scientific basis of ethics, the soul, man's highest good, happiness as the goal of life, rewards and punishments, immortality, the future life, human character, theory of education, the value of the fine arts, duties to the gods and to other men, duties within one's city and within one's family, the rights and duties of women, and duties to friends and to self. There is even a closing chapter on death. One has the feeling, however, that much of this is post-Socratic and that an account of Socrates' ethical position should be somewhat simpler.

The method of philosophic discussion used by
Socrates was characterized by three features: the asking of questions, the profession of ignorance, and
the search for definitions. He may have thought that
definitive knowledge of man or of courage and the
other virtues implied the independent existence of
"forms," such as manhood and courage. If so, then he
actually was the originator of the theory of ideal forms
and Plato merely took it and developed it. Socrates
clearly did think that all the moral virtues are rooted
in practical wisdom. "It is evident," he said, "that justice and every other virtue is wisdom."[26] Most of
his reported discussions emphasize the importance of
self-examination, observation of other worthy men,
reflection on the meaning of our moral convictions,
and moderation in feeling and action. Indeed, as
Plato testified,[27] Socrates personified the two moral
imperatives attributed to the Delphic oracle: "know
thyself" (gnōthi seauton) and "avoid excess" (mēden
agan).

At times Socrates seems to be saying that if one
knows what is right and good one will do it. This sort of
moral intellectualism is probably overoptimistic in its
view of human conduct. Certainly that is what Aristotle thought of it: "Socrates in one respect was on the
right track, while in another he went astray; in thinking that all the virtues were forms of practical wisdom
he was wrong, but in saying they implied practical wisdom he was right."[28]

Socratic well-being *(eudaimonia)* consists in the actual doing of what is good. This is a dynamic theory of happiness and moral success. To do good *(eu–prattein)* is to fare well.[29] Socrates avoided offering a formal standard for the determination of what is good but insisted that earnest discussion and reflection could discover the ideals of temperate, just, and courageous living. Kierkegaard was not wrong when he said: "Socrates was thus a man whose energies were devoted to thinking; but he reduced all other knowledge to indifference in that he infinitely accentuated ethical knowledge."[30]

More than his formal teaching in ethics, the story of Socrates' life has had a tremendous ethical influence. People have admired and wondered at his reported self-control, his reasonableness, his superiority to passing fancies and discomforts, his interest in the views and pleasures of others, his reputation of being warned against evildoing by his familiar spirit *(daimon)*. He is the personification of the pagan "sage." Little wonder that even Christians hailed him as "saint" Socrates.[31]

Three minor schools of Greek philosophy took over and developed diverse aspects of Socrates' teaching and character. The Megarics, founded by Euclid of Megara (fl. 420 B.C.E.), were primarily interested in dialectic. They came to stress the importance of a clear knowledge of the good. Euclid identified the Good with the One, which he also recognized under the names of reason, understanding, and the divine.[32] A century later, another Megarian named Stilpo was teaching in Athens that indifference to feeling *(apatheia)* is the special virtue of the good men. Stilpo taught Zeno the Stoic who in turn exploited this idea of apathy. In another such school, the Elean–Eretrian group, Menedemus of Eretria taught that virtue is one with knowledge.

More important in the history of ethics was the Cynic school, named perhaps from the Greek word for dog, because of the Cynics' disdain for conventional behavior. The founder, Antisthenes (fifth century B.C.E.) studied under Gorgias the Sophist and knew Socrates. He admired the independence and self-sufficiency of Socrates' personal character. The Cynic ideal of virtue thus became *simplicity* of living, a renunciation of wealth, pleasure, adornment, and ambition. The Cynic paragon was a sort of pagan ascetic represented in popular legend by the fourth-century Diogenes of Sinope, who was said to have lived in a tub. Diogenes was an Athenian beatnik, imitating a dog in disdain for the amenities of life and the rules and customs of polite society. Cynicism became another name for vulgarity and at its lowest ebb was a moral skepticism as extreme as any to be found in the ancient world. As late as the fifth century C.E., Augustine testified that there were still Cynics wandering about imitating the behavior of Diogenes.[33] He even tells the old story that the ancient Cynics went so far in imitating the "naturalness" of dogs as to copulate openly in public places. Crates of Thebes (fourth century B.C.E.) was a more cultivated Cynic who influenced the development of Stoic ethics. Cynicism was a negative kind of ethics that stressed a lack of interest in personal and social satisfactions.

Aristippus of Cyrene (ca. 435–355 B.C.E.) founded the third Socratic school. After studying under Protagoras, he attended some of the discussions conducted by Socrates in Athens, and on his return to Cyrene, taught there in the Cyrenaic school. Aristotle considered Aristippus a Sophist.[34] He thought that personal pleasure was the thing to aim at in life: any act that tends to secure such satisfaction on the sense level would be good. This is the first known occurrence of egoistic hedonism in the history of ethics. Aristippus seems to have started from the Socratic ideal of well-being *(eudaimonia)* and independence of the person *(autarkia),* eventually concluding that personal pleasure is the highest good.[35] Later, this theory was to be developed by the Epicureans but there is no known connection between Aristippus and Epicurus. Little more than the names of later Cyrenaics remains: Theodorus the Atheist (who is said to have identified pleasure with mental satisfaction), Hegesias, and Anniceris.[36]

If these three Socratic schools offer only partial appreciations of the ethical thought of Socrates, there is no question that his moral views were given ample development in the next school of ethics, the Platonic. Plato (427–347 B.C.E.) was the first Greek philosopher to write on nearly all the problems of philosophy and to leave us almost his entire literary product. With various interruptions for travel and political activity in Sicily, he taught in his school in Athens (the Academy) for about fifty years. Around twenty-five authentic dialogues are extant plus a number of letters. There is a strong tradition that Plato delivered a famous lecture *On the Good (Peri tagathou)* which was recorded by Aristotle when he was Plato's pupil.[37] This lecture is not now extant, of course, but the final lines of the *Eudemian Ethics* imply that it identified the one and the Good. This would mean that Plato was already attempting to identify fullness of being (unity) with moral perfection (good) and was thus inaugurating a type of self-perfection ethics. It is probable that the sixth book of Plato's *Republic* offers a closely related doctrine.

As already noted, one group of Platonic dialogues *(Apology, Crito, Phaedo)* deals with the last days of Socrates and his thoughts before death. Socrates was not afraid to die: he looked forward to some sort of life after death. One of the chief arguments for personal immortality of the human soul *(psychē)* is found in the *Phaedo:* the soul is the principle of life within each man, death is the opposite to life, the process of change from one opposite to another always entails a return from one extreme to the other, thus the soul always reverts from the extreme of death to that of life, hence "the souls of the dead are in existence and the good souls have a better portion than the evil" *(Phaedo,* 72D). There are several such arguments for immortality offered in this dialogue. It is likely that they represent something of the actual thought of Socrates, as revised by his pupil, Plato.

Another set of Platonic dialogues present Socrates as the dominant speaker and are probably closely related to some of the actual discussions that Socrates held in Athens and its vicinity. Nearly all of these Socratic dialogues deal briefly with the nature of certain virtues, or with definite moral problems. In the *Euthyphro,* for instance, Socrates talks about the virtue of piety (respect for one's parents and country, and the gods), hears a standard definition from Euthyphro ("piety is that part of justice which gives the gods their due") and then criticizes this definition as a trivial account of man's dealings with the gods. As in most of the dialogues, no positive conclusion is reached, no dogmatic teaching is offered, but the discussion raises many moral and ethical problems and stimulates the serious reader to do some personal thinking. Similar debates are found in other early Platonic dialogues: *Laches* deals with courage, *Charmides* with temperance or the moderating of sensual desire, *Lysis* treats friendship, *Euthydemus* covers prudence or practical wisdom. Some scholars think that the early books of the *Republic* (in which several definitions of justice are reviewed and criticized) date from this first Socratic period and were incorporated into the longer dialogue during Plato's maturity.

More general ethical questions are discussed in later dialogues where Socrates is still the main character. We have seen that the *Protagoras* presents the problem of the teachability of moral virtue. Socrates argues that, if virtue is knowledge and can be taught, then all successful and wise men would certainly teach their sons to live as they do *(Protagoras,* 319–326). The discussion turns to the problems of whether wisdom, temperance, courage, justice, and piety are reducible to one key virtue that could be acquired by education. There is some suggestion that a theory of the good life would have to pay some attention to pleasure and pain and that knowledge is not the only factor in moral character. "Socrates" in this dialogue ends by arguing that no man voluntarily chooses evil: "to prefer evil to good is not in human nature" *(Protagoras,* 358). The implication is that one will always do what one thinks good—and that education helps one to make reliable judgments on what is good. In other dialogues this discussion is related to the exploration of the "good life" (in the *Gorgias)* and to the problem of voluntary and involuntary error (in *Hippias Minor).*

A group of dialogues extending from the middle of Plato's writing career to his old age provide outlines of his personal thinking on the nature and problems of ethics. He does not reject the moral intellectualism of Socrates but expands it and places it in the context of a developed view of reality and of man's psychic functions. These dialogues include the *Sympo-*

sium (on the good and the beautiful), the *Republic* (on justice, both individual and social, and on many other matters), the *Phaedrus* (on love and the relation of man's appetites to reason), the *Philebus* (on pleasures and the good for man), and the *Statesman* (on the division of sciences into practical and theoretical, the problems of political rule, the doctrine of the mean, the origin of state laws, and the importance of reason in all areas of virtue). Finally, the longest and apparently the last of Plato's dialogues is the *Laws,* which offers a less idealistic and more practical consideration of most of the questions that had been raised in the *Republic.* Politics is there *(Laws,* I, 650B) identified with the art of managing the natures and habits of men's souls—a notion that is easily transformed into totalitarianism. Many readers think that the *Laws* reproduce the thought of an aging, or even senile, Plato.

Very distinctive in the background of Plato's ethics is his theory of the "parts" of man's soul. These are not precisely faculties, nor are they mere functions: they are divisions of psychic reality and activity but certainly not physical parts. In the *Phaedrus* (246, 253) he compares the soul to a pair of winged horses plus a charioteer. One horse is ill-bred and ignoble, inclined to pursue brutish pleasures: this one symbolizes the appetitive or concupiscent part of the soul *(to epithumētikon).* The other horse is well-bred and noble, inclined to soar upward toward honor and glory: this is the spirited part *(thumos)* of man's soul. Obviously, they represent two appetites in man, the desire for sensual satisfaction and the aspiration for success and fame. The driver of these two horses must know where he is going, love the better things, and assert his orderly control over his unruly steeds: reason *(logos, to logistikon)* is this highest part of man's soul. Philosophy is designed to train man's soul so that all three parts work together for happiness *(Phaedrus, 254–256).*

The same theory of the tripartite soul is found in the *Republic* (Bk. IV, 431–439). Two levels of psychic activity are there distinguished: the rational and the irrational. The rational *(to logistikon)* is that part which reflects and acquires knowledge. In the irrational are two parts: one feels anger, indignation, and the ambition to excel—it is the spirited element *(thumos);* the other part desires the pleasures of food, sex, and so on—it is the element of desire or appetite *(to epithumētikon).* Each part of the soul has its special perfection or virtue. The rational part is perfected by practical wisdom *(phronēsis, sophia).* Courage or manliness *(andreia)* develops the spirited part. Temperance *(sophrosune)* is the virtue that moderates desire, especially in the concupiscent part, but it perfects all parts of man's soul. Finally, justice *(dikaiosune)* as a virtue of the individual man is that general condition of soul in which each part performs its proper function. The just man only does what is right in his external actions as a citizen of a state—he does the right because his soul is internally well-ordered.[38]

Plato thought that the wise and just man requires some sort of standard, some ideal, on which to pattern his judgments and his conduct. The theory of intelligible "forms" supplies such a criterion. One approach to the ideal forms is through the four levels of cognition described in the sixth book of the *Republic*. Two lower ways of knowing deal with the world of appearances: the lowest is perception of things through images *(eikasia),* it "takes sensible appearances and current moral notions at their face value"[39]; the second level is belief *(pistis)* in the reality of the things perceived by the senses, and also it is belief in the right moral opinions *without understanding why they are right.* Two higher modes of cognition have as their objects certain intelligible realities that are unchanging in character. The objects of understanding (the ideal forms) include mathematical items, such as unity and equality; and moral standards, such as perfect justice, goodness, and so on. These Platonic forms may be known directly and intuitively in themselves; this is the highest level of cognition, called intelligence *(noēsis)* or knowledge *(epistēmē).* Or they may be known indirectly, through other things or acts of knowing, by discursive reasoning, by the process of thinking *(dianoia)* .[40] It may be observed that the *Republic* definitely illustrates this analysis by reference to moral or ethical judgments: some people have moral opinions without seeing the grounds or reasons for these views; other people clearly understand the basis for their moral convictions. Ethics, for Plato, would consist in the second (and highest) kind of cognition.

The allegory of the cave *(Republic,* Bk. VII, 514–521), is another device used by Plato to suggest what the ideal forms are. Men are described as chained in an underground cavern where they can see only the shadows of physical objects cast on one wall. In this condition, they would think that these shadows are all that can be known and all that can be. If one of these cave dwellers were released, he might look at the physical things themselves which cause the shadows and think that reality consists in such bodies. Further, if he is allowed to come out of the cave into the higher world of sunlight, he might be dazzled by the brightness and think that the reflections of visible things are the best objects to look at. Eventually, he might adapt to the upper world so that he could steal brief glances at the sun itself. This higher world symbolizes the realm of intelligibility, the sun is the "essential Form of Goodness." To live well, with clear understanding, one must rise to a vision of the idea of the Good.[41] Many readers see Plato's form of the good as identical with what God would be in a more obviously monotheistic philosophy.[42]

This is not an easy ethics to grasp; it is far from a crude intuitionism. Plato's ideally educated man would be the product of long years of study, particularly of mathematics (here Pythagoreanism is an obvious influence), and years of training in good habits. The Platonic sage would be an elderly, well-balanced character, free from ordinary mundane concerns, enamored of beauty and good order, perfected in intellect so that he might easily and accurately see the principles of good living. This may well be an idealization of the personality of Plato's teacher, Socrates.

But Platonic ethics is not simply an intellectualism. The notion of well-being *(eudaimonia)* is retained and explored in the last books of the *Republic*. There had been some suggestion at the beginning of the treatise that injustice, if not detected, might be approvable. This possibility is explored in the story of Gyges, which is told in the second book of the *Republic*. A Lydian shepherd named Gyges happened to find a gold ring and he put it on his finger. At the monthly meeting of the royal shepherds Gyges discovered that whenever he turned the setting of the ring inside his hand he became invisible to his companions. With this magic device Gyges went to the royal court, seduced the queen, murdered the king, and took over the throne. Plato asks whether even a just man, equipped with such a ring that would enable him to escape all discovery and punishment for his acts, could be expected to resist all wrongdoing. He even suggests that "people would think him a miserable fool if they found him refusing to wrong his neighbours." This introduces a very important consideration into the history of ethics: whether the moral quality of human conduct is to be determined solely by the consequences of the action. Returning to this theme in the ninth book, Plato there argues that justice pays, that to live justly is to live profitably. He even examines the nature of pleasures and attempts a classification of them. His scale of personal satisfactions depends on the tripartite analysis of the soul: there are pleasures of sensual satisfaction, of competitive achievement, and of rational accomplishment. None is essentially bad or immoral; yet the pleasure associated with the perfect use of reason is obviously held to be best.[43]

Plato's ethics is fundamentally eudaimonistic. He saw the good life for man in terms of the personal attainment of well-being; in this condition man's reason would regulate and order all the functions of the irrational appetites. The movement within each man toward the ideal personality is an original version of self-perfection ethics. The development of the basic virtues is a personal process, of course, and varies from one man to the next. Yet Plato, like most of the Greeks, was well aware of the social dimensions of human life and well-being. A good life requires association with other persons. Ethics is but a part of politics—which deals with how to live well in the state *(polis).* In the fourth book of the *Republic* the descriptions of personal kinds of virtue are paralleled by the accounts of the functions of the three classes of citizens. The lowest class is productive and acquisitive: its social virtue is temperance. A second class is spirited, competitive, and warlike: its distinctive virtue is courage. The highest class (the rulers or guardians) is distinguished by its rationality: its special virtue is practical wisdom. When all three classes work well together, the state is marked by the virtue of justice. In the *Laws* Plato offers a very detailed and less idealistic description of the good society. There are to be precisely 5040 households in this state. A council of 360 members is to be in charge. The guardians of the law are to number thirty-seven. Such precisions are based on a sort of numerology: the number 5040 is chosen, for instance, because it has fifty-nine divisors! This dialogue, written in Plato's last years, maintains the parallelism between personal moral goodness and political good order but it stresses throughout the superiority of political virtue over the attainments of the individual. Since state "morality" is identified with the divine good, the *Laws* offer a suggestion of totalitarianism. Even in the *Republic* Plato had taught that the rulers may lie, if it is for the good of the state as a whole. This is one of the least attractive features of Plato's social ethics.

Another dimension in Plato's ethics involves the afterlife. There is little question that he taught that man's soul is immortal. We have already noticed how the *Phaedo* offers dialectical arguments to show that the *psychē* cannot end with physical death. Several other dialogues *(Gorgias, Symposium, Phaedrus,* and *Republic)* contain myths suggesting something of the nature of the afterlife of the soul.[44] The most impressive is the Tale of Er, which is told in the last book of the *Republic*. This man, Er, is pictured as going after death to a place of judgment, from which he eventually returned to earth to tell his story. Er saw many souls of the dead being offered the choice of various sorts of lives: they were free to choose what they thought best. This choice depended on what each man felt the good life should be. Obviously, Plato considered it most important to be ready to make this choice: "Each of us should lay aside all other learning, to study only how he may discover one who can give him the knowledge enabling him to distinguish the good life from the evil."[45]

Chapter II
Teleological Eudaimonism: Aristotle

P LATO'S EMPHASIS ON the good life for the individual man is continued and expanded in the ethical thinking of his pupil Aristotle. The eudaimonism of Aristotelian ethics, however, is teleological: it stresses the purposiveness of human nature. For Aristotle the goal of moral activity is achieved when man develops his understanding and appetitive powers so that he can habitually act in accord with the moral virtues. His early studies in biology doubtless influenced Aristotle's conception of maturity as an ideal stage in the development of any living being. His father was a physician named Nicomachus who served as court physician to a Macedonian king in the town of

Stagira in northern Greece, where Aristotle was born in 384 B.C.E. After studying with his father, he went to Athens at the age of eighteen and worked in Plato's school for about twenty years. Aristotle eventually established his own school in Athens and taught there from 335 B.C.E. until shortly before his death in 322.

The philosophic writings of Aristotle are numerous and extensive, covering almost all the divisions known to classic philosophy: logic, philosophy of nature, psychology, metaphysics, ethics, politics, rhetoric, and poetics. Indeed, these names and many others that have become traditional to philosophy are due in great part to Aristotle. He is likewise the originator of much of the terminology that is still used in ethical discussions. Several ethical writings are attributed to Aristotle and accounts of his moral philosophy differ, depending on which treatise is emphasized. Three popular treatises stem from his youthful period (ca. 355 B.C.E.) and they were ethical in character. The *Protrepticus* was an essay in praise of philosophy as a way of life, stressing the view that *eudaimonia* consists in intellectual contemplation.[1] In the dialogue *Eudemus* Aristotle discussed the nature, origin, and destiny of the human soul in Platonic terms. The contents of another early dialogue, *On Justice,* are not now known. In fact, we have only fragments and indirect reports on these early works.

Aristotle's two main works in ethics are the *Eudemian Ethics* and the *Nicomachean Ethics.* Books IV, V, and

VI of the *Eudemian* are identical with V, VI, and VII of the *Nicomachean Ethics*. Although there is still some dispute on the matter, most Aristotelian scholars now think that Aristotle wrote the *Eudemian Ethics* in his early period and used some of the same material when he compiled the *Nicomachean Ethics* later.[2] It is possible that the former work was a compilation made for or by a person named Eudemus and that the latter was dedicated to Aristotle's father or son, both of whom were named Nicomachus. The *Nicomachean Ethics* is the most complete, and apparently the most mature, ethical treatise. Most of our discussion of Aristotle's ethics will be based on it.

A third version of Aristotle's ethical teaching is printed among his works, under the title *Magna Moralia*. This has but two books (both quite long) and they duplicate material from the *Eudemian Ethics* and *Nicomachean Ethics*. It is generally agreed that the *Magna Moralia* is a compilation made after the death of Aristotle and that it adds nothing to his thought. The same thing may be said of the short treatise *On Virtues and Vices,* found in the collected works of Aristotle. Some of the other authentic works of Aristotle (such as the *Rhetoric, Politics, De Anima,* and *Metaphysics)* contain passages which throw light on his ethical position.

Before turning to Aristotle's main ethical teachings, a few preliminary observations on his theory of human nature are in order. As a long-time pupil and assistant teacher under Plato, Aristotle was much influenced by Platonism. The key role assigned to *eudaimonia* and the concept of the regulation of the irrational movements of the soul by the rational are two important examples of this debt. There are other similarities: the description of the moral virtues, the picture of the ideal moral person as an Athenian aristocrat, and of course the basically intellectual approach to moral life.

However, Aristotle is also very critical of certain aspects of Plato's thought. Generally speaking, he is less otherworldly and more naturalistic than Plato. This is very evident in the critique of the theory of ideal forms: Aristotle thinks that the world of sensible things is the real world and that there is no realm of intelligible entities. Instead of "forms" as constituents of another and higher world Aristotle speaks of forms as co-principles with matter of all physical substances. Dogs are not such by virtue of a Platonic participation in an idea of dogness; rather, each dog has the formal and specific nature of dogness within him. Such natures are the sources of various activities characteristic of their species. Trees grow and reproduce but do not see; dogs include sense perception and locomotion among their activities; men have all of these plus the ability to reason. The natures of things are dynamic, that is, they are equipped with various powers *(dynameis)* to act and to be acted upon. Such activities are the operations or workings of these powers, movements from potency to act. Appropriate activities tend to perfect their powers by bringing them to the condition of habituation *(hexis)* and, in turn, this process perfects the beings to which the powers belong. A dog's use of his sense and motor powers is generally self-perfective and the same may be said about human activity. It is clear that the ethics stemming from such a view of dynamic natures is going to be a type of naturalistic self-perfectionism.

The psychology of Aristotle's *De Anima* is an application of the foregoing to specifically human functioning. The soul *(psychē)* in man is the principle or source of his vital activities: growth, assimilation of food, sexual reproduction, self-movement, appetition, sensory and intellectual cognition. Man's soul is never very clearly described by Aristotle; some of his immediate followers thought that he understood the *psychē* as simply the orderly arrangement *(harmonia)* of the living body—which would disappear at death. Other interpreters (especially medieval Christians) noted how the third book of *De Anima* spoke of human intelligence as separable, impassible, and unmixed—and when "set free from its present conditions it appears as just what it is and nothing more: this alone is immortal and eternal" (III, 5, 430a17–24). Whatever Aristotle personally thought about the possibility of immortality, he made no use of this notion in his ethics: the good life that he tried to describe is the life of men on earth. Unlike Socrates and Plato, he did not teach anything about rewards or punishments in a future life.

One other feature of Aristotle's theoretical view of human nature is important here. All natures are thought to be tendential, inclined toward a certain optimism of activity, end-directed. This is Aristotelian teleology. As a biologist, Aristotle thought chiefly in terms of living things and he was convinced that they are always tending toward a goal or end *(telos)*. Each living thing is born with a set of unused and undeveloped potencies: as it moves through its life cycle, it inclines toward mature perfection and reproduction within its kind. This ongoing process includes the notion of internal finality: the final cause (purpose) of each man's activities is the continued perfect use of his potencies. This end is not some goal outside the man's own nature: it is the condition of "entelechy," of having reached the full perfection of the *telos* within the individual person. Such self-perfection is, of course, not incompatible with the welfare and perfection of the human species and of society.

It is with the foregoing in mind that we should read the famous opening sentence of the *Nicomachean Ethics:* "Every art and every inquiry, and similarly every action and pursuit, is thought to aim at some good; and for this reason the good has rightly been declared to be that at which all things aim." Aristotle proceeds to argue that some such ends or goods are external products and others are immanent activities. It is generally agreed that what men aim at above all else is *eudaimonia;* this includes the notions of living well and doing well. As noted in the terminology of Socrates and Plato, the Greek word *eudaimonia* is often translated as "happiness." Literally, it does mean being in good spirits but Aristotle gives it a much more dynamic signification. For him, *eudaimonia* is not a state or possibility of enjoyment or even of well-being: it is perfect *activity (energeia)* performed for its own sake.[3] One misses the point of Aristotle's ethics if he does not grasp this claim that immanent action is an end in itself. What all men desire, as Aristotle sees it, is not some product or consequence of action, nor some conformity of activity with a law or sense of duty, nor even some highly rewarding pleasures. Aristotelian *eudaimonia* is (1) that to which all men aspire as a fulfillment, (2) a continued and perfect activity, and (3) a whole human life embodying this activity in a favorable context of possessions and friends.[4]

Of course the activity that crowns the successful human life must be of a special kind. Many expositions of Aristotelian ethics simply identify it with intellectual contemplation. There is little doubt that Aristotle did have a very high regard for speculative understanding but it is hardly *eudaimonia* in his special sense. Much of the tenth book of the *Nicomachean Ethics* is devoted to the description of the really good and successful person. Aristotle again emphasizes that human happiness or well-being is an activity and not a habitual state *(hexis)*. Then he argues that it is an activity of intellectual understanding *(nous),* continuous, pleasant, and sufficient unto itself. Suddenly he remarks: "But such a life would be too high for man; for it is not insofar as he is man that he will live so, but insofar as something divine is present in him."[5] We should strive, of course, to cultivate this "divine" factor and to make ourselves immortal. Regretfully, it would seem, Aristotle then proceeds to describe a second-best type of good life: this includes various activities in accord with virtue. Always central to these virtuous activities, of course, is the use of intelligence.

Aristotle's insistence on virtue, in the last book of the *Nicomachean Ethics,* is but the climax of his whole argument in the treatise. His ethics is not a deontology, although he recognized the importance of duty *(to deon).* Nor is his ethics a legalism, although he stressed both natural and legal justice. The truth is that the theory of the virtues is the key to Aristotle's ethics. He distinguishes three factors within the human soul—emotions *(pathē),* powers *(dunameis),* and habitual states *(hexeis)*—and concludes that virtues are good habits.[7] Vices, of course, are bad habits.

This requires Aristotle to explain how one distinguishes between good and bad habits. At times *(Nicomachean Ethics,* 1113a25–30) he suggests that we have to depend on observing what the "good man," the pillar of society *(to spoudaios)* approves and tends to, in order to discover what is morally good. This theory of the wise or prudent man as the measure of morality is reminiscent of later theories of ethical intuitionism but Aristotle is far from intuitionism in his developed theory. Certainly it is not a deductive system, which starts from a certain definition of man and reasons to definite rules governing human activity.[8] Nor does Aristotle agree with Plato that the good is a unity of which there is one great science or wisdom.[9]

The doctrine of the mean *(mesotēs)* plays an important role in Aristotle's study of the moral virtue. As we saw in the Pythagorean view, most human affective attitudes admit of states or feelings which may be excessive on the one hand or defective on the other. The desire for food, for instance, may become habitually too great or too little. The habitual state of such desire in excess would be the vice of gluttony; similarly, habitual disinterest in eating would be a vice of defect. The middle state, or mean, is not one precise point midway between extremes; the moral mean varies for different persons, in different circumstances. What is moderate for an athlete may be immoderate for a sedentary person. In determining the mean of virtue, in the concrete, one uses a capacity for perceptive appraisal rather than formal reasoning.

Aristotle describes in great detail the application of his theory of the mean to many states of moral character. Many later lists of virtues and vices, in classical, medieval, and early modern ethical treatises stem from the Aristotelian descriptions in the second books of both the *Nicomachean Ethics* and the *Eudemian Ethics*. The following table lists the chief moral means with their respective extremes of vice:

EXCESS	MEAN	DEFECT
foolhardiness	courage	cowardice
licentiousness	temperance	insensibility
prodigality	liberality	illiberality
vulgarity	magnificence	meanness
vanity	highmindedness	littlemindedness
ambition	[moderate aspiration]	lack of ambition
irascibility	gentleness	impassivity
boastfulness	truthfulness	mock modesty
buffoonery	wittiness	boorishness
obsequiousness	friendliness	surliness
bashfulness	modesty	shamelessness
envy	righteous indignation	spite

It will be observed that the "means" listed above name virtues which have to do with affective states of consciousness. This is the area of the "passions" in medieval moral treatises. It is the field in which the doctrine of the mean has its most effective application. Moderation, after all, is an obvious ideal in human feelings. Aristotle also uses the notion of the mean in treating intellectual virtues and especially in discussing the moral virtue of justice. Since it deals with transactions between men, justice is the habit of voluntarily doing what is good for other people and of avoiding acts that are harmful to others *(Nicomachean Ethics,* 1129a1–1138b12). There are different kinds of justice, in Aristotle's view, and the mean differs in each. First of all, there is that ordinary kind of justice which is a habitual inclination to act in accord with the recognized laws: this is legal justice. It aims at the good of men in groups—what will in later Aristotelianism be called the "common good" and the public welfare. Legal justice pertains to what is right in most cases and in the ordinary run of things. However, there are extraordinary occasions when to follow the law slavishly is to be unfair. A special virtue is needed enabling one to judge and do what is right in exceptional circumstances. It is called equity *(epieikeia)* and is the best kind of justice *(Nicomachean Ethics,* 1137b9). The mean in these types of justice consists in voluntary action that preserves a reasonable balance in dealing with others.

Aristotle also considers justice as it relates to the good of the individual person (particular justice), and he here describes two kinds. One type is a habit of fairness in distributions of public advantages (or disadvantages) to various individuals. This sort of justice (distributive) recognizes pertinent inequalities among persons and endeavors to adjust honors and monies that are apportioned from the common fund, in such a way that a sort of geometric proportion is achieved. The mean in such transactions is a complicated ratio between the value to the community of the person who receives and the value of the thing allotted to him. A second type of particular justice deals with simple transactions between individual persons (sales, loans, promises, deposits, etc.). In such dealings the private persons are regarded as equals and the appropriate type of justice (commutative) looks to an arithmetic equality in exchanges.[11]

The term "voluntary" has been used in the foregoing discussion of the mean. Aristotle made an important contribution to the history of ethics in his analysis of what voluntariness implies. Although the usual English terminology suggests a close connection with the notion of will *(voluntas)*, Aristotle's language does not. He talks about some of man's actions as being *hekousia,* that is, with the knowledge and approval of the agent. It is such actions that are called voluntary in English. Other activities of man are performed consciously but with a certain amount of repugnance: these Aristotle calls *akousia* (not coming from within the agent, not spontaneous) and we speak of them as involuntary. Obviously, involuntary actions may be partly voluntary. Still other human activities are quite outside his personal control (one type would be those performed as a result of complete ignorance); these Aristotle calls not-voluntary.[12] Obviously, moral actions must be voluntary to some extent. Aristotle's definition of the voluntary as "what is done not under compulsion and not through ignorance" is recognized in contemporary ethics as a still-valid approach to the determination of moral responsibility.

There is no tendency toward legalism in Aristotle's ethics: he does not teach that there is some sort of set of moral precepts which all men are bound to obey. Later Aristotelians, under influences other than the thought of Aristotle, will develop various theories of natural moral law. The *Nicomachean Ethics* has nothing to say about natural law, beyond the basic suggestion that there is a naturally right way of acting; this is the *dikaion* of the fifth book. Rather, it is the theory of the virtues that is characteristic of Aristotelian ethics. Books III, IV, and V of *Nicomachean Ethics* treat the moral virtues, as we have seen. Books VI and VII discuss the intellectual virtues and the concept of right reason.

Five intellectual virtues are studied by Aristotle: all are habits of the intellect described in *De Anima* (430a15) as capable of becoming all things that are intelligible. Three of these habits are theoretical and speculative in character: there is a more or less innate habit of intuiting first principles; there is an acquired habit of reasoning to demonstratively established judgments; and there is philosophic wisdom, the habit of considering the highest objects of knowledge by a sort of fusion of intuitive understanding with demonstrative reasoning.[13] Wisdom in the speculative order (as directed simply to pure knowing) is treated in Aristotle's *Metaphysics*. The sixth book of *Nicomachean Ethics* turns to the other aspect of wisdom: when it is a habit of considering how to act well and rightly, it becomes practical wisdom, prudence *(phronēsis)*. If we speak of *phronēsis* as prudence, it must be remembered that it does not mean a self-seeking astuteness (as in much contemporary usage) but the habit of deliberating and judging well about one's own problems of moral action. Unlike moral science, Aristotle's prudence is not teachable; it is a skill which must be acquired, if at all, by personal effort. In part, Aristotelian prudence is concerned with *knowing* how to act as a human being—but it is also involved in the direction, the rectification, of one's own voluntary activities. In this second sense, prudence governs actions and is a moral virtue.

As a habit of practical understanding, prudence makes it possible to reason to judgments that some actions are good and others are evil. Aristotle takes it that children are born with certain natural tendencies toward virtuous activity: acquired prudence merely develops these inclinations so that they become conscious elements in the living of a good life.[14]

Pleasure is regarded by Aristotle as a sort of satisfaction attendant upon the perfect use of one's powers. There is a pleasure that accompanies sensory perception and one that is associated with the understanding of the most excellent objects. These pleasures are not identical with their concomitant activities but they are, along with perfection of action, constitutive of ideal well-being *(eudaimonia)*. It has been argued that Aristotle's ethics started as a hedonism (pleasure being the ultimate good for man) and moved toward eudaimonism in its later formulations.[15] There is, indeed, greater stress in the seventh book of the *Nicomachean Ethics* on the ultimate desirability of pleasure than there is in the tenth book. However, we do not know enough about the chronology of these books to found any theory of the evolution of Aristotle's thought on such evidence. At best, we can say that he always regarded some degree of pleasure as a proper accompaniment for that perfection of human activity in which *eudaimonia* consists.

The tenth and last book of the *Nicomachean Ethics* tries to restate Aristotle's notion of the good life. Continued intellectual contemplation is the highest activity of man—and the most rewarding. Such activity is the use of "the most divine element in us." Yet Aristotle has some hesitation in concluding that intellectual speculation is by itself the good life for man; "such a life would be too high for man; for it is not insofar as he is man that he will live so, but insofar as something divine is present in him."[16] He then argues that, perhaps, *eudaimonia* consists in activity in accord with moral virtue, requiring also a certain amount of material prosperity, freedom from worries, and the consolations of having some good friends. Such a "good life" is obviously limited to some favored people and is restricted to life on earth.

In the final lines of the *Eudemian Ethics* a somewhat different emphasis is found. Here we are told that all other goods that we may seek are merely means to enable us to advance to the highest good for men. Man's final felicity consists in "serving and contemplating God."[17] Some interpreters think that this terminating passage is an addition by some later scribe, with Christian views on the destiny of man.

The successor of Aristotle as head of the Peripatetic school was Theophrastus (ca. 375–288 B.C.E.), a man who did some work in ethics. In addition to his *Ethical Characters,* he wrote a treatise *On Eudaimonia.* Cicero *(De finibus,* V, V, 12) is our source for the report that Theophrastus emphasized the need for good fortune and material possessions as constituents of the good life. Some historians think that Theophrastus criticized the theological orientation of the ethics of Aristotle.[18] Also, a certain Andronicus (whether this is Andronicus of Rhodes, first century B.C.E., is not known) produced a short treatise *On the Passions* which is Aristotelian in spirit. He may also have written a treatise on the various "parts" or subdivisions of the four chief Aristotelian virtues: prudence, temperance, courage, and justice. The Greek medical doctor Claudius Galen (ca. 130–200 C.E.) produced a treatise, *On Moral Customs,* known through an Arabic summary of the twelfth century. This treatise was one of the first sources of information among Moslem scholars concerning certain elements in Aristotle's ethics.[19] During the Middle Ages a Latin treatise entitled *Liber de Bona Fortuna* was widely circulated as a source of information on Aristotelian morality. It was a compilation from the *Eudemian Ethics* and the *Magna Moralia.*

Greek paraphrases and commentaries on Aristotle's ethical writings were produced at intervals during the first fifteen hundred years of the Christian era. Aspasius (fl. 125 C.E.), the Pseudo-Alexander of Aphrodisias (unknown dates), an anonymous commentator (first centuries, C.E.), Bishop Eustratios of Nicaea (fl. 1052–1120 C.E.), Michael Ephesius (fl. 1070 C.E.), and the Pseudo-Heliodorus (fourteenth to sixteenth century, precise dates unknown) constitute this group. These men are little read and seem to have had but small influence on the history of ethics.

Latin commentaries on portions of the *Nicomachean Ethics* begin to appear in the twelfth century. In the 1240s, Robert Grosseteste made a complete Latin version of the *Nicomachean Ethics* and wrote *Notulae* to explain it.[20] In the ensuing decades of the thirteenth and fourteenth centuries many Christian writers (Albert the Great, Thomas Aquinas, Siger de Brabant, Giles of Rome, Anthony of Parma) produced formal commentaries or series of questions dealing with the *Nicomachean Ethics.* To the extent that they modify Aristotelianism, they belong in the history of medieval ethics. The influence of Aristotle on present-day ethics is evident in some Thomistic works and particularly in the thought of W. D. Ross and Henry B. Veatch.

Chapter III

Hellenistic Ethics: Stoic, Epicurean, and Neoplatonic

THE LAST THREE centuries before Christ witnessed the development of three different schools of ethics: Stoicism, Epicureanism, and Neoplatonism. This Hellenistic period actually extended well beyond the time of Christ. The last great figure in pagan Greek philosophy, Proclus, lived in the fifth century of the Christian era. We have, then, eight centuries in which there were many students and teachers of ethics. Many scholars wrote commentaries on the thought of the earlier Greek philosophers but some original thinking was done in ethics. With the growth of Roman culture, Greek philosophy was translated into Latin and adapted to the problems and interests of the new Roman empire. Christianity was born in the middle of this period and it introduced a new outlook on the good life for man. However, we shall postpone our treatment of Christian ethics until the next chapter. In the present one we shall concentrate on the ethical views of the thinkers who represent the last stages of Greek philosophy.

In general, later Greek philosophy was less speculative and more practical in its interests than the thought of the early Greeks. While problems of knowledge and reality continued to be investigated, the main thrust of Hellenistic philosophy was toward the discovery of how men might live well. Religious teachings became part of these philosophies. Man's ultimate destiny and his possible relations with the divinity now came to the forefront of attention. Some philosophers, particularly in the Stoic and Neoplatonic schools, became the equivalent of religious leaders. In the first centuries after Christ, an intellectual brand of neopaganism appeared, for a time, to rival Christianity. All these developments left their effects on ethics.

Stoic Ethics

Stoicism began early in the fourth century B.C.E., when Zeno of Citium (336–264) came to Athens to teach at a place that had a porch *(stoa),* whence came its name. Zeno wrote a number of treatises—*On Human Nature, On Living in Accord with Nature,* and *On Duty*—but except for fragments in later writings these works have been lost.[1] Zeno's successors, Cleanthes (331–232) and Chrysippus (282–204), also were important in the history of the ethics of the first Stoics. Roman Stoicism falls in a much later era, the first and second centuries C.E.; its leading ethicians were Seneca, Epictetus, and Marcus Aurelius.

The Stoic view of reality was thoroughly materialistic: all that exists is matter. Stoicism taught the usual ancient theory of four elements (earth, air, fire, and water) but regarded fire as the ultimate substance. Souls and God are subtler kinds of fire than that of crass bodies. Growth and change are due to certain seedlike rational forms *(logoi spermatikoi)* which are present in matter. There is a pattern, an understandable plan *(logos),* for everything that exists and happens in the nature of things. Knowledge is fundamentally sense perception: Stoicism is usually classified as a sensism. However, the Stoics obviously thought that men are able to understand the orderly character of mundane events, so they recognized the function of reason. Stoic logic was a highly sophisticated theory of reasoning that differed radically from the Aristotelian syllogistic. In particular, the Stoics maintained that certain general notions are given to men prior to sense experience, so their theory of knowledge bordered on innatism.[2] Although the Stoics were generally deterministic in regard to causality, this did not prevent them from granting a certain personal freedom to human agents. A man is not able to control the general course of events in the world but he is able to control his own inner acts of assent, his own desires, and his affective responses to internal experience.

Ethically, the Stoics still thought in terms of Greek eudaimonism. Their concept of *eudaimonia,* however, was more static than that of Aristotle. The end, or ultimate goal, to which they looked was a condition of undisturbed happiness, "a calmly flowing life." The Stoic sage would be a person who had acquired such a degree of rational control of his feelings that he would rarely, if ever, be inclined to any excess of emotion. Affective movements of consciousness, pleasure *(hēdonē),* sorrow *(lupē),* desire *(epithumia),* and fear *(phōbos)* are irrational and incompatible with human nature. The ideal of virtue is *apatheia,* a condition in which passionate feelings are not merely controlled but virtually eradicated. It is good to live in accord with nature; nature is fundamentally rational in character; hence, the second Stoic maxim, that the good life is in accord with reason. The highest instance of reason is God *(Zeus)* and divine law orders and governs all events universally. This respect for the universal and natural law of reason was evident in one of the earliest writings, Cleanthes' famous *Hymn to Zeus.* It is worth reading in its entirety.[3]

Most glorious of the Immortals
many-named
almighty forever
ZEUS
ruler of nature
that governest all things with law.
Hail! for lawful it is that all mortals should
    address thee.
For we are thy offspring
taking the image only of thy voice
as many mortal things as live and move upon the
    earth.
Therefore I will hymn thee
and sing thy might forever.
For thee doth all this universe that circles round
    the earth obey
moving whithersoever thou leadest
and is gladly swayed by thee.
Such a minister hast thou in thine invincible
    hands—
the two-edged blazing imperishable thunderbolt.
For under its stroke all nature shuddereth
and by it thou guidest aright the universal Logos
that roams through all things
mingling itself with the greater and the lesser
    lights
till it have grown so great
and become supreme king over all.
Nor is aught done on the earth without thee
O Zeus

nor in the divine sphere of the heavens
nor in the sea
save the works that evil men do in their folly.
Yea, but thou knowest even to find a place for the
    superfluous things
and to order that which is disorderly
and things not dear to men are dear to thee.
Thus dost thou harmonize into one all good and
    evil things
that there should be one everlasting Logos of
    them all.
And this the evil among mortal men avoid and
    heed not
wretched ever desiring to possess the good
yet they neither see nor hear the universal law of
    Zeus
which obeying with all their heart
their life would be well
but they rush graceless each to his aim:
some cherish lust for fame
the nurse of evil strife
some bent on monstrous gain
some turned to folly and the sweet works of the
    flesh
hastening indeed to bring the very contrary of
    these things to pass.
But thou
O Zeus
the all-giver
dweller in the darkness of cloud

lord of thunder
save thou men from their unhappy folly
which do thou, O Father, scatter from their souls
and give them discover the wisdom
in whose assurance thou governest all things with
    justice
so that being honoured
they may pay thee honour
hymning thy works continually
as it beseems a mortal man
since there can be no greater glory for men or gods
    than this:
duly to praise forever the universal law.

In this compendium of early Stoic ethics several points may be noticed. For the first time in Greek ethical teaching, the notion of an all-pervading "law" is introduced. Some of the pre-Socratics, it is true, spoke of *nomos* as a principle of regularity and harmony in change; but the view that a divine Ruler governs all events, including human activities, under universal law is an important innovation in Greek thought. This is the nearest approach to a theory of divine providence that we will find outside the Judaeo-Christian teaching. Cleanthes is saying that all things are ordered according to a rational plan *(logos)* which is implanted in the material universe and which is, at the same time, implicit in the Reason of God. Christian moral writers for many centuries were impressed by this Stoic doctrine of the law of nature. It is one of the chief sources of natural-law ethics.

The third head of the Greek Stoic school was Chrysippus of Soli (ca. 280–204), who is sometimes credited with turning the attention of Stoicism to the nature of man as opposed to its original interest in the nature of the universe.[4] However, because we have practically no source materials, it is impossible to assess the personal contributions to ethics of the earliest Stoics; beside those mentioned there were: Persaeus, Aretus, Sphaerus, Aristo, Zeno the fourth scholarch, Diogenes of Seleucia, Antipater, and Crates. They bring the school down to the second century B.C.E.

The name "middle Stoicism" is given to the teaching of a group of Greek thinkers who combined the original views of the school with parts of the philosophies of Plato and Aristotle and who transmitted this eclectic but practically oriented philosophy to Roman students and writers. Panaetius of Rhodes (ca. 189–109) taught for a time in Rome but became scholarch (head of the Stoic school) in Athens in 129 B.C.E. Due to the influence of Panaetius, the Stoic ethics that the Romans learned in the second century before Christ was less insistent on the ideal life of the sage, less interested in the restrictive virtue of *apatheia*—and more favorable to the view that the good life consists in a reasonable moderation in all things. One of Panaetius' pupils, Poseidonius (ca. 135–51 B.C.E.), taught Cicero at Rhodes and so made a profound impression on Roman culture.

Two important ethical ideas came to the Romans from middle Stoicism. The first was a development of the original Stoic teaching that all nature is rationally ordered under the supreme Reason of the Deity, and that man is morally obliged to conform his conscious life to the force of universal reason.[5] Second, Stoicism provided Roman and early Christian moralists with a practical psychology that emphasized the distinct functions of various cognitive, appetitive, and motor faculties *(dynameis)* of the soul.[6] In this theory there is a growing emphasis on the function of willing *(boulēsis),* viewed as rational wishing. Moreover, middle Stoicism introduced the concept of the *hēgemonikon,* a faculty that rules and governs the other powers of the soul. In various versions of Christian ethics, the role of the *hēgemonikon* will sometimes be played by the will, sometimes by the intellect.

Roman Stoicism begins to develop in first-century (B.C.E.) reports found in Latin writers who do not fully share the ethical positions of the Stoics. This is probably true of M. Terentius Varro (116–27 B.C.E.), whose encyclopedic writings are mostly nonextant. Through references and quotations in Augustine of Hippo *(City of God,* XIX, 1–3), we know that Varro transmitted 288 Greek views on the end of man and the nature of happiness. We also have the works of M. Tullius Cicero (106–43 B.C.E.), in which there is a great deal of information about Stoic ethics. Books III and IV of *De finibus* contain a lengthy exposition of the ethics of Stoicism, in the words of a Roman spokesman, Cato Uticensis. He was a real person and a contemporary of Cicero in Rome. One feature of this version of Stoic ethics in Rome was its social-mindedness. Even the Greek Stoics were noteworthy for their concern about the common good of humanity: if they had lived in the twentieth century, the Stoics would have been strong supporters of the United Nations. Cicero further emphasized the importance of human brotherhood in his personal revision of Stoicism.[7]

Of all the moralists of ancient Rome, L. Annaeus Seneca (ca. 4 B.C.–65 C.E.) was one of the most voluminous and widely read. His *Letters* and *Moral Essays* show no great interest in ethical *theory* but develop a practical doctrine of human virtues. Long lists of these good qualities of the human person are found in his works. Self-control, moderation of desire, rational reflection, and self-sufficiency *(per se sufficientia)* are typical Senecan virtues. He wrote with great respect for the higher mental aspects of man's nature, as well as for the influence of the Deity on human life, with the result that later Christian moral writers make abundant use of his descriptions of virtue and the good life.[8]

The greatest ethician among the later Stoics was Epictetus of Hierapolis (ca. 50–138 C.E.). A Greek slave in Emperor Nero's service, Epictetus was freed and taught philosophy in Rome and in Nicopolis. One of his pupils, Flavius Arrianus, made records of Epictetus' lectures and these reports constitute the four extant books of *Discourses (Diatribai)* and the little manual called the *Enchiridion*. As a pupil of the lesser Stoic, Musonius Rufus, Epictetus returned to the epistemological and physical views of early Stoicism: a sensistic explanation of knowledge (with a special insight into first principles, *syneidesis),* plus a generally materialistic notion of reality which did not exclude freedom of choice and assent within the consciousness of each man. Extramental things and the activities of the body are not under the control of one's will and it is the mark of the wise man to recognize this. As the opening lines of the *Enchiridion* put it:

> Of things some are in our power, and others are not. In our power are opinion, movement towards a thing, desire, aversion, turning from a thing; and in a word, whatever are our acts. Not in our power are the body, property, reputation, offices (magisterial power), and in a word, whatever are not our own acts. And the things in our power are by nature free, not subject to restraint or hindrance; but the things not in our power are weak, slavish, subject to restraint, in the power of others.[9]

Yet Epictetus thought that all men have enough natural ability and information to govern their internal dispositions according to right reason *(orthos logos).* The original notions *(prolēpseis)* of good and evil are innate but the study of philosophy and ethics is necessary to assure a reasonable development of moral judgment and a fair application of principles to various concrete problems of life. Epictetus retained the earlier teaching of a ruling power *(hēgemonikon)* in man whereby one knows the difference between good and evil, makes choices, and controls the activities of the lower psychic powers. This governing power is almost identical with will. All human evil reduces to a perversion of will. Personal contentment *(ataraxia)* comes from learning to accept the course of external events and the divine regulation of men and the universe. Epictetus succinctly states this in his *Discourses:*

And will you be angry and peevish at the ordinances of Zeus, which he defined and ordained together with the Fates who spun in his presence the thread of your begetting? Do you not know how small a part you are compared with the whole? That is, as to the body; for as to the reason you are not inferior to the gods, nor less than they; for the greatness of the reason is not determined by length nor by height, but by the decisions of its will.[10]

Much the same point of view is found in the *Meditations* of Emperor Marcus Aurelius (121–180 C.E.). He is, perhaps, less materialistic in his teaching on man's nature. He divides the human person into three parts: body *(sōma),* soul *(psychē),* and intelligence *(nous).* The last is the ruling power *(hēgemonikon)* for Marcus Aurelius. Each man's personal intelligence is his guiding spirit *(daimon)* or conscience: in turn, this guiding power is subject to the will of God.[11]

The practical ethics of Marcus Aurelius may be summed up in the following nine rules of conduct: (1) be ready to forgive your neighbor when he offends you, since we all exist to serve each other; (2) reflect on the unfortunate effects which the bad actions of others have upon these others; (3) avoid making moral judgments on other persons; (4) remember your own moral defects; (5) remember that you do not know the internal attitudes of your fellow men; (6) when the occasion for anger arises, remember that you will soon be dead; (7) it is not the sins of others that really bother us but only our own opinions about others; (8) remember that anger and grief can be worse for a person than the external consequences of another man's actions; (9) remember that kindness and friendliness to others are best for all concerned.[12]

In popularized versions such as the foregoing, Stoic ethics was the dominant school of thought in pagan Rome and continued to be so during the first two centuries of Christianity. Platonism was too lofty and difficult; Aristotelianism was not well known and was felt to have little literary appeal. Besides Stoic ethics the only important contemporary moral philosophy was Epicureanism, and it was never anything more than a minority view, as we shall see.[13]

Epicurean Ethics

Among the post-Socratic schools, the Cyrenaics had taught that personal satisfaction is the test of the morally good act. This is hedonism in its simplest form. The line of connection between Epicurus (341–270 B.C.E.) and the Cyrenaics is not clear but it is evident that Epicurean ethics is also a hedonism. Where the Stoic located the focal point of moral good and evil in the conscious attitude of the moral agent (and so, remotely, anticipated certain deontological or intuitionistic types of modern ethics), the Epicurean ethician looked to the consequences of man's actions for his criterion of morality (and so, equally remotely, presaged modern utilitarianism in its individualistic versions). For some unknown reason, most of the writings by Epicurus have been lost: we now have three letters and some fragments, mostly from a work *On Nature.*

Like the Stoics, Epicurus divided philosophy into three parts: theory of knowledge, physics, and ethics. He was, however, comparatively uninterested in the logic of discursive reasoning and had no teaching that compares with Stoic logic. Epicurus' theory of knowledge is sensistic. He concentrates on sense perception *(aisthesis)* and the judgments consequent upon it. There are no innate notions: all knowledge comes through sense experience. The test of true knowledge is clarity. Concepts are memory images, usually following many sense perceptions.[14] Epicurus' theory of the nature of things was a version of the earlier materialistic atomism found in Democritus. Only bodies exist and all bodies are constituted out of innumerable little particles. It is possible that Epicurus originated the notion of the "swerve" in the falling of the atoms, to account for the various configurations of collections of atoms and possibly to allow room for some sort of freedom in an otherwise rigidly mechanistic explanation of the universe.

It was ethics that interested Epicurus most and he may simply have adopted from his predecessors those epistemological, psychological, and metaphysical views which were calculated to form a basis for his moral theory. He thought that most of the evil and suffering in man's world is due to the ignorant and superstitious acceptance of polytheism. He may not have been an atheist, in any fundamental sense, but he was very critical of the popular paganism of his day. Epicurus believed that most men live in terror of death and in fear of the gods. Hence he taught that there is no personal survival after death and that the gods are not concerned with human affairs. Epicurean ethics is naturalistic, then, in a special sense: it endeavors to deal with moral good and evil without any recourse to the divine will of Zeus, or to any supernatural laws or ideals of duty.[15]

Just as clearness of perception is the test of truth in the acquisition of knowledge, so the feeling of pleasure or pain is the criterion of right choice and action. Pleasure is the "first good innate in us," but this does not mean that all pleasures are equal in value, or that every pleasure is to be chosen. Sometimes the wise man will choose a present pain to secure a future pleasure. In any case, pleasure does not mean to Epicurus "drinking's and revellings, nor the satisfaction of lusts . . . but sober reasoning, searching out the motives for all choice and avoidance, and banishing mere opinions, to which are due the greatest disturbance of the spirit." The goal of morally good activity, then, is peace of mind *(ataraxia),* freedom from mental perturbation.[16] Epicurus held that study and personal effort will enable a man to acquire the virtues that lead to the equanimity of the sage. Primary among these are prudence *(phronēsis)* and friendship *(philia)*: the former is more precious even than philosophy and is the root of all other virtues; the latter is the crown of the perfected life.[17] Evidently, Epicurus was far from teaching libertinism or the selfish pursuit of sensual satisfactions. Indeed, in the long run, the Epicurean and the Stoic ideally good men were not too different. Both were supposed to be men controlled by reason, interested in their own true good and that of other persons, pursuing a high-minded ideal of natural human perfection.

The most complete treatise, still extant, from Roman Epicureanism is Lucretius' poem *On the Nature of Things.* T. Lucretius Cams (ca. 96–55 B.C.E.) introduced Latin readers to the teachings of Epicurus. At the beginning of several of the six books *On the Nature of Things,* Epicurus is addressed in glowing terms as the wisest and best of men.[18] Epicurean atomism and sensism are explained at great length by Lucretius— who does not seem to have added anything to the basic theory. Epicurus' "atheism" and critique of popular religion are much stressed by Lucretius; it is possible that the Roman poet was more anti-religious than the Greek philosopher. Lucretius shows himself to be a great admirer of the philosophy of nature. The more we know about physical realities, the more we realize that we should not crave any special satisfactions in life. "Nec nova vivendo procuditur ulla voluptas" (by living we cannot forge for ourselves any new pleasure).[19] The key attitude of the morally good man, according to Lucretius, is resignation, based on an understanding of the way things are. Like Epicurus, Lucretius insisted that friendship *(amicitia)* is the bond of the good human society.[20]

Neoplatonic Ethics

In the first five centuries of the Christian era, several types of ethics were developed by Greek writers who were more or less under the influence of Platonism. The common denominator in this Neoplatonic ethics is the view that the good life consists in a flight from the world of sense experience to a closer relationship with a supreme principle. These Neoplatonists use a variety of ways to explain the culmination of this other-worldly ethics. Chief among these were Philo Judaeus, Plutarch of Chaeronea, and Plotinus.

Philo Judaeus (ca. 25 B.C.E.–40 C.E.) was a Jewish scholar who lived in Alexandria and wrote about forty works in Greek.[21] Most of these writings are allegorical commentaries on the Old Testament. He was convinced that the same basic truths are found in Scripture and in Greek philosophy. The higher forms (or ideas, as in Plato) are created by God in the divine Reason *(logos)*. In turn, the material things of the universe are fashioned from the four elements after the pattern of the forms.[22] Man is a creature with a mind ruling his body in somewhat the way that God rules the universe. Man's soul is made in the image of God and, while on earth, is on a journey away from God. It is the destiny of the soul to free itself from the burden of matter and to rise to a union with the divine wisdom. This "flight from the body" is what should be the aim of the perfected and good man.

> Depart out of the earthly matter that encompasses thee: escape, man, from the foul prison-house thy body, with all thy might and main, and from the pleasures and lusts that are its jailers. . . . if thou desire to recover the self thou hast lent and to have thine own possession about thee, letting no portion of them be alienated and fall into other hands,

> thou shalt claim instead a happy life, enjoy-
> ing in perpetuity the benefit and pleasure
> derived from good things not foreign to
> thee but thine own.[23]

Clearly, this poetical description of a mystical journey of the soul to rejoin its God is not a philosophical ethics. Yet there are adaptations of the Platonic vision in Philo's thinking and he exercised a good deal of influence on Plotinus and many Christian moralists.[24] His ethics would seem to stand at the opposite pole to the this-worldly naturalism of both Stoics and Epicureans.

Plutarch of Chaeronea (ca. 46–120 C.E.) was another ancient moralist who built a sort of practical ethics on a modified Platonic view of man. He combined an acceptance of much of the popular Greek religion with a desire to know God in a purely intellectual manner. His God is transcendent and in no way the cause of evil: the World-Soul is the source of mundane evil, even though it emanates from God. The intelligence *(nous)* in man is superior to the soul *(psychē)*. It is the intelligent mind that may, by living virtuously and possibly by the practice of certain religious rites, achieve happiness in a future life after separation from the body. Unlike most of his contemporaries, Plutarch showed some acquaintance with Aristotelian ethics. He embraced the theory of virtue as a mean between excess and defect. Like the Stoics, he advocated the brotherhood of man as an ideal for the organization of human society.[25]

There is a sort of ethics in the group of Greek writings emanating from Alexandria, Egypt, and purporting to be the teachings of Hermes Tresmegistos. One discourse speaks of a rebirth of the soul and a mounting to some sort of culminating vision in the afterlife.[26] This teaching is expressed in very obscure myths and cannot be called a formal ethics but it serves to illustrate a point of view in paganism during the first Christian centuries. It placed the good for man in a nonterrestrial happiness.

Plotinus (205–270 C.E.) was the greatest philosopher in these centuries—yet he is rarely mentioned in histories of ethics. He studied at Alexandria and began to teach in Rome when he was about forty. Partially blind, Plotinus devoted much of his time to solitary meditation. He knew the philosophies of Plato, Aristotle, and the Stoics and used all of them in his personal thinking. His lectures were edited by his pupil, Porphyry, in six books with nine chapters in each and so were called the *Enneads* (the "Nines").

The whole of things is viewed by Plotinus as originating from a supreme principle, the One. This unitary beginning is beyond all predicates: one cannot even say that It *is,* for it is beyond being. Some interpreters identify the One with a personal God: Plotinus uses both personal and impersonal pronouns in speaking of It and he does suggest that It is divine. From the One there issues a first hypostasis, Intelligence *(nous).* This first emanation contains the Ideas (like Plato's ideal forms). In turn, the Intelligence gives rise to a second emanation, Soul *(psychē)*. This is a cosmic soul: in itself it is not associated with the corporeal, it is the nous thinking itself. On a lower level the world soul animates the whole physical universe. Matter is the limit of the process of emanation: as such, matter is relative nonbeing. Each human being is a composite of a portion, as it were, of Soul plus some bodily matter. Man is poised, then, in a precarious position of existence, capable of going up or down in the scale of reality. If he goes down, by becoming more material, his life becomes evil. If he goes up toward his origin in the One, he is perfected and becomes a better man. The whole of reality is in process: what is real is not static substance but dynamic energy of an incorporeal sort.[27]

The process of emanation from the One is a necessary movement from goodness to evil, a descent into the imperfection of matter. Much of the first Ennead is dedicated to the proposition that the good life for man consists in a voluntary ascent of the individual soul toward the One: this is why these chapters are called the "ethical treatises."[28] The fourth chapter, for instance, is a discussion of *eudaimonia*: Greek ethics is eudaimonistic even in its last stages. Plotinus offers a review of his predecessors' notions on well-being; he covers the views of Plato, Aristotle, the Stoics, and the Epicureans. Like Aristotle, Plotinus insists on the active character of *eudaimonia* and is quite critical of the Stoic restriction of final happiness to the rational soul alone. All life is capable of eudaimonia and, just as there are different levels of life, there are different degrees of happiness. Similarly, the sixth chapter in Ennead I shows how the beautiful (*to kalon*) provides a starting point from which the soul may rise to the contemplation of its own beauty and eventually of the ideal Beauty. This description of the ascent of man's soul toward a peak of perfection is a moral reworking of the thought of several of Plato's dialogues, notably the Phaedrus *Symposium*, and *Theaetetus*.[29] In another place, Plotinus suggests that this ascent of the soul toward the highest Beauty is a mystical phenomenon which he has experienced himself.

> Often I awaken to myself by escaping from my body: thus cut off from other things, in the intimacy of my self, I see a beauty that is as marvelous as can be. Above all, then, I am convinced that I have a higher destiny; my activity is the highest degree of life; I am in union with the divine and, once I have reached this peak of activity, I fasten to It above the other intelligible beings.[30]

In the immediately preceding chapter (7), Plotinus is very insistent on the incorruptibility of man's soul (he offers several arguments from Plato's *Phaedo)* and on the generic similarity between the life of the soul and the divine life. What makes it possible for the spirit of man to ascend to union with the divine is a purification *(catharsis)* from material concerns, an advance in the knowledge of the soul itself and intelligible things, and a process of self-perfection through virtues such as temperance and justice. The second chapter of *Ennead* I is an exposition of a highly developed theory of moral virtue *(aretē)*. There are four levels: (1) the virtues required to live well among men in society *(aretai politikai)*: these are temperance, courage, justice, and prudence; (2) the virtues needed to cleanse the soul from interest in the body and sense objects *(kathartikai)*; (3) the virtues of the already purged soul *(virtutes purgati animi* in the fifth-century summary made by Macrobius, *In Somnium Scipionis,* I, 8); and (4) the exemplary virtues *(aretai paradeigmatiká)*, which qualify the soul for the intelligible vision of the One.[31] The following passage from the sixth *Ennead* shows how this fits into the ethics of the soul's ascent:

For the soul by its nature refuses to go down to absolute nothingness; when it descends it goes as far as evil, which is a non-being, but not as far as absolute non-being. In going upward, it does not ascend to a being different from itself; rather, it returns into itself and dwells in nothing other than itself. As soon as it lives within itself alone and not in lower being, it is by that fact present in It. For It is a reality which is not an entity *(ousia)* but beyond entities; to this the soul is united. If a person is aware of his self becoming It, he sees his self as an image of It. If he goes beyond this stage, moving from the image to the reality Itself, he thus reaches the end of the journey. When a person falls back from such contemplation, it is possible for him to revive the virtue *(aretē)* that is within. Then he understands his internal orderliness and rediscovers the upward tendency of his mind: thus, through virtue one moves up to the Intelligence *(nous),* and through wisdom *(sophia)* ascends to the Highest. Such is the life of the gods and of godlike and morally successful men *(anthropōn theiōn kai eudaimonōn bios):* to free oneself from things here below, in a life finding no value in lower things, in a solitary flight toward the One.[32]

From the foregoing it will be evident that Plotinus' ethics is a remarkable version of self-perfectionism. It is a teleological theory, for the quality of good action depends on its being rationally directed toward the attainment of a contemplative and loving union with a supreme End. However, since the perfection achieved in this final union is the highest degree of incorporeal life, and since man's soul is life itself, this ultimate *eudaimonia* is but the final stage in the perfection *(aretē)* of the soul itself. Plotinus' ethical vision fascinated many spiritual-minded thinkers in the ensuing centuries: Greeks, like Dionysius the Areopagite and Maximus the Confessor; Latins, like Marius Victorinus, Augustine of Hippo, Scotus Erigena, Meister Eckhart, and Nicholas of Cusa; Moslems, like Avicenna and Al-Ghazzali; Jews, such as Avicebrón; and a host of Renaissance "Platonists."

Plotinus' immediate followers among the pagan Greek philosophers did not improve the ethics of Neoplatonism. Porphyry of Tyre (233–ca. 305 C.E.) edited his master's *Enneads* and wrote his life and also produced personal treatises which attempt a combination of Plotinus' ethical mysticism with a rather crude version of polytheism. Porphyry came to see himself as the prophet of a revived neopagan religion, in which the intelligible universe of Plotinus was filled with demons and spirits who required to be propitiated and managed by magic and esoteric rites. He was a forceful critic of Christianity. One of Porphyry's pupils was a Syrian, Iamblichus of Chalkis (d. ca. 330 C.E.). He adopted the four-level theory of virtue and even added a higher type: the priestly virtues, through which the soul is united in ecstasy to the divine One. Iamblichus pushed Neoplatonic ethics further toward a cult in which were practiced divination, theurgy, and magic.

The Greek Neoplatonic school ends with Proclus Diadochus (410–485 C.E.). He was a serious philosopher: his *Elements of Theology* is a highly systematized version of the metaphysics of Plotinus. His more personal writings on *Providence and Fate, Problems concerning Providence,* and the *Subsistence of Evil* are now preserved in Latin versions made in the thirteenth century by the Christian translator William of Moerbeke. Proclus was interested in the theory of the soul's ascent; he distinguished in this process these three stages: the initial *love* of the beautiful, *true knowledge* of reality, and *faith* in the union with the One.[33]

As we shall see in our next chapter, Neoplatonic psychology and ethics were adapted to Christian use by both Greek and Latin writers. The first thousand years of philosophical teaching in Christian centers were characterized by a dominant preference for Neoplatonism.

Part Two

Patristic and Medieval Theories

Chapter IV

Patristic and Early Medieval Ethics

IN THIS CHAPTER we propose to treat the ethical position taken by key figures in the Christian tradition during the period from the first to the twelfth century C.E. This is actually about a thousand years, for the first Christian writings (apart from the New Testament) that could be called ethical in any philosophical sense, were produced toward the end of the second century. The first part of this millennium is termed the patristic period from the fact that the Fathers *(Patres)* of the Church lived and taught then. While the term is used with some vagueness, it is agreed by most authorities that a "Father" is marked by three special characteristics: he must be orthodox in his religious doctrine, he must be of considerable influence in his teaching and writing, and he must be noted for the personal holiness of his life. Men like St. John Damascene in the Greek Church and SS. Ambrose and Augustine among the Latin writers are universally recognized as Fathers.[1] Boethius, on the other hand, although a Christian and an outstanding writer, was never called a Father; he was not a member of the clergy. We shall examine, then, the views of these patristic and medieval Christian teachers to see what they contributed to the history of ethics. It is significant that none of these teachers knew Aristotle's *Nicomachean Ethics* (which became very influential from the thirteenth century onward). Their contemporaries in the Islamic and Jewish schools knew Aristotelian ethics long before the Christians did. We shall reserve for the next chapter our examination of these non-Christian schools of medieval ethics.

The relation between the sort of moral teaching found in the Bible and philosophical ethics is not understood in the same way by all present-day writers on the subject. To some scholars, morality that is based on belief in God's commands is not ethical theory at all.[2] To others, no ethics presuming to offer guidance for real living is possible without some reference to right and wrong as determined by God's Law or Will. As the outstanding contemporary Protestant theologian Emil Brunner puts it: "The Good consists in always doing what God wills at any particular moment."[3]

Without attempting to settle this metaethical problem, we will take it that a moral teaching based on a well-promulgated set of precepts backed by divine authority does involve an ethical position, provided it makes some effort to relate its views to recognized positions in moral philosophy. We do find such "theological approbative theories"[4] in the writings of Christians before the thirteenth century and feel that they have a place in a historical survey of ethics.

The earliest Christian moral writers made no complete break with ancient Jewish traditions in which it was claimed that God had conveyed directly to Moses ten general commandments to regulate human conduct. This "Decalogue" was known and accepted by Christians from the beginning. For them, as for the Jews, the reason why a man was obliged to honor his elders, or to avoid killing and stealing, was simply that God had so commanded. New Testament morality did not negate the precepts of the old Jewish law but rather suggested a greater emphasis on love as the inner motivation of the believer who wished to live righteously. The two Christian precepts of charity (Matthew 22:37–40, "Thou shalt love the Lord thy God" and "Thou shalt love thy neighbor as thyself") are usually understood as fulfillments of divine law (Romans 13:8) and not as cancellations of the traditional rules of the Old Testament. In the Sermon on the Mount it is clearly stated: "Do not think that I [Christ] have come to destroy the Law or the Prophets: I have not come to destroy, but to fulfill."[5]

It can hardly be denied that there was a certain tension in early Christian writings between a strictly *juridical* approach to moral problems and a contrary tendency to emphasize mercy, love, and good will. Although the latter is what is typical of the spirit of Christian morality, the Fathers and medieval writers on ethics all accepted a code of moral precepts as imposed by divine command. This sort of legal view of moral obligation is unlike anything in Greek or Roman philosophy. The closest approach to it is in the universal "law" of the Stoics, but that was not a set of precepts promulgated by a transcendental Deity.

Actually, the first speculation about ethical obligations and their relation to laws may have taken place among Christians who were neither Greeks nor Latins. We sometimes have a tendency to forget that the "Oriental" Church, in the Near East and in North Africa, had many learned men during the first Christian centuries. Quite recent studies have thrown light on the work of an early Syrian Christian, Bardaisan of Edessa (154–222), who faced the problem of reconciling classical philosophy with Christian doctrine.[6] His *Book of the Laws of Countries* admits that man's bodily activities are subject to external controls, and even to fate, but Bardaisan argues that man is internally free to choose right or wrong actions. Unlike some later Christian writers who tended to stress similarities in the laws of great nations (as evidence of their dependence on one natural law), Bardaisan found a certain support for moral freedom in the fact that laws in various countries differ and are easily changed. The full ethical significance of this early Christian thought in the Near East has not been properly studied as yet.

Greek Christian Writers on Moral Theory

Much the same admission would have to be made concerning our lack of knowledge of the beginnings of philosophy in the Greek Christian schools. We lack not only technical studies of the ethical thought of these people but also critical editions and good translations of their writings. There was, for instance, a Greek writer named Hippolytus whose precise dates are unknown but who was "probably a pupil of Irenaeus." This would place Hippolytus in the last half of the second century. He is thought to be the author of a treatise entitled *Philosophumena* in which much of classical Greek philosophy is appraised from the viewpoint of Christianity.[7] It contains an approving survey of Plato's ethics: the immortality and tripartite character of the human soul, the notion of rewards and punishments in a future life, the four virtues described in the *Republic,* and the notion (as suggested in the tale of Er) that our lives are only partly in the hands of fate and that we have some choice as to our destiny. This early Christian treatise also treats evil as a privation of goodness in a being where such goodness would be expected. The impressive feature of Hippolytus' thought is his unquestioning acceptance of the practical philosophy of Plato.

In the same period, a very active and productive school of Greek Christian thought was developing at Alexandria. This was a very cosmopolitan city: it had a famous library and outstanding Greek schools from the third century B.C.E. The first Alexandrian Christian writer to turn his attention to philosophy was Clement of Alexandria (ca. 150–215 C.E.). One of his writings, the *Miscellanies (Stromata),* offers many comparisons between pagan philosophy and Christian teachings. Clement was a noted classical scholar before his conversion to Christianity but he generally took the position that many of the same truths are found in philosophy and in religious revelation. He criticizes the Epicureans, however, as atheists and materialists. Such unfavorable appraisals of the school of Epicurus are common in early Christian writers. In the sixth book of the *Miscellanies* Clement develops a theory of practical wisdom *(phronēsis)* as a universal principle of beings and of the functions of the human soul. This appears to be an adaptation from the rationalism of Platonic ethics and the right reason theory of the Stoics. We should strive to live in such a way that we will become more and more like God (a rule also found in Hippolytus), even though, as Clement frankly admitted, we can know with certainty little or nothing about God's nature.[8] He does discuss certain moral problems concerning moderation in eating, drinking, and clothing but is little inclined to speculate about the philosophical basis for making ethical judgments. Perhaps Clement's greatest contribution was to have given a certain respectability to philosophy by virtue of his incorporation of some of its teachings in a widely read Christian work.

Another Alexandrian who produced Greek works with ethical content was Origen (185–254). His treatises *Against Celsus* and *On First Principles* contain some teachings similar to those of Plotinus; this is probably due to the fact that they studied under the same teacher, although Origen was at least twenty years older than Plotinus. Origen is less optimistic than Clement about the value of philosophy: it is alien to Christianity. In his psychology, Origen has some views that are generally considered unorthodox for a Christian and these teachings affect his moral theory. He is certain that each human soul is immortal but he speculates on the possibility that the soul may exist before union with its body, that it may sin in this pre-existence, and that it may be punished by being bound to a body in earthly existence.[9] This is a Christian version of something like the Plotinian descent and eventual ascent of the human soul. Man is free to go up or down: the soul "may either descend from the highest good to the lowest evil or be restored from the lowest evil to the highest good." Reason and free will are present in each soul and make it possible to control base tendencies and to live a good life. The test of what is good or bad action is found in the divine precepts (the Decalogue and certain New Testament injunctions to avoid anger, swearing, and to encourage the fainthearted and support the weak), which are to be literally understood and obeyed.[10] In the final outcome, all things will be restored to their source in God and there will no longer be any evil.

In less radical form, this theory of the ascent of the soul to its God is found in Gregory of Nyssa (335–ca. 394). He rejects the pre-existence of souls but admits the ultimate return of all things to God. Gregory's version of this psychic ascent entails one of the earliest accounts of Christian mysticism. He emphasizes the need for special divine assistance (grace) to enable man to rise to union with God.[11]

The most influential Christian exposition of this flight-of-the-soul ethics is also the most mysterious and historically baffling. At some time during the fifth century a group of five works in Greek come to be known in Christian learning; they were called the *Corpus Dionysiacum* (or *Areopagiticum*). Their writer is unknown but he is called Dionysius the Pseudo-Areopagite. He professed to have lived in apostolic times and to have witnessed certain New Testament events; in reality, these writings are obviously under the strong influence of Neoplatonic philosophy and contain literal passages from Proclus (fifth century). So, they could not have been written in the time of the apostles. These treatises are: *On the Celestial Hierarchy, On the Ecclesiastical Hierarchy, On the Divine Names, Mystical Theology,* and ten *Letters.* They were highly regarded in the Middle Ages—even though their message is obscure and their orthodoxy as Christian teachings is open to suspicion.

The fourth chapter of *On the Divine Names* is devoted to the meaning of "good" as applied to God, and it is in connection with this "name" that Dionysius reveals his predilection for Neoplatonic ethics. Here the problem of evil is raised and treated in terms of the Plotinian claim that evil is merely a privation of goodness.[12] This text is one of the two media (the other, of course, is Augustine) through which the privation theory of evil comes to thinkers of the thirteenth century. Angelic spirits and human souls are called evil, in this view, because of their "deficiency of good qualities and activities and in the failure and fall therefrom due to their own weakness."[13] The positive explanation of good human activity, according to the Pseudo-Dionysius, is given in terms of the soul rising to a personal union with God. In its yearning for the Beauty and Good of its Source, the soul goes through three typical motions: (1) a *circular* turning from the multiplicity of external things inward to itself; (2) a *spiral* movement of discursive and dialectical reasoning; and (3) a *straight forward* movement toward the simple unity of contemplative acts.[14] This theory is tersely and obscurely developed in the short treatise on *Mystical Theology*. Very influential on later moral theologians was a formula used by Pseudo-Dionysius to summarize his views on the good *(to agathon)*: "The good stems from a cause that is one and entire; but the evil comes from defects that are manifold and pertaining to various parts."[15] This is taken to apply to both physical and moral evil, and to mean that a good action must be approvable in every one of its circumstances, while an action becomes immoral if any one of its required circumstances is missing.[16]

Maximus of Scythopolis (580–662) expanded and helped to popularize these views of Pseudo-Dionysius. His treatise on *Ambiguities (Patrologia Graeca 91, 1072–1085)* teaches that man rejoins God through knowing the good and feeling an ecstatic love of the divine Beauty. This terminates in a phase of divinization *(theōsis)* of all things. Man and the universe return to the unity of their divine Ideas. At the end, God will be All in All.[17]

The last Greek writer whom we will consider in this period is John Damascene (ca. 675–749). His large work, *The Source of Knowledge*, has as its third part a section on the basic truths of Christianity that was put into Latin in the twelfth century by Burgundio of Pisa under the title *De fide orthodoxa (On the True Faith)*. In this Latin form, it was very influential in the thirteenth century and much quoted in the

various *Summas* of theology. John Damascene introduces us to a teaching that is different from the Neo-
platonic-Christian flight-of-the-soul theories. There is
an analysis of the powers and functions of man which
Damascene takes from a treatise by the Greek
Bishop Nemesius, *On the Nature of Man* (written ca.
400 C.E.), who in turn adapted his theory from the
pre-Christian teaching of Poseidonius of Apameia.
The following passage shows how John Damascene
understood the moral powers of man; it is translated
directly from Burgundio's Latin version.

We should note that our soul has twofold powers
(virtutes, dynameis), some cognitive, others vital *(zot-
icas)*. Now the cognitive ones are: understanding,
mind, opinion, imagination and sense. The vital or
appetitive powers are counsel [*consilium*, a mistransla-
tion of *boulēsis*, which means volition] and choice
(electio, proairesis). It should also be noted that there
is naturally present in the soul an appetitive power
which is according to nature, and it is directed to
all objects which are associated with nature; it is
called will *(voluntas, thelesis)*. For substance inclines
(appetit) to be, to live, and to be moved, in accord
with sense perception and understanding, craving
its own natural or complete being. Therefore they
describe this natural willing *(thelēma)* in this way:
willing, that is the *voluntas,* is a rational, vital appetite, based on natural tendencies only. The power of
will *(thelēsis),* that is *voluntas,* is itself natural, vital and

subject to reason, an appetite for all the components of nature, a simple power *(virtus)*. There is another appetite for other things and it is not rational, nor is it called will *(voluntas, thelēsis)*. Now volition *(boulēsis)* is in every way natural; thelēsis is the will, the natural and rational appetite for any sort of thing. There is present in the soul of man a power of rational appetition. Since it is naturally moved, this rational appetite for any object is called *boulēsis* [spelled in Burgundio's Latin, *bulisis*], that is will. Now boulesis, that is will, is a rational appetite and desire for any object. It is called *boulēsis,* that is will *(voluntas),* both in regard to objects that are in our power and objects that are not; that is, in regard to possible and impossible objectives.[18]

In this halting and none too clear analysis we have the beginnings of a special moral psychology in which the notion of natural (and so, physically necessary) volition of the good is distinguished from a deliberated, rationally governed (and so, free) movement of the human will. Under the influence of this text, Thomas Aquinas and some other thirteenth-century thinkers taught that there are two kinds of human volition: *voluntas ut ratio,* which is free; and *voluntas ut natura,* which is not free.[19] Moreover, this text from John Damascene introduces the claim that there is more to appetition in man than rational willing. Sensory appetition includes two powers: concupiscible appetite (whose movements are simple desires or aversions in regard to individual things perceived in sensation) and irascible appetite (whose movements are efforts to evade or attack dangerous or difficult aspects of sense objects). This teaching influenced the moral psychology of Aquinas and other writers in the Scholastic tradition so that they adopted a three-appetite view of human activity: will, and irascible and concupiscible appetites.[20]

Latin Writers on Moral Theory

In the period before the thirteenth century, the Western or Latin section of the Christian Church produced a good many writers who touched on fundamental questions of ethics. Of the Latin Fathers, Ambrose and Augustine are the most prominent in this field. Some of their ethical views are still under discussion in the twentieth century. Boethius, as we shall see, had a good deal to say about the moral life in his *Consola·tion of Philosophy*. Erigena and Anselm developed quite different versions of Christian Platonic ethics in the ninth and eleventh centuries respectively. Peter Abelard, however, best typifies the tensions between the subjective demands of personal conscience and the objective requirements of a moral law that transcends human nature. We shall take a look at the more significant ethical theories of key figures in this Latin tradition.

One of the earliest Christian moralists was a North African, Tertullian, who lived from about 160 to 240.

Frequently associated with his name is the phrase "credo quia absurdum" ("I believe because it is absurd"), but it is difficult to decide just what he meant. Quite possibly he was simply saying that faith has its mysteries which lie beyond the scope of reason.[21] In his treatise *On the Soul* (chapter 19), Tertullian suggested that the human soul is of a bodily nature and that the souls of children come from the father's semen. In spite of this apparently materialistic view of man's spirit (few Christian writers have shared it), Tertullian was a strong advocate of personal freedom and did much to make precise the meaning of person.[22] In his moral teaching, Tertullian advocated a very rigid and strict regulation of all aspects of Christian living. Christianity provides a detailed code of conduct: the reward for complete obedience is eternal happiness with God, the punishment for disobedience is eternal suffering. As one patristic scholar sums up Tertullian's legalism: "The God whom he cherished is the inflexible and jealous Judge Who has established *timor* (fear) as the basis for man's salvation."[23]

Less extreme is the position of another African Christian, Lactantius (ca. 250–330), who also wrote in Latin. In his *Divine Institutes,* Lactantius took the position that pagan philosophy has no truth in it (Book III is entitled *De falsa sapientia).* The sixth book in this treatise presents the basic principles of Christian morality and treats these directives as the immediate commands of God. This is a good example of a moderate type of theological approbative ethics in the early Church. While he is little inclined to theorize about ethical problems, Lactantius recognizes the importance of education in practical wisdom.[24]

It is usual to mention Ambrose, Bishop of Milan (340–397), as a practical-minded moralist. His treatise *On the Functions of the Clergy* is indeed a practical application of Cicero's *De officiis* to the Christian setting. In this sense, Ambrose has influenced Christian moral theology.[25] Quite another aspect of his work in philosophy has been discovered recently in connection with research into the background of Augustine's thought. Briefly, Ambrose appears to have had more than a passing interest in Neoplatonic philosophy. The group of sermons gathered under the title *De Isaac et anima* show that he adopted the Plotinian view that evil is nothing positive, but a privation of good, and that he was under the same influence in his treatment of virtues and vices. Furthermore, Ambrose pictured the good life as a flight of the soul from the world to God.[26] He was, then, a medium for the transmission of Greek philosophical ideas to the early Latin Church.

The Latin Father of the Church who has the most completely developed moral theory is Augustine of Hippo (354–430). He had something to say on most of the problems that later ethicians have studied. Augustine's ethical views are still under discussion in twentieth-century ethics.[27] No one work contains his moral teaching. We will use several of the early dialogues, the *Confessions, City of God, On the Trinity, Enchiridion,* and other writings for our exposition.[28]

That all men desire and strive for happiness *(beatitudo),* Augustine did not doubt. His ethical position is as eudaimonistic as any in classical Greek thought. He did not know Aristotle's *Nicomachean Ethics* (except through reports in Latin writers such as Cicero) and his acquaintance with the dialogues of Plato was very limited. He seems to have read parts of the *Enneads* and some of the short moral works of Porphyry. Platonism (under which he included the thought of Plotinus) appeared to Augustine to be the best of the pagan philosophies *(City of God,* VII, chapters 4–7). In his day, however, the popular philosophies were Epicureanism and Stoicism. They were quite wrong in their ethics, Augustine felt. Interestingly enough, Augustine sums up the Epicurean ultimate object of desire as "pleasure of the body," and the Stoic ideal as "steadfastness of spirit."[29] His own view is that man's final felicity cannot consist in some mere perfection of the human person (such as virtue or knowledge) but rather in a special sort of union, after the death of the body, with God.[30]

The really important part of man, as Augustine sees it, is the soul *(anima, animus, spiritus).* Man is a soul using a body as instrument *("anima utens corpore" De moribus ecclesiae,* I, 27, 52). As knowing, this soul is called mind *(mens);* as keeping all objects within it, the same soul is memory *(memoria);* and as the source of any psychic action through the body or apart from it, the soul is called will *(voluntas).* This trinitarian psychology is expounded in Books IX to XIV of the treatise *On the Trinity.*[31] Man's soul is able to direct its attention to various objectives by an act of volitional turning *(versio).* One may turn to concentrate on bodies (all of which are inferior to soul) and this is a perversion. It is not that Augustine considered bodily things evil; they were made by God and are good things *(De natura boni,* 1); rather, he was convinced that the soul as the seat of life, consciousness, and all human effort is obviously better than any inanimate thing.[32] So, the soul only degrades itself by concentrating on corporeal values. When the soul turns in upon itself, it finds a better nature but still something imperfect and subject to temporal changes. Introspection reveals the grandeur of the human spirit, of course (see the famous description of memory, *Confessions,* X, 8–26), but further consideration indicates the inferiority of the soul to God. In looking to God, man's soul finds the source of all reality and goodness.

God will enlighten the minds of men who turn to Him and seek His help. Divine illumination is available to all men, to show them the initial truths of knowing, existing, and acting. God's "Light" is not merely a cognitive principle but also a source of moral information and guidance. Our first notions of equality, order, right thinking *(prudentia),* moderation *(temperantia),* strength of character *(fortitudo)*, justice *(recititudo, justitia)*, and other such ethical ideals, come to us through a personal intuition which is made possible by the divine light.[33] The following passage shows how Augustine presented this intuition of the eternal standards *(rationes aeternae)* of ethical judgment:

> So also among the objects of the understanding, there are some that are seen in the soul itself: for example, the virtues (to which the vices are opposed), either virtues which will endure, such as piety, or virtues that are useful for this life and not destined to remain in the next, as faith, by which we believe what we do not see, and hope, by which we await with patience the life that shall be, and patience itself, by which we bear every adversity until we arrive at the goal of our desires. These virtues, of course, and other similar ones, which are quite necessary for us now in living out our exile, will have no place in the blessed life [in Heaven], for the attainment of which they are necessary. And yet even they are seen with the understanding ... distinct from these objects is the light by which the soul is illumined, in order that it may see and truly understand everything, either in itself or in the light. For the light is God himself. ...[34]

Another way that Augustine has of describing the object of moral illumination puts it in terms of eternal law. As he says in his early dialogue *On Order* (II, 8, 25): "This teaching *(disciplina)* is the very law of God, which ever abiding fixed and unshaken with Him, is transcribed, so to speak, on the souls of the wise, so that they know that they live a better and more sublime life in proportion as they contemplate it more perfectly with their understanding and observe it more perfectly in their manner of living." This eternal law is both the reason and the will of God: *lex est ratio divina et voluntas Dei (Contra Faustum,* XII, 27). It is immutable and universal. In pre-Mosaic times, the eternal law was naturally known through man's reason (and so is occasionally called *lex naturalis* by Augustine) and it was delivered in part, in written form, to Moses: it is said to be "impressed on our minds" or "written in our hearts." Man's conscience *(conscientia)* thus becomes immediately aware of rules such as: Do not do to others what you would not have them do to you *(Enarrationes in Psalmos,* Ps. 57, 1). Many other rules of this kind are naturally known.[35]

Thus far, the ethics of Augustine appears to be a legalistic version of Christian morality. His thought has, however, another important ethical dimension. Despite his insistence on obedience to God's law, Augustine takes second place to no ethical writer in his insistence on personal freedom, the importance of good will, and the need of proper internal motivation. In mature life he wrote a famous treatise *On the Spirit and the Letter (De spiritu et littera,* 412 C.E.) to explain that a person must be moved by the love of God before he can get any credit for acting in conformity with moral law. As he now expresses his view: "If this commandment is kept from fear of punishment and not from love of righteousness, it is servilely kept, not freely, and therefore is not kept at all. For no fruit is good which does not grow from the root of charity" *(De spiritu et littera,* 14, 26). Fear of punishment is not an adequate motive, even for the negative avoidance of immorality *(Epistola* 145, 3, 4). In another letter *(Epistola* 155, 4, 13) Augustine makes the love of God the principle of good living:

In this life, although there is no virtue save that of loving what ought to be loved, prudence lies in choosing it; fortitude in not being turned from it by any troubles; to be allured from it by no seductions is temperance, and by no pride is justice. But what ought we to choose as the object of our principal love but that which we find to be better than anything else? This object is God; and to set anything above or even equal to Him is to show that we do not know how to love ourselves. For our good becomes the greater the more we approach Him than whom there is nothing better.

It is in terms of the foregoing that one should understand the much-quoted Augustinian text: "Love, and do what you will" *(dilige, et quod vis fac).* Augustine did not mean that a good person could break all the laws of God, provided such a person felt a great love for something or other! What he did mean was that a man who truly loves God is of such good will, so well motivated, that he will almost automatically act in full accord with all the precepts of divine and moral law. Such perfection of will and character comes to a man through the gift of divine grace only. The love that motivates all good moral actions is the theological virtue of charity.[37]

In spite of the intensely religious coloring of this teaching, Augustine did think of his wisdom as an ethics. As he formally outlined the matter, in the eighth book of the *City of God,* the third and last part of philosophy is moral, what the Greeks call *ethica* ("quam Graeco vocabulo dicunt *ethiken*"). He proceeds to explain how he understands the field of ethics:[38]

> It deals with the supreme good, by reference to which all our actions are directed. It is the good we seek for itself and not because of something else and, once it is attained, we seek nothing further to make us happy. This, in fact, is why we call it our end, because other things are desired on account of this *summum bonum,* while it is desired purely for itself.

Augustine's ethics is a theocentric eudaimonism: man's ultimate well-being consists in the possession of God *(De moribus ecclesiae,* I, 6, 10). Many people consider it the greatest example of Christian ethics.[39]

Another version of early Christian ethics is found in the next century in the writings of the Roman senator Anicius Manlius Torquatus Severinus Boethius (ca. 470–525). His best-known work is the *Consolation of Philosophy.* Some shorter theological treatises are also sources for his views in ethics. Boethius' psychology is similar to Augustine's but he knew more about Greek philosophy than did Augustine. In particular, Boethius would seem to be the first Latin scholar in the Christian Church who was well acquainted with the *Nicomachean Ethics.* Despite his knowledge of Aristotle, Boethius preferred the teaching of Plato on many problems and was also favorably impressed by many features in the practical philosophy of the Stoics. At the end of the nineteenth century, it was fashionable among historians of philosophy to question the Christianity of this author: today, no serious scholar doubts that he was a Christian.

There are, for Boethius, four levels of cognition: the lowest is sense, which perceives the shapes and qualities of things clothed in matter; the next level is imagination, which views bodily forms without their matter; the third is reason *(ratio),* which penetrates to the universal nature that may be present in many individuals (this is the cognitive power that is distinctive of men living on earth); and the highest power is intelligence, which intuits perfect "forms" existing apart from matter *(intellectibilia)*: this is a divine capacity, men share in it only occasionally, when they get flashes of understanding. Theology is a divine science that cultivates the highest knowledge of God and divine properties.[40] At the beginning of a short treatise on metaphysics which came to be called *De Hedomadibus* in the Middle Ages, Boethius listed nine propositions which he took as axiomatic to the rest of his argument.[41] The first described a "common conception" as a statement which one would approve as soon as it is heard. These are of two types: some, such as the geometric axiom of equality, are understandable to all men; other propositions, such as "incorporeals cannot occupy space," are grasped only by the learned. A second type, such as "equals added to equals result in equals," is knowable to all men. This theory of initial axioms and definitions in philosophy, plus the theory of intuitive intelligence, combine to influence the later Scholastic teaching on first principles of speculative and practical knowledge (including ethics). Taken together with a deductivist emphasis on discursive reasoning (which stems from Boethius' textbooks on syllogistic logic), this Boethian tradition of demonstrative science is the source of much of the system-building that characterized Christian moral philosophy and theology in the later Middle Ages.[42]

Quite a different approach to ethics is suggested in the actual metaphysics of the treatise *De Hebdomadibus*. This is a thoroughly Platonic discussion of how

the many inferior instances of good are good by participation in One, Highest Good. Such metaphysical goodness is not identical with the ethical meaning of good.
At the end of this treatise we are told that "all things
are good but all things are not just." Justice is a species
of activity and there are acts that are not just.[43]

Books III and IV of the *Consolation of Philosophy* give
further evidence of how Boethius attempted to build
a practical philosophy of life by using elements of
Platonism, Aristotelianism, and Stoicism within the
context of a Christian morality. Like the Greeks,
Boethius saw men as striving for the attainment of
ultimate well-being *(beatitudo)*. Different men have
thought that happiness is dependent on obtaining
bodily goods (strength, health, beauty), or goods of
the spirit (knowledge, virtue), or even goods of social
intercourse (fame, political power, good reputation).
Boethius argues that all these ends are imperfect and
not lasting: there must be some Perfect Good which
is the objective terminus of these human aspirations
for happiness. Such reasoning requires one to see that
God exists as the perfect and fullest good.[44] This way
of arguing to the conclusion that God is the objective
goal of all moral striving becomes an important element in the teleological ethics of later Scholasticism.

There are, of course, numerous writings on detailed
questions of practical morality in the centuries
immediately following Boethius. Many of these are
unedited and unstudied. Comparatively unknown, for

instance, is the Bishop of Braga, Martin of Dumio (ca. 515–580). His works are under titles such as *Formula for an Honest Life, The Four Virtues, How to Put Down Pride,* and so on. In general, Martin adopted Seneca's teaching on the leading moral virtues and applied it to Christian living. Much the same could be said of the moral content of encyclopedic writers such as Gregory the Great (540–604) and Isidore of Seville (ca. 570–630). They were not as dependent on pagan sources as Martin, but their ethical views result from a combination of classical humanism with a fundamentally Christian view of life. Gregory's *Moral Exposition of the Book of Job* is much quoted later but it is an exaggeration to call it the classical *Grundwerk* from which medieval ethics sprang.[45]

In the ninth century, John Scottus Erigena (ca. 810–877) put into a Latin work the whole Neoplatonic ethics of the flight of the soul to its Source. His *De divisione naturae* is a vast metaphysical structure purporting to explain how all things, including men, come forth from the one cause and eventually return to this divine Principle. Plotinian emanationism is thus combined in a startling way with Christian creationism. All reality is called "nature" *(natura)*: God as Source is *natura creans sed increata;* the divine Ideas constitute *natura creans et creata;* the universe and men make up *natura increans sed creata;* and finally God as End is *Natura increans et increata*. A human being is initially "a certain intellectual idea formed eternally in the divine mind."[47] At the end of his life on earth each man undergoes another "division" of his nature: the soul divides from the body, and the body disintegrates into its material components. However, in a third step man's body is reunited with his soul and is progressively spiritualized; in a fourth step the spiritualized man rejoins his archetypal Idea in God; and in a final stage of the return all the world will go back to its Source.[48] Man is free to adapt his will to this return, and indeed it is his duty as a Christian to develop his higher capacities so that his whole being is transmuted into pure thought. Divine grace is needed to enable man to rise to this higher state of existence. As Erigena explains in the fifth book *On the Division of Nature,* the man who lives a morally good life not only reunites with God, as all men eventually do, his ultimate condition is a becoming like God *(deifactio).* This deification is granted only to the good.

After Erigena there is no Latin writer on morality of comparable stature until we come to St. Anselm in the eleventh century. Anselm of Canterbury (1033–1109) was an Italian who was trained in a Benedictine monastery in France and became one of the most renowned bishops of the English see of Canterbury. His importance in the history of ethics lies in his emphasis on the personal attitude of the moral agent as the determinant of moral good or evil. One historian goes so far as to say that, with Anselm, "morality is defined independently of any consideration of utility and, generally speaking, of any consideration of ultimate end."[49] This is the first known instance of a medieval ethician who broke away from the eudaimonism of Plato, Aristotle, and the Stoics.

Of course, St. Anselm is very much indebted to Augustine, particularly in his moral psychology. The will is the most important aspect of the soul. Man's will is subject to two possible dispositions *(affectiones)* prior to any moral activity. By one of these predispositions, the *affectio ad commodum,* every man is subjectively inclined to seek various goods that are appropriate to his ordinary state of existence. This inclines him to desire to build a home and cultivate his fields, for instance. The second of these dispositions, the *affectio justitiae,* enables some men to incline volitionally toward a better than natural good. This is the justification of the will by divine grace.[50] To see what this "higher justice" means to Anselm we must look briefly at his theory of truth. In the *Dialogue on Truth* he described many instances of the true *(verum)*: true statements, true opinions, true volitions, true actions, true sense perceptions, true things. Like a good Platonist, Anselm argued that these many instances are true because there is one supreme Truth in which they all share. To be true, then, is to be right *(rectus)* in relation to some immutable standard of Tightness *(rectitudo).* The general definition of truth *(veritas)* is: "rightness perceptible to the mind alone."[51]

Applying this to the problem of morality, Anselm decided that justice is rightness of will that is preserved for its own sake.[52] In other words, a person is just, not so much because of *what* he wills as because of the *reason why (propter quod)* he wills it. Anselm is here broaching the important theme of ethical motivation: he is suggesting that a moral agent is *right,* not because his action achieves a certain result but because of a certain quality of the initial attitude, or volitional inclination, of the person. Since he insists that rectitude must be willed for its own sake alone (true freedom is defined as "the power of preserving rectitude of will, for the sake of rectitude itself"), Anselm is here anticipating something of Kant's theory of the pure and good will.[53] Of course, Anselmian moral rectitude is far from mere subjective rightness; he is not an ethical formalist; one's will is right by conforming with an objective Rightness—which is God.

One of the few writers in the early Middle Ages to use the term "ethics" was Peter Abelard (1079–1142). His treatise *Ethica seu liber dictus scito teipsum* is a landmark in ethical discussions in the Middle Ages. As an opponent of the usual (in his time) realistic approach to universals, Abelard could not maintain that a concrete instance of good *(bonum)* is such by virtue of participation in an existing essence of universal goodness *(bonitas)*. Somewhat under the influence of Anselm, he maintains that sin consists in consent *(consensus)* to what is improper. Since the improper is what is opposed to the laws of God, the consent to sin is equivalent to contempt for God. He proceeds to argue forcefully that what is morally good or bad is not the execution of a given action but the prior disposition of the agent's will. Using an example much favored in present-day situationism, Abelard says: "The sin, then, consists not in desiring a woman, but in consent to the desire." [54]

Abelard had no direct knowledge of the *Nicomachean Ethics* and was thus unable to use Aristotle's analysis of voluntariness. In the key third chapter of his *Ethics* Abelard hesitated to say whether sin necessarily involves an act of willing or not. He discussed several examples of things done "against one's will" and yet seeming to involve responsibility, guilt, and sin. He did much to highlight the important difference between fault *(culpa)* and guilt *(poena)* but his terminology and thought on such points fluctuated. In some chapters the *Ethics* speaks of intention *(intentio)* as the focal point of moral good and evil: in this usage "intention" means the same as consent. Throughout the work he insists that the doing or omitting of an action adds nothing to the moral value of the consent or intention.

Abelard's ethics is not a pure subjectivism: a man's intention must be right, and this means in objective conformity with God's laws. He knows that some people have suggested that an intention is right "when anyone believes that he acts well." [55] He firmly insists that the only good intention is one that actually pleases God. However, he did not indicate how ordinary people can know what does please God, objectively.[56]

The view that morality is a matter of some quality of rightness within the soul of each person (what modern writers would call "intrinsic morality") was rather general in the twelfth century. Even a great critic of the orthodoxy of Abelard's theology, like Bernard of Clairvaux (1090–1153), was in full agreement with the idea that consent to the good is what enables a person to merit an eternal reward in Heaven.[57] St. Bernard was not an ethical theorist: more than any other medieval moralist he simply insisted on the importance of loving God with as pure and exalted motives as are possible. This is the theme of his treatise *On the Necessity of Loving God (De diligendo Deo)*. Of course, this is not moral subjectivism: there is a suprahuman standard to which right willing must conform; this norm is eternal law. Bernard is not juridical-minded, but he is far from saying that goodness is simply having a good feeling. He condemns the man who values merely self-will: "each one made a universal and eternal law."[58] This is a perversion of the desire to imitate God.

During the twelfth century, ethics or moral philosophy came to take an accepted place among the disciplines taught in many Christian schools. Many anthologies *(florilegia)* and eclectic treatises were produced to serve as texts in the training of boys in the monastery schools and in other scholastic centers. Most of these works are anonymous. There is, for instance, the *Teachings of the Moral Philosophers (Moralium dogma philosophorum)*, which has been attributed to William of Conches, Gauthier of Chatillon, and others. There is the *Moral Philosophy of the Good-in-itself and the Useful Good (Moralis Philosophia de honesto et utili)* printed among the works of Hildebert of Tours but of uncertain authorship. And there is the *Oxford Collection of Moral Writings (Florilegium Morale Oxoniense),* only recently edited. What these and other works of this kind have in common is a desire to cull what is best from the classic Greek and Roman moral writers and to adapt these exemplary readings to the requirements of Christian life. This movement is sometimes called "Christian Socratism." The ancient authors who are especially prized are Plato, Cicero, Seneca, and certain minor writers, such as Macrobius and Andronicus. Ethically, these twelfth-century collections represent a spiritually oriented version of self-realization. Instead of emphasizing moral obligation by law, they advise the improvement of moral character by the cultivation of the theological (faith, hope, charity) and the cardinal (prudence, temperance, fortitude, and justice) virtues. These virtues are subdivided into many "parts" and the result is a lengthy listing and description of many good habits (virtues), often accompanied by criticisms of the opposed bad habits (vices).[59]

Certain groups with heterodox religious views appeared on the scene in the twelfth century and may have had some negative influence on the central current of medieval Christian ethics. One such movement was that of the Cathari. In southern France, they had a center in a town called Albi and came to be known as Albigensians. In Italy, two groups of Cathari were found in this century: the *Albanenses* in the Bergamo-Verona area, and the *Concorenses (Garatenses)* in the region of Concorezzo. Basically, Catharism was a revival of Manichaeism, a religious teaching that there are two ultimate Principles: one is the source of all good things and events, the other is the source of all evil. Usually these were regarded as coeternal, and equally powerful, gods. In twelfth-century Catharism the basic dualism of Mani was adapted to several different views of the Christian life. Two effects of this movement may be observed in the ethics of the period. First of all, most of the Cathari embraced a very rigorous and puritanical attitude toward moral behavior. They regarded all sexual activity as morally evil, for instance, and required their perfect believers to abstain from procreation, even in marriage. Extreme asceticism was professed. On the other hand, since the original Manichaeism (of Persian origin, Mani lived in the third century C.E.) held that evil was as real and positive as good, and that there are two wills in every man (one evil and one good), many later followers took it that immorality was inevitable. One could disclaim responsibility for an evil action by saying that it stemmed from his bad will and not from the good will, with which latter he would identify.[60]

Another religious movement with ethical overtones originated in the views of Joachim of Flora (1145–1202), a Cistercian abbot in northern Italy. He advocated a return to the simplicity and rigor of the early years of Christianity. It is probable that he felt that all academic or theoretical ethics is pagan nonsense, so Joachim would represent an odd type of ethical skeptic, critical of such philosophical activity as not pertinent to the salvation of one's soul.[61] His theological and scriptural writings suggest an apocalyptic view of history, which was pushed to an extreme in a treatise entitled the *Eternal Gospel*, written in 1254 by Gerardus de Borgo San Domino. Among many other things, this Joachimist treatise advocated a complete reform of the moral conduct of Christians and stressed a code of behavior so ascetic that it outdid the Stoic ideal of apathy. The results of this work were felt in the lives of religious communities (particularly the Franciscans) in the thirteenth century. It did not produce a formal ethics, but Joachimism was partly responsible for an extreme otherworldly attitude in some varieties of late medieval ethics.

It is obvious that much of the ethical speculation in these Christian writings before the thirteenth century is derivative from the seminal notions to be found in the Bible and in the Platonic and Stoic schools of Greek ethics. However, two important new emphases were brought into the subject during this period. First of all, the view that God's will, or the eternal law, is the ultimate and absolute norm of all ethical judgments now comes to the fore in these patristic and medieval moralists. This norm is equally stressed, as we shall see in the next chapter, by the theistic ethicians in the medieval Jewish and Moslem traditions. Until well after the time of Kant, in the eighteenth century, this conviction that there is a divine source of absolute ethical obligation remained almost unchallenged in the history of ethics.

In the second place, the ethical concept of motivation, of personal attitude toward external events in which one is involved, became a focal point for moral discussions during this period of medieval ethics. As we have seen, men like Augustine, Anselm, and Abelard are quite modern in their ethical claims that what is morally significant is not so much the material character of one's action but rather the inner motivation of the person involved. Perhaps more than we usually realize, this new emphasis is due to the great importance that the medieval Christian attached to the human person as a creature of God. The Augustinian theme of the supreme moral significance of the love of God is but another way of saying this. It typifies Christian ethics up to the thirteenth century— and well beyond it, of course.

Chapter V

Medieval Jewish and Moslem Ethics

THE FIRST FIFTEEN centuries after Christ produced other types of ethics than those taught in the Christian schools. We will examine in this chapter some of the ethical views of scholars associated with two other religions that flourished during the Middle Ages: Judaism and Mohammedanism. Both cultures have been somewhat neglected in general histories of ethics and, indeed, in the usual histories of medieval philosophy. Both, at times, gave a prominent place to ethical thinking and exerted a strong influence on the ethics of Western civilization.

Jewish Ethics in the Middle Ages

Judaism is more a way of life than a special theology or religious creed. There have not been as many philosophers in the Jewish tradition as one might expect. We have already seen the role played by Philo Judaeus in the development of Hellenistic ethics. He felt that he could find many parallels between the wisdom of the Old Testament and the thought of the Greek philosophers. But Philo is the only prominent Jewish philosopher before the medieval period.

While it is quite true that the Bible is not a technical philosophical work it does contain seeds of practical wisdom that continued to grow during the centuries which we are considering. Yahweh orders all things "in measure, number, and weight." Yet the God of the ancient Jews was also a loving deity: "But thou sparest all, because they are thine, O Lord, who lovest souls."[1] He is above all a stern dispenser of justice. His commands are absolute and inescapable. The most famous listing of these divine obligations is found in the Ten Commandments, which are found in the books of Exodus and Deuteronomy. Since these precepts are discussed and used as illustrations by many later writers on ethics, we give the Decalogue in full, here:

> You shall have no gods except me.
>
> You shall not make yourself a carved image or any likeness of anything in heaven or on earth

beneath or in the waters under the earth; you shall not bow down to them or serve them. For I, Yahweh your God, am a jealous God and I punish the father's fault in the sons, the grandsons, and the great-grandsons of those who hate me; but I show kindness to thousands of those who love me and keep my commandments.

You shall not utter the name of Yahweh your God to misuse it, for Yahweh will not leave unpunished the man who utters his name to misuse it.

Remember the sabbath day and keep it holy. For six days you shall labour and do all your work, but the seventh day is a sabbath for Yahweh your God. You shall do no work that day, neither you nor your son nor your daughter nor your servants, men or women, nor your animals nor the stranger who lives with you. For in six days Yahweh made the heavens and the earth and the sea and all that these hold, but on the seventh day he rested; that is why Yahweh has blessed the sabbath day and made it sacred.

Honour your father and your mother so that you may have a long life in the land that Yahweh your God has given to you.

You shall not kill.

You shall not commit adultery.

You shall not steal.

You shall not bear false witness against your neighbour.

You shall not covet your neighbour's house. You shall not covet your neighbour's wife, or his servant, man or woman, or his ox, or his donkey, or anything that is his.[2]

In the second and third of these precepts, Yahweh speaks of himself as a strict Judge who will punish all disobediences. From this attitude arises another aspect of Old Testament morality, the so-called *lex talionis,* which required that the punishment of an injury to another be equal and of like character. It is still quoted in discussions of the morality of capital and other forms of legal punishment: "And he that killeth any man shall surely be put to death . . . as he hath done, so shall it be done to him; breach for breach, eye for eye, tooth for tooth."[3] Balancing this rigid view are Biblical approximations of the golden rule. Thus, Proverbs 24:29 reads, "Say not, I will do to him as he hath done to me"; and Tobit 4:15 (16) states, "Do that to no man which thou hatest."[4]

Judaism has often been accused of excessive legalism. Early rabbinical works distinguished 613 commandments in the law.[5] Yet this juridical tendency was tempered by the spirit of love and forbearance. The

"Great Commandment" enjoining love of God and neighbor is in the Old Testament. Deuteronomy 6:5 says, "Thou shalt love the Lord thy God with all thy heart, and with all thy soul, and with all thy might." Leviticus 19:18 adds, "Thou shalt love thy neighbor as thyself." It has recently been argued that Judaism stresses the love of man for God (and is more interested in ethics and human conduct) while Christianity emphasizes the love of God for man (and thus tends to be more theological).[6] According to this view, the two great themes in ancient Jewish ethics are "holiness" *(kadosh),* expressing both ontological and moral transcendence, and "glory" *(kavod),* expressing the contrary immanence of God in the lives of men, the manifestation of the divine in history.

One of the first medieval Jews to touch on formal problems of ethics was Saadia ben Joseph al-Fayyumi (882–942)[7] who wrote a *Book of Doctrines and Beliefs* at Baghdad in the year 933. His work has much the same purpose as Maimonides' later and better-known *Guide for the Perplexed.* Saadia offers an explanation of the relation between reason and faith, for the enlightenment of educated Jews who may be puzzled by alleged contradictions between what scientists and philosophers say and the teachings of the religious Law.[8] Some men have doubts because of defects in their sense observation of the facts of a problem; others suffer deficiencies in reasoning from sense data, either because they do not understand the method of reasoning or because they are hasty or neglectful in demonstrating their conclusions. Saadia's theory of knowledge and moral psychology are worked out in terms of the attempt to remove such sources of doubt.

He distinguishes two kinds of laws governing human conduct: laws of reason and laws of revelation.[9] He was convinced that mankind *could* have reasoned to a workable code of moral precepts, if divine revelation had not conveyed such a guide to men. However, Saadia thinks that revelation made it possible for men to know their obligations more immediately and more accurately than if they had been left to use unaided reason. Reason "dictates" four points that summarize the moral law: (1) one must return the kindness of every benefactor in some fitting manner; (2) the wise man will refuse to be treated with contempt and, with greater reason, a wise God will expect to be treated with respect; (3) no one should trespass on the rights of another by any sort of aggression; and (4) it is reasonable to employ a workman and to pay him, simply so that he may earn something. In retrospect, these rules of reason rather obviously apply to man's relations to God as well as to his fellow men. Saadia proceeds to list various precepts imposed by God on men (to be just, truthful, equitable, and impartial; to avoid homicide, adultery, theft, tale-bearing, and trickery in dealing with others). Moreover, "the Believer should love his neighbor as he loves himself." These are revealed rules, but "in regard to all the things which He commands us to do, He has implanted approval of them in our Reason."[10] He would appear to say that, given enough experience of life and adequate education of the rational powers, every man may "see" his duty. It is a version of deontologistic ethical intuitionism, with God's law to guarantee it from on high.

Saadia knows about hedonism, that some people argue that the good is that which causes pleasure. Such a view, he claims, ends in manifest contradiction: acts, such as rape, which bring pleasure to one person may be quite painful to another. "But every theory which involves a self-contradiction is invalid." The revelation and moral guidance which come through the prophets are needed, however, to ensure a certain perfection in moral behavior. Though man is the "center of the universe," he must recognize that the Biblical law is eternal and can never be abrogated.[11] Saadia says that reason confirms his Jewish beliefs but does not replace them.

One of the most important ethical treatises in the eleventh-century Jewish tradition was the *Fountain of Life*. Until about the mid-nineteenth century, the author of this *Fons Vitae,* ibn-Gabirol, whom Latin scholars of the Middle Ages called Avicebrón, was not known to be a Jew. Ibn-Gabirol (ca. 1021–1058) wrote in Arabic (as did most medieval Jewish philosophers) and was evidently a theist, so many readers felt that he might be a Christian, possibly Syrian. However, through the research of Solomon Munk we now know that the famous and long treatise called *Fons Vitae (Fountain of Life)* in Latin was written by an eleventh-century Jew. It is under the strong influence of Neoplatonic emanationism. All things in the universe, including men and angels, are compounds of matter and forms. God is the Creator but works through Universal Will which efficiently produces lower things by a progressive descent of forms. Man is a microcosm in which all features of the subhuman world are formally contained.[12] As in any version of Neoplatonism, the good life consists in a process of self-perfecting within each man, whereby he renders himself less corporeal and more fitted for union with the higher forms. This is not treated at any length by ibn-Gabirol but it is clear that education, intellectual improvement, and good will are requisite to the movement back to the source of all. Eventually, the good man returns not to God (who is so transcendent that He is inaccessible) but to the Universal Will which appears to be God's Power *(Virtus)*. The nature of this Will is not clear in the *Fons Vitae*.

Each medieval religious tradition has one thinker who bluntly rejects philosophy as a study that is not helpful for salvation: Islam has its al-Ghazzali, Christianity its St. Bernard, and Judaism is represented by Judah Halevi (b. ca. 1080). His *Sefer ha-Kuzari* is a dialogue in which the chief speakers are the King of the Khazars (a convert to Judaism) and a learned Rabbi. In the course of their discussion two things are brought out that have some bearing on the history of ethics. First of all, Judah Halevi insists that there is no other source of obligation or moral guidance for men than the will of God as conveyed through divine law in the Bible.[14] This, then, is a purely religious type of morality. Judah Halevi does say that there are "rational laws" that are present and needed in every society, but that these general principles, as well as the more detailed rules of legal and ceremonial behavior found in the Old Testament, are all issued by the absolute divine will.[15] In the second place, Judah Halevi taught that "intention" is not enough to merit a moral reward: wherever action is possible, "actions must be perfected to claim reward."[16]

A more detailed system of morality is found in the *Duties of the Heart* by Bahya ibn Pakuda (eleventh to twelfth century). The treatise has ten "gates" (chapters), each discussing a distinct duty. Thus, the first duty is to recognize God as existent, one, and uncreated; the second duty is to meditate on the evidences in creatures of the divine wisdom. The third chapter deals with the duty to serve God in physical actions, thus stressing with his contemporary, Judah Halevi, that good intentions must be completed by good deeds. The remaining nine duties are not novel but it soon becomes clear that Bahya sets philosophy in a much higher place than does Judah Halevi. Besides faith in divine revelation, chapter 4 presents three other sources of information: sensory observation, intellectual intuition, and logical inference. In this theory of knowledge (which owes something to Saadia), insight into the requirements of moral duty falls on the second level, that of intellectual intuition. The tenth chapter treats the duty to love God and argues that awareness of this obligation arises from an innate urge in the mind. Divine grace is needed for the perfection of this love but there is a natural and philosophical preparation for it. The love of God grows in man's soul "when the believer's heart has been emptied of love of this world and freed from its lusts, as a result of perception and understanding."[17]

The greatest Jewish ethician in the Middle Ages was, of course, Maimonides. Born in Córdoba, Rabbi Moses ben Maimon (1135–1204) had a distinguished career in Spain before moving to Cairo, where he spent his mature years. Maimonides was a rabbi, legal expert, and physician. His best-known writing is the *Guide for the Perplexed* but his *Mishneh Torah* and a *Letter on Astrology* are also important sources for his ethics. He was convinced that the rational investigation of morality is incumbent on the educated person.

Much of Maimonides' thinking and writing was devoted to the problem of the relation between religious belief and philosophical rationalism. His best-known work, the *Guide for the Perplexed,* was written to inform Jewish believers who were disturbed and in doubt concerning this point. Although he was quite ready to criticize the "philosophers" (Aristotle's facts are useful, his theories are not), Maimonides had great respect for the life of understanding.[18] The opening pages of the first and second parts of the *Guide* offer an elaborate explanation of the role of divine revelation (the law) in contrast with the use of natural reason. In sum, he argues that but few men are equipped intellectually to probe the depths of metaphysics and, even among those who can be philosophers, the road to philosophical truth is long and paved with errors.[19] Maimonides' acquaintance with the philosophers was broad: he knew the teachings of all the major schools of Greek philosophy but particularly valued Plato and Aristotle. Much of his detailed information came through the encyclopedic writings of the Moslem scholars, such as al-Farabi and Avicenna.

The moral psychology used by Maimonides is an adaptation of Aristotelianism. Man is equipped with cognitive and appetitive powers. External sense experience is retained in imagination. The power of understanding with which man is born is minimal: the "hylic" (material) intellect is little more than the passive capacity of the imagination to receive actual understanding from above the soul. Study, sense experience, and a righteous moral attitude prepare some men for "acquired intellect."[20] Personal freedom is much prized by Maimonides: "Free will is bestowed on every human being. If one desires to turn towards the good way and be righteous, he has the power to do so. If one wishes to turn towards the evil way and be wicked, he is at liberty to do so."[21]

The ethical views in the third part of the *Guide* are almost identical with the teaching of the *Mishneh Torah,* usually called the *Code.* There is so much discussion of the law and its many precepts (as mentioned above, 613 commandments are enumerated in the rabbinical tradition) that one gets the initial impression of a strict legalistic ethics. However, this juridical emphasis is tempered in Maimonides by the idea that joy and love are the proper dispositions for the morally developed person. Righteousness *(sedaqah)* and loving-kindness *(hesed)* are more important than formal compliance with rules.[22] This is evident in a frequently quoted passage from the *Fundamental Principles of the Torah, Repentance,* X:

Whoever serves God out of love occupies himself with the study of the Law and the fulfillment of the commandments and walks in the paths of wisdom, impelled by no external motive whatsoever, moved neither by fear of calamity nor by the desire to obtain material benefits; such a man does what is truly right because it is truly right, and ultimately, happiness comes to him as a result of his conduct.[23]

This text shows clearly that we are still dealing with a type of ethics which is eudaimonistic. The ultimate end of man is happiness or well-being. Both the welfare of the body (orderly social intercourse) and the well-being of the soul (correct opinions in the multitude concerning their capacities) are aimed at in the divine law.

Moral virtues are, of course, important aids to a good life. The doctrine of the mean between extremes of excess and defect establishes the right way of feeling and acting. Saints may be more scrupulous and incline toward extreme dispositions but the ordinary person should strive to follow a middle path.[24] Moral rules are not made to cover exceptional people or cases; they are directed to "things that occur in the majority of cases." Maimonides seems to admit that natural moral law is knowable to people who have not received divine law but revelation is necessary for those who wish to attain to complete personal perfection.[25] It is in the acquisition of the "rational" virtues, however, that this highest human perfection lies. There are passages in Maimonides that suggest that intellectual development is all-important, at least for those favored few who are highly intelligent and able to secure a good education. The following text is but one among many such.

His ultimate perfection is to become rational in actuality, I mean to have an intellect in actuality; and that is to know everything concerning all the beings that it is within the capacity of man to know in accordance with his ultimate perfection. It is clear that this ultimate perfection does not comprise either actions or moral habits and that it consists only of opinions arrived at through speculation and made necessary by investigation.[26]

Such a development of theoretical understanding requires a prior acquisition of moral virtue, and even a moderate freedom from bodily discomforts, but it remains speculative and theoretical in character. This intellectualist tendency was due in part, at least, to Maimonides' explanation of prophecy. Some men can prepare themselves by study, experience, and good moral conduct, to receive an infusion of special information into their perfected imaginations.

Know that the truth and essence of prophecy consist in its being an emanation from God, the Mighty and Majestic, through the mediation of the Active Intellect to the rational faculty in the first place and thereafter to the imaginative faculty. This is the highest degree of man and the ultimate perfection that can exist for his species; and this state is the ultimate perfection of the imaginative faculty. This is something that can in no way exist in every man.[27]

Certain judgments of Maimonides on more specific moral questions have had an important influence on the history of ethics. He made an influential contribution to the theory of mental reservation in his *Letter on Apostasy* (written ca. 1160). In connection with persecutions of the Jews by the Moslem community at Fez, he was asked whether a Jew might repeat the formula expressing praise for Allah as the only God and Mohammed as his Prophet, provided the Jew thought in his heart that this prayer was not true. With some qualification, Maimonides replied that one might do so, under coercion.[28] This judgment that it is not immoral, under certain circumstances, to express something different from what one thinks to be true, was taken over by various Christian Scholastic ethicians and developed into the theory of mental reservation.

Concerning the view of the astrologers that a man's life is determined by the position of the stars at the time of his birth, Maimonides vigorously rejects such fatalism and argues that both religion and Greek philosophy support the personal freedom of every man to work out his own destiny.[29] He was well aware of the difference between scientific astronomy and the pseudoscience of astrology. Similar reasonableness is indicated in Maimonides' views on ascetic practices. For the average man, he advised moderation in this area, as in all others.

The Sages accordingly enjoined us that we should only refrain from that which the *Torah* has expressly withdrawn from our use. No one should, by vows and oaths, inhibit to himself the use of things permitted. 'Do not the prohibitions of the *Torah* suffice thee' say our Sages, 'that thou addest others for thyself?' Our wise men prohibited self-mortification by fasting.[30]

There is no question that Maimonides' ethics is a version of theological approbatism. Man's moral obligations stem ultimately from divine law. Such law is not the arbitrary expression of God's will: it springs from divine wisdom, as well as divine will, and is the essence of fairness and reasonableness.[31]

After Maimonides there were other medieval Jewish ethicians of secondary importance. Hillel ben Samuel (1220–1295) commented on and defended the views of Maimonides. His chief treatise was *The Rewards of the Soul (Tagmule ha-Nefesh)*. He does not diverge from the teaching of his master. At the beginning of the fourteenth century, Levi ben Gerson (Gersonides, 1288–1344) produced a treatise in Hebrew, *Milhamot Adonai (Wars of the Lord),* which touches on ethical questions in its early, psychological section. Hasdai ben Abraham Crescas (1340–1410) showed some interest in ethics in *Or Adonai (Light of the Lord)*. Crescas opposed the use of Aristotelian philosophy in Jewish schools, while Gersonides favored it.[32]

A very interesting treatise was written in fifteenth-century Spain by Joseph Albo (ca. 1380–1444). This was the *Sefer ha-ikkarim (Book of Principles)*. Its fifth chapter accords more importance to natural law than Maimonides had wanted. This natural law is required to preserve justice in all human societies and to eliminate wrongdoing. As Albo saw it:

This order [in society] would comprise protection against murder, theft, robbery, and the like, and in general, whatever would preserve the political association and arrange it so that people might live in a proper manner. This order the wise men called by the name of natural law—that is to say, that it is something that man needs in respect of his nature—whether it is ordered by a wise man or by a prophet.[33]

He further argues (chapter 6) that divine law is also necessary to lead people to the attainment of happiness. His very systematic treatment of various types of laws (divine, natural, and conventional) suggests that Albo may have borrowed some things from the Latin writers of his period. With his work, the story of Jewish ethics in the Middle Ages comes to a close.

Islamic Ethics in the Middle Ages

Before the Prophet Mohammed (ca. 571–632 C.E.) founded the religion of Islam there were some learned Christians writing in Persian, Arabic, or related languages, who helped to preserve and translate Greek ethical writings. This Syrian Christian activity continued throughout the Middle Ages. In the ninth century, for instance, Hunaïn ibn-Ishaq translated Porphyry's *Commentary on the Nicomachean Ethics* into Arabic. Both the Greek and Arabic versions of this *Commentary* are now lost but something of its content is preserved in Moslem ethical treatises.[34] The Jacobite Christian, Yahya ibn-Adi (d. 974 C.E.), wrote an ethical treatise entitled *The Correction of the Dispositions (Tahdhib al-Akhlaq)* that was an epitome of Greek moral thought; it served as a source for later Moslem writers, such as Miskawaihi.[35] As late as the thirteenth century we find a Syrian Christian, Gregorius

Abu al-Faraj (known to the Latins as Abulfaragius and Bar-Hebraeus), producing a moral treatise *(Book of the Dove)* and a work entitled *Ethikon* (written in 1278) which incorporated much of the ethical teaching from al-Ghazzahi's *Ihya al-Ulum.* Little historical work has been done on this school of Syrian ethical scholars but it is suspected that they knew classical writings no longer extant today in the original.[37]

Early in the seventh century the Koran (Qur'ān) appeared as the writing of the Moslem religion. According to Moslem belief, it was divinely revealed to Mohammed through the angel Gabriel. Mohammed was regarded as the last and greatest of the prophets: his chief predecessors were Adam, Noah, Abraham, Moses, and Jesus. As a prophetic religion, Islam occasioned many studies—religious, psychological, and philosophical—of the act of prophecy. From the ninth century onward, an important school of philosophers associated with Islam developed. There were many more Moslem "scholastic" philosophers than there were Jewish philosophers in this period. And long before Latin Christians had translations of the key works of the major Greek ethicians the Mohammedan teachers were familiar with these classics. The moral code of duties imposed in the Koran included five basic obligations: (1) to profess the faith daily; (2) to pray five times in every twenty-four hours, facing Mecca; (3) to give alms to the poor; (4) to fast from dawn to dusk in the holy month of Ramadan; and (5) to make a pilgrimage to Mecca once in one's life. Teaching and discussion of these and other religious duties induced Moslem teachers to investigate the grounds and nature of moral judgment and obligation. Their study of prophecy contributed to the growth of remarkable analyses of the psychic functions of man.[38]

In the ninth century a theological movement called the *kalam* ("word" or "speech") developed within Islamic thought: this is the school of thinkers called *Loquentes* in later Latin treatises. These Moslem theologians gave a place to both reason and faith, and they differed from the stricter interpreters of the Koran in affirming the freedom of man, the justice of Allah, and in denying rigid predestination. A certain appreciation of the possibilities of philosophy stemmed from this school. We find al-Kindi (ca. 796–866), for instance, writing treatises in the ninth century on nearly all the problems of classical philosophy. Within a few decades, Mohammed ibn-Zakariya al-Razi (865–925) wrote two ethical treatises which gave a very important role to natural reasoning. Using the Platonic psychology of the tripartite soul, al-Razi argued that reason should control the passions and the virtue of justice should balance the interests of all three parts. Moderation is stressed as the keynote to a good moral character. The problem of telling a lie is already taken as an example of the influence of intention on moral activity. Al-Razi decided that a lie is bad, if directed to a bad purpose.[39]

Though these thinkers made important contributions to Islamic philosophy, the first really great

Islamic philosopher was al-Farabi (d. 950). He studied in Baghdad under the Christian teacher Yuhanna ibn-Haylan (a Syrian), who was a link with the traditions of the earlier school at Alexandria. The writings of al-Farabi are encyclopedic in scope and character and they were used for the next four centuries, not only by Moslems but also by Jews and Christians, as sources of information concerning the philosophies of Aristotle, Plato, and other Greek schools.[40]

Plato's *Republic* and *Laws* are of primary importance in the practical philosophy of al-Farabi. He tries, however, to effect a harmony between Platonism and Aristotelianism. One view which he finds in both is the notion that ethics is but a part of the architectonic science of politics. In the fifth chapter of the *Enumeration of the Sciences,* al-Farabi lists three practical sciences: politics, jurisprudence, and theology *(kalam).* This does not mean a downgrading of ethics. He simply sees the moral life of man as but one aspect of political and religious life. Good and bad actions are distinguished to the extent that they promote or hamper the attainment of happiness. It is in a future life, after the death of the body, that true happiness may be achieved. As al-Farabi expresses it: "Distinguishing the actions and ways of life, it [political science] explains that the ones through which true happiness is attained are the goods, the noble things, and the virtues, while the rest are the evils, the base things, and the imperfections."[41]

From Aristotle and al-Kindi comes a complicated theory of the stages of human understanding which, with modifications in Avicenna and Averroës, continues to ground the moral psychology of medieval Aristotelianism up to the thirteenth century. As Aristotle did in his *De Anima,* al-Farabi distinguished sense perception from intellection. Sensation receives impressions from individual aspects of bodies; these "phantasies" are retained in sensory memory; eventually sense experience provides a preparation for personal understanding of the universal meanings of the objects experienced through the senses. The power of understanding with which man is born is, for al-Farabi, *'aql hayulani (intellectus materialis),* the passive potency to receive understanding. Above all men there exists a higher Intelligence which is always knowing; this is the *'aql fáal,* the Dispenser of Forms *(Dator Formarum,* in the Latin versions). We have here an interpretation of the two intellects (potential and agent) that are obscurely described in Aristotle's *De Anima* (III, 4–5). When the passive power of understanding is informed from above by the Dispenser of Forms, man's soul achieves actual understanding, *'aql bi'l-fi'l (intellectus in actu).* One is in this actuated condition when actually thinking of the conclusion to a theorem in geometry, for instance. Actual understanding of any given universal notion is but temporary: even Einstein could not always think about one universal truth. So, the basic power of understanding, after being actuated, reverts to an intermediate state from which it may more easily and promptly be actuated the next time; this state of habitual understanding is called *'aql bi'l-malaka (intellectus in habitu)*. It is the way in which all higher learning, skills in arts and sciences, remain in man's soul; habitual understanding is intellectual memory, science, wisdom. Other stages of the basic power of understanding are distinguished by al-Farabi and his followers in psychology. There is, for instance, that special skill that enables some people to teach others; and there is an even higher intellectual perfection, which enables a few men to receive and transmit special information from above, concerning future events, the higher meaning of the sacred writings, and so on: this is the understanding of the prophet. From the point of view of ethics, al-Farabi's theory of the stages of human understanding is of primary importance. Since it implies that even rather ordinary men are informed from above, from a higher Intelligence, concerning the meaning of items such as happiness, virtue, goodness, and so on, this teaching suggests that the standards of ethical judgment have a suprahuman origin which is, nevertheless, not outside the realm of nature. The suprahuman Dispenser of Forms is not Allah but simply a higher kind of spirit, an angel. In some versions of the theory, this Intelligence is identified with the Mind of the Prophet, Mohammed.[42]

It is in the light of the foregoing that we must interpret al-Farabi's account of the attainment of happiness.

His view of the personal perfection of man is thoroughly intellectualistic. There are five generic faculties in man: theoretical reason, practical reason, appetitive power, imagination, sensory power. "Happiness, which only man can know and perceive, is known by the theoretical-rational faculty and by none of the remaining faculties."[43] Education is for the few who can profit from it; they are people with the capacity to become happy.

A similar ethical teaching is found in the work of al-Ameri (d. 992). His book *On Seeking and Causing Happiness* has not been translated but the editor of the original text reports in his introduction that it combines the moral positions of Plato and Aristotle.[44]

The outstanding Moslem ethician before the thirteenth century was Ahmad ibn-Muhammad-ibn Yaqub Miskawaihi (932–1030). His *Tahdhib al-Akhlaq (Correction of the Dispositions)* has been printed many times and is still influential in the Islamic schools. He is not well known outside his own culture. Like the other early Mohammedan thinkers that have been mentioned, Miskawaihi was from the east; he served as a librarian at Shiraz and Ray, in what is now Iran.

In his psychology, Miskawaihi distinguished three faculties of the human soul: (1) the power to exercise thought *(al-fikr)*, discrimination *(al-tamyiz)*, and observation *(nazar);* (2) the power which gives rise to anger *(al-ghadab)*, firmness *(al-najda)*, and initiative *(al-iqdam);* and (3) the power of sensual desire *(al-shahwa)* for food, sexual pleasure, and similar goods.[45]

Obviously, these powers are the equivalents of reason, and irascible and concupiscible appetites, in the terminology of contemporary Latin thinkers in the Aristotelian tradition. Chapter 3 of Miskawaihi's *Tahdhib* offers an almost verbatim passage from a work of Aristotelian origin called *Fada'il al-Nafs*. This would seem to be the *De Virtutibus et vitiis* composed by some follower in the later Greek school of Aristotle. A pupil of the Syrian translator, Hunaïn ibn-Ishaq, named abu-Uthman al-Dimishqi (809–877), had translated the Aristotelian treatise into Arabic.

Miskawaihi uses his theory of three powers or parts of the soul to expound a teaching on the four virtues— wisdom *(hikma)*, purity *('iffa)*, courage *(al-shaja'a)*, righteousness *('adala)*—that is close to that in Plato's *Republic,* Book IV.[46] He then distinguishes seven "species" of practical wisdom: acuteness of intelligence, quickness of intellect, clearness of understanding, facility of acquisition, precise discrimination, retention, and recollection. This is followed by a description of eleven species of courage, twelve species of temperance, and nineteen species of justice. We are obviously in the midst of a typical Aristotelian exposition of the "parts" of each of the cardinal virtues. There are dozens of virtues *(fada'il)* and vices *(radha'il)*. Virtue is a mean between extremes of vice. The fifth chapter of Miskawaihi's *Tahdhib* offers an analysis of different types of love. Man's ultimate end is happiness. This complete good is that to which all men aspire: health, wealth, fame, honor, success, and right thinking. Some degree of this happiness is attainable in this life; Miskawaihi is not as completely otherworldly as some of his colleagues.[47] However, he insists that divine justice is supreme in the realm of morals. It is a religious ethics that has incorporated a good deal of Greek naturalism.

Avicenna, abu-ʿAli al-Husayn ibn-Abdallah ibn-Sīna (980–1037), was the greatest of the Eastern school of Moslem philosophers. An almost universal genius, poet, medical doctor, theologian, lawyer, this man would be ranked by many historians with the ten greatest philosophers of all time. The year 1952 marked the millennium of his birth, according to Moslem chronology, and witnessed the publication of many studies of the life and thought of Avicenna. His *Shifa (Book of Healing)* is an encyclopedic work treating all the branches of speculative knowledge available in the eleventh century. Its four parts cover respectively logic, physics, mathematics, and metaphysics. Ethics receives only occasional mention. The *Najat (Salvation)* is a shorter version of the *Shifa*. It was the *Shifa* that was translated into medieval Latin and which gave Christian scholars some idea of the riches of Moslem learning, particularly in the fields of psychology, physiology, and physics.

The psychology of Avicenna was a development of the same basic Aristotelianism that we encountered in al-Farabi. His analysis of the human soul and its functions is found in the sixth book of the Physics section of the *Shifa;* it became known in Latin as *Liber Sextus Naturalium,* or simply *De Anima.* Five internal senses are distinguished by Avicenna: common sense, phantasy, cogitative (imaginative), estimative, and memorative *(De Anima,* I, cap. 5). In the functions of cogitation and estimation man knows and makes judgments of a particularized sort concerning individual bodies and their concrete meanings. Thus, if a man were attacked by a snarling dog and came up with the decision "This animal is dangerous to me," he would make this judgment in his estimative power, not in his intellect. Understanding for Avicenna, as for most Aristotelians, looks to universal objects only. He did not put much emphasis on the ethical significance of this teaching but it had a profound influence on Latin Scholasticism. In the thirteenth century, ethics as a science of universal judgments concerning human conduct was kept quite distinct from the habit of prudent reasoning about one's own concrete problems of morality. The latter involves judgments made in "particular reason" (an internal sense power to cogitate under the general direction of the rules of intellectual reasoning). Avicenna is, in good part, the source of this position.[49]

Part of Avicenna's ethical position is discernible from his writings on the mystical life. One such work is the *Story of Hajj Son of Yaqzan.* This enigmatic description of Moslem mysticism has recently been shown to involve most of the philosophical teachings of Avicenna.[51] Briefly, man's soul starts on a journey and encounters a guide named Hayy (living) son of Yaqzan (awake). This guide seems to be the Universal Agent Intelligence. Man's soul is conducted to various places in the West (the realm of matter) and in the East (the realm of form). Various temptations are encountered by the soul in its quest for knowledge and peace; it struggles with external and internal impediments; a variety of helps are provided it. Finally, it reaches the King, is enraptured with admiration and love, and achieves an ineffable peace.[52] The meaning of the work is veiled in symbolism and romantic imagery.

Perhaps this is the "ethics" of Avicenna. He obviously thinks that there are two classes of people: the many unlearned and material-minded, the few who are educated and spiritual-minded. The souls of the many face downward to the world of sensory images: for such people it is good to follow the guidance of an imam, a spiritual and religious leader. In the case of the intellectual elite, their souls face in a different direction and are ordered to a higher perfection. What is good for them is the acquisition and development of personal understanding, a process which begins with the study of science, philosophy, and religious teachings, in this life—and which continues to develop in a future life, in the company of the angels and the divine presence. As he says, "Through this science [ethics] one knows how man ought to be in his moral habits and his actions so as to lead a happy life here and in the hereafter. This part is contained in Aristotle's book on ethics."[53]

In the Eastern school, the last great personality in medieval Islam was al-Ghazzali, abu-Hāmid Muhammad (1059–1111). He came to be known in Latin as Algazel. This man was generally critical and suspicious of pagan philosophy. His *Tahafut al-Falasifa* was a vigorous refutation of twenty philosophical conclusions, mostly taken from Avicenna. Al-Ghazzali's autobiographical *Deliverance from Error* tells how he studied the philosophers and decided that their views were not in accord with Moslem teachings. This negative aspect of his doctrine is usually emphasized in histories of philosophy. Other works of al-Ghazzali show him as one of the greatest of Mohammedan theologians, by no means an obscurantist but much concerned to preserve the original spirit of the Koran. The *Ihya al-Ulum al-Din (Revivification of the Religious Sciences)* and the *Risalat al-Laduniyya (Inspired Treatise)* show that he was in the early twelfth century the "best known writer on ethical subjects."[55]

The *Risalat* offered ten rules of personal conduct: (1) maintain a good intention; (2) aim to serve Allah only; (3) conform to truth; (4) oppose procrastination; (5) avoid innovation and follow established practice; (6) cultivate humility toward others; (7) seek salvation through faith, fear, and hope; (8) pray devoutly; (9) banish all but Allah from your heart; (10) seek the knowledge that leads to the vision of Allah.[56] This is a purely religious ethic in which values such as gratitude, repentance, trust, and fear of God are stressed in a manner quite foreign to the moral philosophy of the Greeks.[57] For al-Ghazzali all ethical problems can be answered by consulting the will of Allah as revealed in the Koran and as interpreted by orthodox theologians. This is theological approbative ethics at its purest.

In his discussion of lying,[58] al-Ghazzali used an example that appears in many later treatments of the same problem, notably that of Immanuel Kant.

> Understand that falsehood in speech (al-kidhb) is not forbidden (haram) in itself, but because of such injury as may be in it to the speaker, or to others. . . . Maimun ibn al-Mohr said that falsehood is at some times better than truth (al-sidq). For example, if you see that a man is trying to fall upon another man with a sword in order to kill him, that he has entered the gate and has come to you and has said, 'Have you seen such a person?' You will not say, 'I have seen him' but you will say, 'I have not seen him' This type of falsehood is required, for we say that speech is but a means to an end.

In addition to the interest of the illustration, this passage shows the forthright position of a Moslem theologian who thinks that, in this problem, the end does justify the means.

Al-Ghazzali's influence in ethics extended beyond his century and outside his religious culture. In the thirteenth-century *Ethikon* by Bar-Hebraeus there is a series of chapters (on the soul, its training, wantonness, the tongue, anger and envy, worldly desires, avarice, hypocrisy, pride and boasting) that parallel ten chapters in al-Ghazzali's *Ihya.*

Another Persian moralist contemporary with al-Ghazzali but with a different notion of the happy life was Omar Khayyam (d. ca. 1123). His poems, gathered under the title *Rubáiyát,* have provided in the English paraphrase by Edward FitzGerald (1859) one of the most quoted expressions of ethical hedonism.

> A book of Verses underneath the Bough,
> A jug of Wine, a Loaf of Bread—and Thou
> Beside me singing in the Wilderness—
> Oh, Wilderness were Paradise enow!

> Some for the Glories of This World; and some
> Sigh for the Prophet's Paradise to come;
> Ah, take the Cash, and let the Credit go,
> Nor heed the rumble of a distant Drum!

A member of the sufi sect, Omar was not an epicurean ethician but used lyrical imagery to convey his mystical and somewhat pessimistic views.[60]

Western Islamic philosophy centered in southern Spain. One of the first ethical treatises was written there by ibn-Hazm, abu-Muhammad Ali ibn-Ahmad iba-Sa'id (994–1064). This was the *Kitab al-Akhlaq Wa-l-Siyar (Book of Dispositions).* Just as "ethics" comes from a Greek word *(ethos)* meaning custom or habitual disposition, and "morals" from a Latin word *(moris)* with the same meaning, so does the Arabic *akhlaq* have the same meaning, and it has come to be used for the discipline of ethics. Ibn-Hazm's work is a moral essay advising zealous study in order to develop a spirit of repose, good manners and conduct, friendliness, and practical honesty in dealing with others.[61] It contains information on how to heal broken characters and how to profit from study sessions.

More influential was ibn-Bajjah, abu-Bakr Muhammad ibn-Yahya (ca. 1087–1138), known in Latin as Avempace. He was learned on many subjects (music, medicine, astronomy, mathematics, as well as all divisions of philosophy) but most interested in moral philosophy. He knew the major works of Aristotle quite well, including the *Nicomachean Ethics.* For the unlearned, ibn-Bajjah had no concern; their interests are base. His treatise *Governance of the Solitary* is directed to the cultured Moslem who had time and ability to study philosophy.

> The man of wisdom is therefore necessarily a man who is virtuous and divine. Of every kind of activity, he takes up the best only. . . . When he achieves the final end— that is, when he understands simple essential intellects, which are mentioned in the *Metaphysics, On the Soul,* and *On Sense and the Sensible*—he then becomes one of these

intellects. It would be right to call him simply divine.[62]

With ibn-Bajjah, we are obviously in an ethics that
is Aristotelian and intellectualistic. Human actions
are clearly distinguished from nonvoluntary, animal
functions. Appetition is quite different from cognition. Right opinion based on the study of speculative
philosophy (note the metaphysical and psychological
works of Aristotle mentioned in the quotation) is
the norm of ethical judgment.[63]

In the short work *Fi ittisal al-'aql bi-l-insan (On
the Union between the Intellect and Man)*, ibn-Bajjah used the term *ittisal* to name that conjunction
(which is cognitive, moral, and ontological) between
the internal sense power of a man (prepared by the
acquisition of phantasms and by study) and that separate Agent Intelligence which dwells in the sphere of
the moon and is available to all humans as a source of
actual understanding. This is fundamentally an intellectual perfection. It is necessary for any real advance
on the road to happiness.[64]

Less Aristotelian but open to the value of practical
philosophy is the Spanish Moslem, ibn-Tufail, abu-Bakr
Muhammad ibn-'Abd-al-Malik (ca. 1100–1185), known
to the West as Abubacer. His only known work is a sort
of philosophical novel bearing the same title as Avicenna's mystical treatise, *Hayy ibn Yaqzan*. Ibn-Tufail
starts his much longer story with the solitary birth of

a boy on a deserted island. Unaided by other humans, this child learns to care for himself and to deal with his material environment. From the death of a gazelle that had helped to mother him, Hayy grasps the notion that a life spirit has departed from this dead animal. Observing the upward movement of flame suggests that this hot vapor may have some kinship with the principle of life and that it strives to rise into the celestial regions. He meditates on his own body-spirit constitution and rises to the thought of a Perfect Being. Eventually he meets two humans from a neighboring island and gets some experience of social life. He comes to realize that most men "are like irrational animals" but that "all wisdom, guidance to the right path, and good fortune reside in the utterances of the apostles of God and what is set forth by religious Law."[65] There is also the implication at the end of this romance that there is a secret meaning to the story and that men of intelligence will know what it is.

The story has fascinated people through the ensuing centuries and has been read in many languages. Apart from its obvious literary influences the story of Hayy was an important source of inspiration for the greatest Moslem thinker of the West, Averroës, and probably affected the thought of radical Aristotelians in the Latin schools of the thirteenth century, such as Arnold of Brescia and Siger of Brabant. When the Bishop of Paris, Etienne Tempier, condemned as religious errors (in 1277) two propositions saying that happiness is attainable in this life through the intellectual and moral virtues, he was objecting to a position originally taken by ibn-Tufail. The implication of the story of Hayy is that "the philosopher, left to his inner light, is capable of attaining to supreme bliss."[66] More amazing is the claim that ibn-Tufail was an inspiration to George Fox (1624–1691), the founder of the Quakers.[67]

The greatest Aristotelian scholar in the history of Islam was Averroës: he was named *the* Commentator (on Aristotle), even in the Christian writings of the later Middle Ages. Ibn-Rushd, abu-al-Walīd Muhammad ibn-Ahmad (1126–1198), wrote commentaries of three types (epitome, middle, and long) on most of the major writings of Aristotle. Averroës was not as interested in ethics as in speculative philosophy and produced only a middle commentary on the *Nicomachean Ethics*. This is extant in Hebrew and Latin versions but not in the original Arabic. His explanation of Aristotelian ethics follows the original closely and need not be detailed here.

Averroës' more personal treatises have some bearing on ethics. The *Fasl al-maqal (Decisive Treatise)* deals with the problem of the role of philosophy in the studies and life of a learned Moslem. He was accused, from the thirteenth century onward, of teaching the doctrine of the "double truth": that a conclusion may be true according to reason but false according to religious belief, or vice versa. Modern historians point out that he actually rejected such a view.[68] Throughout the *Decisive Treatise,* Averroës insists that al-Ghazzali did not understand the peripatetic philosophers and was mistaken in his condemnation of them.[69] He argues that the study of philosophy is quite useful for those intelligent enough to profit from it and that it is, indeed, obligatory in the religious law.

Since all this is now established, and since we, the Muslim community, hold that this divine Law of ours is true, and that it is this Law that incites and summons us to the happiness that consists in the knowledge of God, Mighty and Majestic, and of His creation, that [end] is appointed for every Muslim by the method of assent that his temperament and nature require.[70]

Some men, he proceeds to explain, base their assent on demonstrative reasoning: philosophy is useful to them, of course. A second kind of men are convinced by dialectical arguments, and a third type reach assent through rhetorical arguments. For each the appropriate arguments may be used by religious teachers; without question Averroës places the first kind of men in the highest place. He is simply saying that, where it can, faith should seek understanding.

There has been a great deal of controversy as to whether Averroës denied or supported personal immortality for man. He interpreted Aristotle's *De Anima* much as al-Farabi and Avicenna had. However, where Avicenna seemed to grant a potential power of understanding to each human soul at birth, Averroës is rather definite in saying that the highest cognitive potency that man has at birth is the cogitative power *(fikr)*, which is not the same as Avicenna's estimative. Whether the Averroistic cogitative is originally an intellect or merely sensory is a disputed point.[71] Those who read Averroës as saying that, at birth, man is little more than a beast, conclude that he denied personal immortality for all except those few who merit everlasting life by study and good behavior. Actually, the *Decisive Treatise* states that the knowledge "of happiness and misery in the next life" is available to each of the three classes of men named above.[72] He did think, then, that philosophic demonstration of the future life for the individual person is possible. For Averroës, as for most Mohammedan ethicians in the Middle Ages, the good life culminates in a personal union in actual understanding with the Agent Intelligence, which is always knowing and offering information to men.[73]

The most representative treatise on ethics by a medieval Moslem philosopher was the *Akhlaq-i Nasiri (The Nasirean Ethics),* written in Persia about the year 1235 C.E. The author, Nasir ad-Din Tusi (1201–1274), was a scholar and man of affairs in thirteenth-century Persia. It must be admitted that Nasir was not a great speculative mind but he did write a work which gives "a conspectus of most of the significant moral and intellectual preoccupations of the medieval Islamic world."[74] His book is actually an exposition of the three traditional divisions of Aristotelian practical philosophy: ethics (morality of individual conduct), economics (right and wrong in family life), and politics (moral direction of the state). Most of the following analysis will be confined to the ethical theory in Nasir's first *Discourse*.

In the first division of Discourse One, Nasir describes the three souls present in man: vegetative, animal, and human. The vegetative soul has three basic faculties, the nutritive, augmentative, and generative powers. The animal soul has two generic faculties: organic perception and voluntary motion. The first is divided into two sets of subfaculties: (1) external senses—sight, hearing, smell, taste, touch; (2) internal senses, which are common sense, fantasy, reflection, estimation, and recollection. Voluntary motion is assigned two sub-faculties: concupiscible and irascible powers. The human soul has one generic faculty, rationality, which apprehends without an organ and discriminates among the objects thus known. Rationality is subdivided into speculative intelligence, through which one knows existent beings and various types of intelligible objects; and practical intelligence, through which one directs the control of objects, distinguishes good from evil actions, and exercises discovery in the sphere of the arts. There is no special faculty called will; volition on the level of desire and emotional reaction to irritants and dangers are the functions of the concupiscible and irascible powers of the animal soul; volition, which is expressive of rational motivation and choice, is the function of practical intelligence.

Nasir next describes: (1) faculties whose operations come under control of will and reason and that lead to meritorious effort; (2) faculties whose functions work by nature and receive no added perfection from their use. The first kind are obviously the sort of actions that would be called voluntary by Nasir's Latin contemporaries; these are the operations that are ethically interesting. Three of the previously listed faculties initiate acts of this ethical kind: rationality, concupiscible power, and irascible power. Through the concupiscible one experiences attraction for benefits, or pleasures (food, drink, women); through the irascible a person reacts to injuries, faces perils, yearns for authority and fame.

In the fourth section of the first discourse, Nasir introduces the basis for the discrimination between good and evil. Even the vegetative soul has the ability, he explains, to be attracted to the wholesome and to shake off the unwholesome. One date palm may show affection for another tree! It is in brute animals, however, that one finds a certain voluntariness and the power to sense. Similarly, the distinguishing features of human acts are their ranks of perfection determined according to volition *(irada)* and reason *(ru'yat)*. It is possible that the latter term simply means cogitation or mental perception.[75]

Next, Nasir describes three levels of human perfection: (1) that of people skilled in the mechanical arts and the use of instruments; (2) that of people skilled in knowledge, the sciences, and virtues; and (3) that of persons skilled in receiving knowledge of truths and laws from above. Man is originally stationed in a middle position, able to go up or down. To know what to do, most people need guidance from prophets, philosophers, and other wise teachers. The wise man is called rational, which signifies:

> the faculty of perceiving intelligibles and the power of distinction and reason, by which one discriminates between fair and foul, reprehensible and praiseworthy, and disposes of them according to the will. It is on account of this faculty that Man's actions are divided into good and bad, and fair and foul, and that he is characterized by felicity or affliction, as against the other animals and the plants. Thus, whoever applies this faculty properly, and by will and endeavour reaches that virtue towards which he was directed at creation, such a one is good and blissful; but one who neglects to tend that property, either by striving in an opposite direction or by sloth and aversion, is evil and afflicted.[76]

At this point, Nasir approximates a "right reason" theory of ethics, not far removed from the contemporary views of Christian moralists in the Latin tradition.

The difference between the theoretical faculty and its speculative perfection and the practical faculty with its perfection in activity is further discussed in the sixth section. Both speculative and practical perfection are needed for felicity: "Theory without practice is abortive, and practice without theory is absurd." The most sublime happiness is found in the divine Presence. Nasir is very critical of hedonism, whether directed to sensual pleasure in this world or the next: people who cherish such a goal "are the companions of the dog and the pig." Two moral feelings promote good moral judgment, shame occasioned by the unfitting and love of a fair action.

At times, Nasir is concerned to show that his ethics is in accord with the teachings of the Koran. Thus he cites passages in the sacred writings to show that his threefold division of souls is supported by the religious doctrine of the Imperative, Reproachful, and Peaceful souls. He is well aware that Plato's *Republic* has much the same division of psychic parts. In other places Nasir echoes some teaching of Aristotle: "Every action is in order to attain a purpose," for instance. Or, the "Absolute Good" is that to which all men must aim. The attainment of future felicity "is vested in reason and the intelligence." Long passages are quoted almost verbatim from the *Tahdhib al-Akhlaq* of Miskawaihi.[77]

The second division of Discourse One is devoted to Ends. The three moral faculties are again described, with the enumeration of many species of virtue perfecting each. These virtues are habitual dispositions that serve as means to the achievement of good ends. He has the doctrine of the mean: "Every virtue is, so to speak, a middle-point." As a science, ethics is "to give fundamental principles and rules, not to calculate particulars."[78] Rather specific moral questions are treated in connection with the virtues of temperance and courage. Suicides, for instance, are judged to be cowards.

In the seventh section of the second division, Nasir discusses justice and stresses the idea that its central notion is equivalence (the Aristotelian "equity," *epieikeia*). Other types of justice are distributive, commutative, and legal. Nasir even claims that the *Nicomachean Ethics* teaches that the greatest law may be from God.

Intellectual union of the soul with Truth *(ittisal)* is the end of the cultured and perfected man, viewed subjectively. Various sorts of felicity are discussed, bodily, psychic, and civic. This portion of the treatise parallels the discussion of goods of the body, soul, and society, in the tenth book of the *Nicomachean Ethics.*

Moral vices are described as "sicknesses of the soul." There are many more of them than there are virtues, for there is an indefinite number of ways of going wrong. Nasir cites Master Miskawaihi to show that it is not reasonable to grieve at the death of relatives. Suppose a certain prince and all his descendants were to remain alive for four hundred years. They would number more than ten million people in this one family! The surface of the habitable earth would not permit them space to stand. Eventually, they would have to stand on each other's heads. Thinking on something like this shows how ignorant and absurd it is to wish that people would live forever.[79] Obviously, the possibility of overpopulation of the earth did occur to medieval thinkers.

There is a sort of humorous and even earthy quality to Nasir's examples and conclusions that served to make his work popular. He cites al-Ghazzali to the effect that the concupiscible faculty is like a revenue agent, inclined to take everything. To men whose attention is wont to stray from their wives to other women, Nasir points out that all women are basically rather similar: why not be satisfied with what you have at home? On the same subject, in the second discourse (which deals with problems of family life), Nasir says that the main thing that a husband should instill in his wife is awe. He offers four "stratagems" which may be used to rid oneself of a bad wife. Here, and in many of the later sections of the treatise, the discussion descends to mere details of etiquette. Ethical notions that occur in the third discourse (on Politics) are not novel: the influence of Aristotle's *Politics* is evident.

In the fifteenth century another popular treatise on ethics was written in Persia by Jalal al-Din Muhammad ibn-Asad Dawani (d. 1502). His *Aklaq-i Jalali (Jalal's Ethics)* is merely an abbreviated and somewhat corrupted version of Miskawaihi and Nasir ad-Din Tusi.[80] The work is still read; numerous editions in modern India attest to its popularity in that country.[81]

Despite the difficulties of communication and translation in the Middle Ages, particularly from various Middle Eastern and Semitic languages into Latin, it is clear that the ethical learning of the Jews and Moslems did reach their Christian contemporaries. The twelfth century saw many versions from Jewish and Mohammedan writings made at two busy translating centers: Toledo in Spain and Naples in the Sicilian Empire. It was from these translations that Latin scholars of the thirteenth century got their first taste of Aristotelian ethics. Before long, the Christian scholars were clamoring for complete translations from the Greek text of Aristotle. The continuing influence of Avicebrón, Maimonides, Avicenna, and Averroës is everywhere evident in the Christian schools of philosophy in the last part of the Middle Ages. Greek rationalism and eudaimonism became part of medieval culture through these intermediaries.

Chapter VI
Right Reason Theories

FROM THE EARLY thirteenth century to the fifteenth century a very large number of men were interested in ethics. This was the period when the first universities of Europe came into being; their courses in liberal arts usually included some study of ethics. It was a time in which two religious orders (Dominicans and Franciscans) were founded and gave opportunities to their members for study and writing in this field. Aristotle's *Nicomachean Ethics* became generally available in Latin at this time and stimulated much discussion of ethical problems. Christian theology was highly organized in the thirteenth century and this doctrinal study always included sections on moral theology that paralleled the contemporary work in ethics. There were even certain popular fads (such as the vernacular poetry of courtly love) that challenged established academic and ecclesiastical moral teachings. In the present chapter we will examine some of the main contributions made to ethics by Latin writers between 1200 and 1500. The dominant ethics of the period centered around the theory of right reason but there were other interesting positions.

The *Nicomachean Ethics* of Aristotle was not known to the Latin scholars of the early Middle Ages. Its second and third books were put into Latin during the twelfth century and became known as the *Ethica vetus (Old Ethics)*. Book I was translated early in the thirteenth century and was called *Ethica nova (New Ethics)*. Together, these three books were used as texts in *scientia moralis* in the Arts Faculty of the University of Paris between 1230 and 1250. By March 19, 1255, the statutes of the Arts Faculty at Paris required the reading of four books of the *Nicomachean Ethics*. About the year 1240, Robert Grosseteste produced a complete Latin version directly from the Greek. At about the same time, at Toledo, Hermannus Alemannus translated an Arabic paraphrase of the *Nicomachean Ethics* into Latin. It was Grosseteste's version which became the base for commentaries by Albert the Great (1245–1252), Thomas Aquinas (1265–1272), Giles of Rome, and many others in the thirteenth century. The next century saw similar commentaries by Walter Burleigh, Gerardus Odonis, Jean Buridan, John Baconthorpe,

and others. Leonardo Bruni d'Arezzo (1369–1444)
made a new translation of the *Nicomachean Ethics* in
the fifteenth century. The *Magna Moralia* was translated by Bartholomew of Messina at Naples (1258–
1266) but the only book of the *Eudemian Ethics* that
was in Latin in the thirteenth century was the seventh, through the compilation called *De bona fortuna*.
We shall see later in this chapter how extensively the
thought content of Aristotle's ethics affected the writers of the later Middle Ages.

Apart from academic writings in Latin there was in
the vernacular poetry of the troubadours a romantic
view toward life and love that exerted a certain influence on medieval ethics. It is probably too much to say
that "courtly love is an ethics, a religion, an obsession."[1]
Many people in the thirteenth (as in any other) century were fascinated with the ideal of unrequited love.
This was the publicly professed admiration of a knight
for his unattainable lady love. What made courtly love
different was the claim that the lover was ennobled,
morally improved, by his unfulfilled love. In spite of
efforts to fuse it with spiritual love of God, courtly
love was essentially an idealized form of sensual love.
It may have some background in Moslem philosophy
(Avicenna's mystical love) but this romantic movement
in popular European literature indicates one important
fact in the thirteenth and following centuries; many
medieval people sought happiness in this life and
in the pleasures of the flesh. In 1277 the Bishop of Paris

condemned a long list of erroneous teachings. Among the errors noted by Bishop Etienne Tempier were the following: "that happiness is possessed in this life and not in another; that there are fables and falsehoods in the Christian law just as in others; and that simple fornication, namely, that of an unmarried man with an unmarried woman, is not a sin."[2] That the bishop had in mind the courtly love ideals is evident from his prologue to the list of errors; in it he expressly mentions the treatise *On Love* with its opening and closing lines. This is the *De amore* written about the year 1185 by Andreas Capellanus; it was probably the most influential treatise produced by this movement.

The theme of human love found different emphasis in Franciscan spirituality. Many people consider St. Francis of Assisi (1182–1226) the typical medieval man: otherworldly, impractical perhaps, guided by feelings. He was typical of but one tendency in a complex period. No scholar himself, Francis founded a religious community (the Order of Friars Minor, started about 1208) which, within a few decades, included professors at Paris, Oxford, and other university centers, St. Francis produced no technical writings on ethics and, indeed, the *Flowers of St. Francis* is a fourteenth-century compilation incorporating materials from the early days of the Franciscans. He is mentioned here only because of his influence on the moral attitudes of many late medieval Christians. Brand Blanshard calls his exaltation of feeling over reason "an immensely important experiment in morality."[3] Francis did feel that love is all-important and his spiritual disciples in their later and more learned works always retained something of his respect for the affective and volitional approach to moral and religious values.

More distinctive of the ethical thinking of these centuries was the contrary tendency. From the thirteenth to the sixteenth century most writers on the theoretical basis of moral judgment espoused some version of right reason *(recta ratio)* as the ethical standard. To avoid repetition, we will first state the general character of this theory and then indicate the individual attitudes of key thinkers in this period toward the common teaching. The background of right reason ethics is complex. Patristic and medieval Biblical scholars produced many commentaries on the Book of Genesis (the usual name for such a work was Hexaëmeron, "On the Work of the First Six Days"). In these there developed the teaching that God as Creator had a divine Plan *(Ratio)* in mind for all things that He created. Each creature was known eternally to God and thus the eternal Idea *(ratio aeterna)* of every distinct thing served as an exemplar or archetype for the existence and functioning of that thing. In this sense there is a "reason" for each human person and this reason is present eternally in the creative mind of God *(in arte Dei)*. The first chapter of Genesis describes how God finished making all things on the sixth day: "And God saw everything that he had made, and behold, it was very good." This was understood to mean that God compared the products of His creative activity with their exemplars in the divine mind and judged that these creatures were well made and pleasing. This is divine exemplarism; it is accepted by all medieval Christian thinkers. According to this view a man performs good actions when he functions in accord with the requirements of his "eternal reason" in God's mind. This is the religious element in the doctrine of right reason.

Most medieval philosophers also knew about the theory of ideal forms, as found in Platonic dialogues such as the *Symposium, Republic,* and *Theaetetus.* In this tradition, there was a perfect archetype for each and every *species* of things in this world. In some sense, all men were thought to share in the ideal form of man. This is Platonic participation of the many in the One. As a theory, it also carried the implication that a good horse will act in conformity with the archetypal "horseness"—and the good man will act in accord with the ideal "humanity." In Latin versions of paraphrases of Plato, these ideas are often called "reasons" *(rationes).* Thirteenth-century Latin writers came to know the way in which Aristotle modified Plato's teaching without entirely rejecting it. Aristotelian metaphysics and philosophy of nature rejected the supposition of a separate world of ideal forms but retained the view that all members of a real class (or species) of things have the same specific form.

These "forms," whether substantial or accidental, are not things in themselves but they are constitutive factors in the existing being of each individual thing. Thus, for Aristotle, there is in each horse the substantial form of "horseness"—not existing as a universal essence but individuated and proper to each horse. Each man is similarly constituted of substantial form and prime matter. The substantial form of a man specifies the way in which this individual person exists and operates. Reason, the ability to understand and make inferences *(logos* in Greek, *ratio* in Latin), is the *specific difference* that distinguishes man from brute animal. Man acts in a good way, according to Aristotle, when he realizes as fully as possible in his operations the potentialities of his formal nature as a *rational* animal. This clearly includes the suggestion that the good man must think rightly about his proposed activities. Such practical reasoning is right reason *(orthos logos),* when carried out in a manner befitting a human nature. This Platonic-Aristotelian teaching is the second element in the constitution of medieval right reason ethics.

From the Stoics came the third and last influence. As much as Hegel, these Greeks thought that the world is completely rational in character. There is a reason *(logos)* for everything that occurs. If men were completely wise, they would be able to grasp all these "reasons" and would not hesitate to adjust their interior, conscious attitudes and judgments to the requirements of reason. This is another way of saying that law *(nomos)* is simply what reason, as universalized, dictates. What characterizes the lawmaker is not a will to bind his subjects to the performance of certain actions. Such a voluntaristic account of universal law never occurred to the pre-Christian Greeks. "To order is the function of reason," Thomas Aquinas wrote,[4] and he was echoing both Stoicism and Aristotelianism. Now, the Stoics saw all things as interrelated in a comprehensible manner: some things are useful or suitable for other things, some are not. Such suitability is a relation, an order, a "ratio" in the mathematical sense. In Greek it is a *logos.* The order of nature is a vast complexus of such intelligible relations. As part of that natural order, each man is able to discern those things and actions that are really fitting for him. It is reasonable enough for a stone to stay in one place for all its existence: this behavior is not fitting or suitable for a man. Such a judgment ultimately rests on an intelligent appraisal of what a man is and how he stands in relation to other things. There is a rational order in which man finds himself. Moral law is nothing but the expression of what is fitting for human agents in view of their significant relations with other beings. Right reason is simply another name for a correct or justifiable understanding of the natural order. Universalized, right reason is expressed in general rules; applied to particular actions right reason is a personal decision as to the suitability or unsuitability of this individual action in its present conditions.

We have noted how a certain amount of Stoic ethics entered the Christian tradition through writers
such as Ambrose and Augustine. St. Jerome (340–
420) was probably the first to introduce into Latin
the term *synderesis,* which may be a corruption of the
Stoic word for insight *(syneidesis)* .In a Biblical commentary[5] Jerome spoke of synderesis as the spark of
conscience *(scintilla conscientiae)*. At the start of the
thirteenth century this terminology was picked up by
theological writers and developed into a special teaching.[6] Generally speaking, synderesis came to mean the
human ability (variously interpreted) to distinguish in
a general way between moral good and evil, while conscience was reserved for the personal discrimination
between good or evil in individual action. In other
words, the deliverances of synderesis are universal, the
decisions of conscience are particular. Moral reasoning is considered by most medieval thinkers as starting with the general rules or laws grasped through synderesis and as proceeding step by step through various
other judgments derived from religious faith or rational experience, or both, to conclude in: (1) more specific but still general judgments concerning right and
wrong types of actions (these would be conclusions of
"moral science," *scientia moralis,* either ethics or moral
theology, depending on whether one used natural reason and information only, or along with supernatural
revelation and divine law); and (2) completely particularized moral judgments about the goodness or bad-

ness of an individual human action in its context of actual circumstances (such a decision or judgment is called conscience, *conscientia*). The process of practical reasoning to individual (nonuniversal) decisions concerning moral problems is not part of ethics; but when well done it is called right reason *(recta ratio)*. The virtue of prudence, or practical wisdom *(prudentia)*, is the good habit of reasoning rightly to good practical judgments about individual actions. It reaches its term in good actions. Thus, right reason in its most concrete form is translated from the sphere of mental experience (which may be both cognitive and affective) into the order of action or *praxis*. There are many variations in the explanations of how such a transition is effected but the general pattern is suggested in the foregoing.

Of course the theory of prudential reasoning owes a great deal to the *Nicomachean Ethics*. The versions used in the thirteenth century were, as we have seen, a twelfth-century translation of the first three or four books and the complete translation made by Robert Grosseteste (ca. 1168–1253). Grosseteste also produced a fragmentary commentary *(Notulae)* on the *Nicomachean Ethics* and its Greek commentators. These "Notes" are partly printed with a commentary made by Walter Burleigh in the fourteenth century.[7] In addition to his pioneer work as translator and commentator, three things may be remembered in connection with Grosseteste's contribution to ethics. First, he was one of the first lecturers on the liberal arts in the schools at

Oxford. The university was granted a charter there in 1248 but long before that time Grosseteste was teaching at the Franciscan house of studies, although not himself a member of that order. From 1229 to 1235, he was the first lecturer in theology for the Oxford Franciscans.[8] In 1235, he became Bishop of Lincoln (and thus is often cited as *Lincolniensis*). So, Grosseteste was doubtless one of the first to lecture on ethics in England. The second thing for which Grosseteste is important in this field was his general emphasis on natural science, mathematics, and the observation of nature. He is thus partly responsible not only for the continuing British interest in the philosophy of science but also for an emphasis on empirical information as an important source of ethical judgment. He was convinced that natural experience is a necessary element in all learning and that mathematics supplies the key to the interpretation and understanding of the speculative and practical significance of such experience. Grosseteste's third contribution was a blunt explanation of right reason as a direct conformity between a thing or an act and its exemplar in the divine mind. His version of *recta ratio* is a simple theological approbative theory, as the following text shows.

> This rule [of rightness, *rectitudo]* is nothing other than the eternal reason *(ratio aeterna)* of the thing in the divine mind. . . . But if it be said that this is the right reason accord-

ing to which the thing should be thus, it is asked again: where is this reason seen to be the right reason of this thing and such as it should be, except, in turn, in its reason? And so there will always be a regress until the thing is seen to be as it should be in its first reason which is right according to itself. And, therefore, the thing is as it should be because it conforms to that. All created truth, then, is evident in so far as the light of its eternal reason is present to the person observing, as Augustine testifies.[9]

Grosseteste's most famous pupil and admirer was Roger Bacon (ca. 1214–1292), who entered the Franciscan Order in 1257 after teaching liberal arts at Oxford and Paris for many years. Bacon was highly critical of most of his contemporaries and advocated a complete reform in Christian learning. (Both Grosseteste and Bacon anticipated by several centuries the more famous "idols" and "new method" of Francis Bacon.) While in Paris, Roger Bacon had met a canon lawyer named Guido Fulcodi and told him of his plans for reform. Roughly, what Bacon wanted was more emphasis on natural science, mathematics, and the study of ancient languages as aids for the interpretation of Scripture. In 1265 Guido became Pope Clement IV. He wrote to Bacon requesting a copy of his writings and ordering that this be sent regardless of any Franciscan regulation to prevent the publishing of Bacon's views.

This is the first intimation that Bacon was in some difficulty with his superiors.[10] He had written various short treatises but he now began the *Communia Naturalium* (a *Summa* of all types of knowledge). Soon he saw that this grandiose work could not be finished in time to satisfy the pope's interest in a plan for the reform of Christian education, so Roger started the *Opus Majus (Greater Work)* to cover much the same ground but more briefly. With a few other writings, the *Opus Majus* was dispatched by messenger to Rome in the year 1268. The treatise is of some importance in the history of ethics, since the seventh and last part of the *Opus Majus* is an essay on moral philosophy.[11] Somewhat in the manner of Auguste Comte in the nineteenth century, Roger Bacon argued that ethics should be placed at the peak of the sciences and that all other disciplines should be propaedeutic to it. Indeed, Roger also shared with Comte a sort of positivistic attitude toward ethics: he was quite frank in saying that canon law is an important source of moral judgment, along with the Scriptures.

However, Roger Bacon had little else in common with Comte. One has only to read a few pages of the *Opus Majus* to realize that, like Augustine, Bacon takes "philosophy" as Christian wisdom and makes little distinction between philosophy and theology. The Bible, canon law, and the "philosophers" are all sources of moral instruction. Among his favorite authors were Augustine, Seneca, and Avicenna. Many parts of the essay on moral philosophy are verbatim extracts from one or the other of these writers. In the third section of this treatise *(Opus Majus,* VII, 3) Bacon argues that the views of the ancient philosophers are frequently superior to the practices of Christians —yet he frequently asserts that Christian revelation is needed for a really good life. He is very close to Grosseteste's position that moral goodness consists in direct conformity with the law of God as manifested in the Scriptures. God's will is the standard of moral judgment. Most people learn what their moral obligations are through the dictates of canon law. There is also a moral illumination that comes in the inner mental experience of at least some men, but it is difficult to ascertain the extent and content of this sort of special communication. Some texts suggest that it is a theory of innate ideas.

In connection with his discussion of politics (civil science, which he takes as a part of moral philosophy) Roger Bacon introduces a threefold division of man's moral relations which is retained by some later Scholastic ethicians (notably Francis Suárez). First of all, man is considered in relation to God; then in relation to his neighbor; and thirdly in relation to himself.[12] On each of these levels, Bacon feels man has certain rights and responsibilities. He does not seem to see that the third relationship (of man to himself) is not interpersonal, as are the other two, and can hardly involve "duties" in the same sense as the two external relations. In spite of his protestations concerning the high role of moral philosophy in Christian education, Bacon did not actually contribute much to the development of the theory.

The Franciscan school at Paris was also active in the realm of practical philosophy. From about 1236 onward they had one or two of their members teaching continually as theology professors at the University of Paris. Alexander of Hales (ca. 1186–1245) was an elderly Parisian professor (though born in England) before entering the Order of Friars Minor in 1236–1237. His admirers in the order compiled in his honor a large encyclopedic work of theology which came to be known as the *Summa Fratris Alexandri*. It contains the first treatise on law in the *Summa* literature and exerted some influence on Aquinas' better-known discussion of various types of law.[13] One of Alexander's successors as a Franciscan professor at Paris was the French scholar John of La Rochelle (died in 1245). His treatise *On the Soul* became the standard exposition of Franciscan psychology in the thirteenth century.[14] Many of the teachings of this type of psychology (no real distinction between the soul and its powers, a different mode of cognition for corporeal things and for immaterial beings, and much stress on the affective-volitional functions of the human soul) become influential in the work of later Franciscan moral writers, such as Bonaventure, Duns Scotus, and even William of Ockham.

The great figure in Franciscan thought at Paris in the thirteenth century was Bonaventure (ca. 1217–1274). Born Giovanni di Fidanza in Italy, he joined the Franciscans at an early age, studied theology and liberal arts in Paris, received his doctorate in the same year as Thomas Aquinas (1256–1257), and was made general minister of his order at that time. As an administrator for the rest of his life, Bonaventure wrote mostly short treatises and sermons. However, he had definite views on the role of philosophy in Christian life and represented a very distinctive approach to the ethical theory of right reason.

Psychology is most important in Franciscan thinking. In the thirteenth century their analysis of the human soul and its functions embodied elements from Augustine, Damascene, and Aristotle.[15] Starting with Alexander of Hales and John of La Rochelle, continuing with Bonaventure and Matthew of Aquasparta (ca. 1240–1302), Franciscan psychology insisted on the unity and simplicity of man's soul (and so refused to make radical distinctions between powers such as intellect and will), and this psychology further maintained that volitional activity and affective experience are more distinctive of man than is any cognitive activity. Bonaventure would say, for instance, that man is a "rational" animal but he would understand rationality as expressed in volitional decision and activity. The test of this view is found in Bonaventure's notion of ultimate beatitude: the good man's final union with

God is essentially an act of love, and not an act of intellectual knowledge as Aquinas was teaching in the same years at Paris. This is what is meant when Bonaventure is called a voluntarist. He is not extreme in his views but he is opposed to the idea that the intellect is man's highest power.

It was as a consequence of this psychological position that Bonaventure decided to place synderesis in the function of volition. As he explained in his lectures on Peter Lombard's *Sentences:*

Just as from the very creation of the soul the intellect possesses a light which is for it a natural seat of judgment *(naturale judicatorium),* directing the intellect in its acts of knowing, so also does the affective capacity *(affectus)* have a sort of natural weight *(naturale quoddam pondus),* directing it in its acts of appetition . . . and in this way, synderesis only denotes this weight of the will (or the will plus this weight) in the sense that it has the function of inclining toward that which is good in itself *(ad bonum honestum).*

He goes on to say that conscience *(conscientia)* is different from synderesis. As a habit in the order of cognition, conscience belongs to practical understanding and even has a certain moving character *(rationem motivi),* inasmuch as it prompts and inclines the soul to action.[17] So, for Bonaventure conscience is a habit of the practical intellect which inclines a person to know both general principles of moral rectitude and the particular character of good or bad actions.

The source of this "rightness" is a moral illumination which involves the light of sacred Scripture. In one of his shorter treatises, the point is expressed as follows:

Accordingly, in the consideration of rectitude there is seen the rule of life. For he indeed lives rightly who is guided by the regulations of the divine law, as is the case when the will of man accepts necessary precepts, salutary warnings, and counsels of perfection that he may thereby prove the good and acceptable and perfect will of God. And then is the rule of life right when no obliquity can be found therein.[18]

Obviously, then, the moral philosophy *(philosophia moralis)* of St. Bonaventure employs the data of religious faith and is a moral theology.

At the same time that the Franciscans were developing their affective approach to moral theory the Dominicans were beginning to emphasize the role of practical reason in the moral life. The first teacher in the Order of St. Dominic to develop an ethics was Albert the Great (1206–1280). He was accused by Roger Bacon of teaching philosophy without having had any teacher in the subject. This was probably correct: Albert taught liberal arts courses based on his own voracious reading of all the ancient, patristic, and early medieval treatises that he found available in Latin. At the beginning of several of his commentaries on works of Aristotle, he stated his intention to make Aristotelian philosophy known to the "Latins." However, Albert's views in speculative philosophy are not simply Aristotelian: he combined Neoplatonism, Christian Platonism, Avicennism, and Augustinism with his own meditations. His metaphysics is not identical with that of his pupil Thomas Aquinas: Albertinism is a complicated theory that has not yet been fully investigated.

On moral questions, Albert's writings are very extensive and their chronology is not yet completely established. However, the following works are important: *Tractatus de natura boni* (written before 1240), as yet unedited, treats detailed moral questions; *Summa de creaturis* (1244–1249), one part: *De homine,* has information on the moral psychology and theory of knowledge, another part, *De bono,* contains data on moral science; *Commentaria in libros Sententiarum* (1244–1249), Albert's theology lectures on Peter Lombard's *Sentences:* books two and three are important for ethics; *Lectura in libros Ethicorum Aristotelis* (1248), a course of lectures on the *Nicomachean Ethics,* recorded in the handwriting of Thomas Aquinas; *Commentaria in libros Ethicorum Aristotelis* (1256–1270), a much later paraphrase of the *Nicomachean Ethics;* and the *Summa Theologiae* (1270–1280), a very late work with much material on moral science but frequently incompatible with the earlier views of Albert.[19]

It is evident that Albert was one of the first thinkers in the thirteenth century to develop a moral philosophy based in good part on man's natural experience and reasoning. He believed that there is an eternal law in the mind of God, of course, but was quite anxious to investigate what the Greek and Arabian philosophers had to say about ethics. The theory of right reason *(recta ratio),* as outlined earlier in this chapter, is central to Albert's thinking. Synderesis is the intellectual capacity to understand the first principles of moral reasoning—which are general rules of natural law *(jus naturale).* In his *Lectures on the Ethics* (1248) he explained:

Just as there are in speculative thinking certain general principles from which one reasons to particular conclusions, so in moral considerations there are some general principles by which one discovers rules for actions, such as "theft is forbidden" and similar rules; every man is expected to know these and he can, because he has the process of reason for this purpose, and these rules are called the natural law.[20]

The process of practical reasoning starts with such a general rule and moves through more particular judgments (factually grounded in experience) to individual conclusions. Conscience *(conscientia)* is the name that Albert uses for these concluding judgments of practical reasoning.[21]

The expression *jus naturale* (in both Albert and Thomas Aquinas) is usually translated as "natural law." This may cause misunderstanding in English. Other modern vernaculars have a special word for *jus (Recht, droit)* as opposed to *lex (Gesetz, loi).* In authors such as Albert and Aquinas, *jus* means what is objectively right (adjusted) in the concrete. So, it is *just* for a male and female of the same biological species to reproduce and care for their offspring. This is not because some lawmaker has so willed but because there is in the real relation between male and female a certain suitability *(convenientia)* which is not present between male and male, or between members of two different species. Provided other circumstances are reasonable, it is thus good for male and female to engage in reproduction. Man apprehends this good quality of his actions by observing what is in accord with his nature and what flows from his nature as a reasoning being.[22]

According to Albert, the most general rule known through synderesis is: "Good should be done; evil should be avoided" *(bonum faciendum; malum vitandum)*. However, Albert thought that other broad rules of conduct (such as: honor your parents, help those in need, do no injury to any man, avoid fornication, commit no theft or murder, love God, etc.) are known to all men by natural insight. These are *jura,* i.e. right things. His whole approach to law, moral or otherwise, is intellectual and realistic. Command is the work of reason.[24] The expression of such an intellectual order is a law (called either *jus* or *lex),* and the will of the lawmaker is no more active in declaring a moral law than it would be in a mathematician who states that equals added to equals must result in equals. After hundreds of years of emphasis on the notion that a law must be enacted by the will of the legislator, it is difficult for a twentieth-century man to appreciate this intellectual view of law which characterizes one line of late medieval ethics, starting with Albert and running through Thomas Aquinas, Soto, Medina, and Robert Bellarmine.

Thomas Aquinas (1224–1274) remains the outstanding ethician of the thirteenth century and perhaps of the whole Middle Ages. A colleague of Albert in the Order of Preachers, Thomas had studied liberal arts at the royal University of Naples before becoming a Dominican. After further studies in philosophy and theology, under Albert at Cologne and in the University of Paris, Thomas taught philosophy and theology at Paris, in several study centers of his order in the vicinity of Rome, and finally as a professor at the University of Naples. His writings with important ethical content are: *Commentary on the Sentences* (1252–1256), *On the Truth of the Catholic Faith* (*Summa Contra Gentiles,* 1259–1264, Book III is on moral science), *Commentary on the Nicomachean Ethics* (at any time from 1263 to 1272), *Disputed Questions on Evil and on the Virtues* (1268–1272), and the first and second sections of Part II of the *Summa Theologiae* (1268–1272).

Broadly speaking, the ethical theory of Thomas is similar to what we have seen in Albert; the Thomistic position is much more thoroughly developed, however, and is more internally consistent than the Albertinian ethics.[25] Thomistic ethics is often classified as a "natural law" theory,[26] but this is unfortunate for two reasons. In recent terminology, law implies a command with an origin in the will of a legislator: this is not Thomas' view. He defined law as "an ordinance of reason promulgated by someone in charge of the community for the common good."[27] Second, the meaning of "natural law" has been so diversified in late medieval and modern discussions that the term is no longer accurately descriptive. Thomas' ethics is eudaimonistic and teleological; it stresses internal motivation as well as the consequences of moral action; it is, moreover, a self-realization theory.[28]

Man as a moral agent is analyzed in great detail by Aquinas. Human functions range from vegetative acts of assimilating food, growing, and reproducing, through the range of animal activities of sense perception, appetition (concupiscible and irascible emotions), and kinesthesis, to the typically human actions of understanding simple meanings, reasoning discursively to logical conclusions, and intellectual appetition (also called volition). Important in this complicated moral psychology is the distinction between man's sensory experience (cognitive and affective), which is concerned with the *individual* aspects of bodies; and man's rational experience (cognitive and appetitive), which deals with the *universal* meanings of reality. Moral actions must be voluntary, that is they must come under the control of human understanding, must be done (or omitted) with some end in view, with some knowledge of the nature of the act under consideration, and with some approval on the part of the agent himself. This excludes from the domain of voluntary action purely accidental actions, merely physical or biological functions, and acts resulting wholly from external violence. It should be emphasized that, in Thomism, voluntary does not mean volitional. There are four powers in man which are the centers of moral activity: concupiscible appetite (feelings of sensual desire and the contrary), irascible appetite (emergency feelings in response to threats from sense objects), intellectual appetite (personal inclinations toward or away from the universal objects of intellection), and potential intellect (the functions of understanding, judging, and reasoning about universal objects). Each of these moral powers is open to being perfected by an appropriate moral habit: temperance *(temperantia)* may be acquired in the concupiscible appetite, and is the moral virtue of reasonable *moderation* in sense desires; courage *(fortitudo)* is the chief habit of the irascible appetite, and brings a *firmness* to one's emotional responses to emergencies presented in sense experience; justice *(justitia)* may habituate the intellectual appetite *(voluntas)* so that it customarily wills what is good for other persons, and *equality,* either simple or proportional, is the keynote of justice; and fourthly, prudence *(prudentia)* or practical wisdom is the chief practical habit of man's intellect, and is the moral virtue of reasoning well about, and commanding, good moral actions. Only one of these cardinal virtues is a habit of the will. This is a fundamental difference between the ethical theory of Thomas Aquinas and that of the other scholastics: most others think that will *(voluntas)* is the only essentially moral power in man.[29] As to Thomas' particular approach to right reason and the distinction of morally good from evil action, he did, of course, think that God knows all the rules of morality and has perfect judgment of individual human actions. But Aquinas did not teach that we humans know all that God knows.[30] Some part of God's moral wisdom is conveyed to men by way of revelation (as in the case of Moses and the Decalogue); other partial knowledge of eternal Justice is acquired by ordinary natural experience and rational reflection on it (as in the case of thoughtful pagans like Aristotle and Cicero but also in philosophers of every era). Aquinas was convinced that "God is not offended by us except by what we do against our own good."[31] In other words, actions are not morally right or wrong because of some arbitrary fiat of divine will: what is good for man is what may be understood as fitting *(conveniens)* to this kind of agent, under certain concrete circumstances, in relation to the purpose that this agent intends to accomplish, in the real environment of the actions including other persons individually and collectively. This complicated set of relations is what Thomas Aquinas means by right reason. As expressed in universal judgments about the kinds of actions that are morally appropriate or inappropriate for a human agent, the conclusions of right reasoning are identical with the rules of natural moral law. As applied by the prudent person to practical decisions about individual moral problems, right reasoning terminates in moral conscience, a practical judgment of choice, and right action.

Thomistic ethics, in its original form, is a eudaimonism but it differs from the theory of Aristotle in that Thomas regards the ultimate end of a good human life as not merely internal well-being *(eudaimonia)* in the moral person but also as a positive approach to an external and real objective: the Perfect Good which is God. Thomism is not simply a self-realization ethics, then; it has certain resemblances to "good will" ethics (as found in Anselm, or later in Kant) by virtue of the emphasis on right intention. On the other hand, Thomas' stress on a prudent consideration of the purpose and predictable results of each voluntary action has something in common with utilitarianism and naturalistic pragmatism.

Some of Thomas' contemporaries were even more naturalistic, however. At some time during the 1260s a movement began at the University of Paris that has been variously called Latin Averroism, and heterodox or radical Aristotelianism. It was basically an attempt by certain teachers in the Arts Faculty (all of them Catholic priests) to give a great deal of autonomy to naturalistic philosophy. Leaders in this school of thought were Siger of Brabant (ca. 1240–1284) and Boethius of Dacia (fl. ca. 1270). As far as their ethical teaching is concerned, these professors were Aristotelians who attempted to philosophize without using the data of their Christian faith. Our information on their views is defective, because we have very few of their writings today and because our reports on them are mostly derived from their thirteenth-century critics and opponents. Siger wrote a *Book on Felicity,* now nonextant. Boethius produced a short treatise on the highest good.[32] It appears that they taught that the good life for man consists in the cultivation of speculative understanding. In his famous *Condemnation of 219 Propositions* (1277 C.E.) Bishop Etienne Tempier was concerned about the teachings of these Aristotelian professors. Among the "errors" to which he objected were these:

> That there is no more excellent state than to study philosophy; that all the good that is possible to man consists in the intellectual virtues; that happiness is found in this life and not in another; that a man who is ordered as to his intellect and his affections, in the manner in which this can be sufficiently accomplished by means of the intellectual and moral virtues of which the Philosopher [Aristotle] speaks in the *Ethics,* is sufficiently disposed for eternal happiness.[33]

At least three anonymous *Commentaries on the Nicomachean Ethics* from the late thirteenth century have been discovered as evidences of the spread of this naturalistic ethical trend in the period.[34]

Giles of Rome (ca. 1247–1316) shows the continuing influence of Aristotelian ethics in the latter part of the thirteenth century. His letter on the *Distinction of Rhetoric, Ethics and Politics* simply repeats peripatetic doctrine.[35] One distinctive view in Giles's work is the subordination of politics to moral philosophy, on the theory that the latter is the complete science of human action. This same view carries over into Giles's famous treatise *On Ecclesiastical Power,* where he argues for the subordination of civil authority to that of the Church: "The duty of earthly power is to prepare the materials in order that the ecclesiastical ruler may not be hampered in spiritual matters."[36]

It is in this second half of the thirteenth century that we find the beginnings of ethical voluntarism. We have already noted how Franciscan psychology emphasized the affective and volitional side of man's nature. Peter John Olivi (d. 1298) was one of the first Franciscans to teach that "either the will is free, or it is not a will."[37] Prior to this in patristic and medieval thought there is no discussion of free will *(libera voluntas)* but only of free choice *(liberum arbitrium).* From the time of Olivi onward, more and more people insist that the human will is an essentially free power.[38]

This emphasis on volition is not confined to the Franciscan thinkers. Henry of Ghent (ca. 1217–1293) was a prominent professor in arts and theology at the University of Paris who taught that the will of man is in every way the most distinctive human power. Will directs the intellect in its functioning but the will "by its own power of knowing can direct itself."[39] As a result of this view, Henry thought that moral law and obligation issue directly from the will of the legislator. While he may still speak of right reason, Henry of Ghent stands at the beginning of a different theory of moral and legal obligation. To command now becomes a function of a will that is autonomous and undetermined by external judgments of intellect. What the lawmaker wills to be done is what is right and no other justification is required.

Associated with this "Neo-Augustinian" trend in thirteenth-century thought is the remarkable Catalan writer Ramón Lull (ca. 1232–1315). A layman and married, Lull devoted the last part of his life to the project of converting the Moors to Christianity. On the island of Mallorca he founded a university which continues to this day as a center of Catalan culture and Lullism. His psychology is that of St. Augustine: the human soul has no separate powers, it is utterly simple but has three main functions—memory, understanding, and willing. Of these the last is most distinctive, and volition reaches its peak in love. Lull's famous "Great Art" was simply the teaching that man

intuits (by means of divine illumination, as in Augustine) a number of self-evident notions. These principles
are: goodness, greatness, eternity, power, wisdom, will,
virtue, truth, and glory. The foregoing may be used as
predicates with various basic concepts and relations to
form true and useful judgments in the practical order.[40]
Although Ramón Lull was not a theoretical ethician, he has some importance in ethics as an advocate
of a rather simple version of intuitionism. One might
even suggest that his semi-autobiographical novel,
Blanquerna, has many of the attitudes that character-
ize recent phenomenological ethics. The following passage illustrates Lull's emphasis on concrete emotions:

> "Justice," said Blanquerna, "what thing
> desirest thou in my will?" Memory answered
> for Justice: "I desire therein contrition
> and fear; I desire tears in thine eyes, in thy
> heart sighs, and in thy body afflictions." "And
> thou, Liberality, what desirest thou in my
> will?" Understanding answered for Liberal-
> ity: "I desire to possess it wholly, for love, for
> repentance and for the despising of the van-
> ities of this world." "And thou, Mercy, what
> desirest thou of my memory and understand-
> ing?" Will answered for Mercy: "I desire
> thy memory wholly, for remembrance of
> the gifts of Mercy and her pardon, and thine
> understanding wholly for comprehension of
> the same, and these yet more for the contem-

plation of Mercy herself." So Blanquerna gave himself wholly to that which the virtues of his Beloved desired of him.[41]

From these lines it will be obvious that existential commitment is not without its medieval antecedents and that "irrational man" found a place in the century of right reason.

Another very unusual thinker at the end of the thirteenth century was Meister Johannes Eckhart (ca. 1260–1327). He was a Dominican, as were Albert and Thomas Aquinas, but Eckhart's philosophy was a complicated blending of Neoplatonic speculation with Christian mysticism. The peak or spark of the soul *(scintilla animae)* is the highest part of man, above both reason and will. It is in this "citadel" that God contacts man in mystical union. As one historian describes Eckhart's theory: "The gradual purification of the soul from contact with matter by its turning toward God, its final liberation by union with him in a region beyond knowledge and being-all this reminds us of Plotinus' flight of the soul to the One and its absorption in it."[42] It is in his *Sermons* that we see Eckhart developing a "good will" doctrine of human conduct that owes something to the right intention theories of Abelard and Anselm and that anticipates the famous teaching of Immanuel Kant.

> If you have good will, you shall lack for nothing, neither love, humility, nor any other vir-

tue; what you will with all your strength you
shall have, and neither God nor any creature
can deprive you—if, again, your will is sound,
divine and wrapt in God. . . . Good will is
not less powerful for good than bad will is for
evil. . . . With a will that is purely bad, I
commit as great sins as if I were to murder
all the people in the world, even though I did
not lift a finger toward the crime. Why should
not the same power reside in good will?[43]

Still another nonacademic personality who should be
mentioned briefly is the poet Dante. Dante Alighieri
(1265–1321) was widely read in philosophy and introduced much of his learning into his literary works.
He was not, of course, a professional in the field of ethics
but deserves mention here for two reasons. He agreed
with Thomas Aquinas and the Aristotelians that reason in man "is especially his life and the actuality of
his noblest part."[44] Moreover, Dante offers in the
Divine Comedy and *De monarchia* an instructive picture of the moral attitudes of the Christian non-
cleric in the thirteenth century.

Comparatively little historical work has been
done on the ethics of the fourteenth century—yet it
was rich in its thought and exerted no little influence
on the Renaissance and early modern period. Most of
the ethical writers who treated the subject in the sixteenth and seventeenth centuries studied some type
of fourteenth-century philosophy. The outstanding

schools were either Scotistic, terminist, or Thomistic in orientation.

John Duns Scotus (ca. 1265–1308) was a Franciscan who taught for only a few years at Oxford and Paris. He died before he could say his best word on the problems of ethics. Until recently his writings have been badly edited and they are not yet wholly available in critical texts. The *Ordinatio* is Scotus' own edition of his several series of lectures on Peter Lombard's *Sentences.* In the Prologue to the first book of the *Ordinatio* we find a great deal of his philosophy expounded, including his ethics. There is some information on ethics in the *Quodlibetal Questions,* which were conducted in Paris and contain his most mature thought. Duns Scotus is known as the "Subtle Doctor." Very intelligent and learned, he was one of the most brilliant intellects produced in the British Isles. He differed on fundamental points of philosophy from Thomas Aquinas. Perhaps the most important items in the speculative thought of Scotus are his doctrine on the object of the human intellect *(ens in quantum ens,* being without any qualification) and his teaching that the will is free and rational by nature and is superior to the intellect.[45]

In spite of his general opposition to the philosophy of Thomas Aquinas, Duns Scotus supports the view that right reason is the basis on which to judge good human action. He offers, in fact, one of the clearest explanations of the meaning of *recta ratio,* in these lines from the first book of the *Ordinatio:*

Just as beauty *(pulchritudo)* is not some absolute quality in a beautiful body but is the aggregation of all items that are suitable to such a body (that is, matters of size, shape and color) and also the aggregation of all the relations (which pertain to these suitable aspects) in regard to the body and among themselves—so also the goodness *(bonitas)* of the moral act is something like the decorous character *(decor)* of the act, including the aggregation of due proportion to all items to which it is to be proportioned (for instance, to the power, to the object, to the end, to the time, to the place, and to the manner of acting) and this especially according as they are dictated by right reason *(ratione recta)* to be suitable to the act. Consequently, we may say in all cases that the suitability *(convenientia·)* of the act to right reason is that which, once it is present, renders the act good. For since every act is concerned with a definite kind of object, if the act is not in accord with right reason in the agent (that is, if he does not have right reason in acting), then the act is not good. Primarily then, the conformity of the act to right reason—fully dictating concerning all the proper circumstances of this act—is the goodness of the moral act.[46]

There is no question that Duns Scotus upheld the standard of right reason in ethics. "The moral goodness of the act," he explains elsewhere, "is the entirety *(integritas)* of all those items which right reason judges to be required to fit the act itself, or to be suitable to the agent involved in his action."[47] However, unlike Aquinas, Scotus teaches that every moral action is an act of willing, either completed within the will *(actus elicitus voluntatis)* or performed by some other power under command of the will *(actus imperatus voluntatis)*. Every deed *(praxis)* for which man is morally responsible is a will act.[48]

The notion that will, either in God or man, is the source of moral law is rejected by Scotus. He carefully reviews the teaching of Henry of Ghent to the effect that conscience *(conscientia)* resides in the affective part of man's soul and is like a universal mover prompting man to action ("universalis motor stimulans ad opus"). But this view is subjected to severe criticism by Scotus.[49] Then he proceeds to explain that synderesis is the habit whereby practical principles are known—and it is in the intellect, not the will. Furthermore, Scotus treats conscience as the habit of the practical intellect which elicits judgment as to the conformity or nonconformity of concrete actions with the principles of right reason.[50] In the next distinction he repeats his explanation of what right reason means: a reasonable agreement *(convenientia)* of a proposed action with the end the agent has in view, with the free character of the agent *(efficiens)*, with the generic character of this kind of action, with the manner in which the action is executed, and finally, with various extrinsic circumstances of time, place, and other such conditions.

If Scotistic ethics is a right reason theory that insists on the intrinsic character of the good or evil moral action, the next great thinker in the Franciscan school does not agree. William Ockham (ca. 1280–1349) marks the beginning of ethical extrinsicism: the theory that moral good and evil have nothing to do with the internal character of man or his action but rest on the external attribution of a moral quality. Moreover, Ockham is the first prominent ethician to reject eudaimonism. He did not think that man is naturally ordered to the pursuit of personal well-being or happiness. The only objective which can satisfy the human will is God; but ethics cannot show that there is such an ultimate end for men. Hence, Ockham also rejected the medieval theory of the finality of man's nature. He *believed* that God is the ultimate goal of human aspiration but he stoutly maintained that he did not *know* this philosophically. This is the start of the "modern way" *(via moderna)* in ethics.

William Ockham's works with ethical content are the *Ordinatio* (a commentary on the first book of Lombard's *Sentences,* written by Ockham himself); the *Reportatio* (a written record by listeners at Ockham's lectures on the last three books of the *Sentences;* the *Seven Quodlibets;* and the *Treatise on Predestination and Divine Foreknowledge.* His political writings deal chiefly with the Church-state problem and the internal frictions in the Franciscan Order arising from the efforts of a group desiring to return to the pioneer poverty and spirituality of St. Francis.

The speculative philosophy of Ockham sets the stage for his moral views. He has a logic and a philosophy of nature but no metaphysics. The only realities are existing individuals, material or immaterial things. Universals (humanity, goodness, justice) are general words and, in a special sense, generalized concepts. Sometimes Ockham explains the universal concept as a *fictum,* that is, a mental construct produced by intellectual abstraction to represent several similar individuals. In his later period he gave more reality to the universal concept by identifying it with the abstractive *act* of understanding.[52] In any case, the real objects of human understanding are individual things. It becomes difficult for Ockham to assign a difference between sense perception and understanding, since both types of cognition are concerned with individuals.

Ockham's logic includes his epistemology. He has a very strict notion of the requirements of demonstrative science, being convinced that the philosopher could not prove all the things that Thomas Aquinas, or even Duns Scotus, had tried to demonstrate. For instance, Ockham flatly denied that a person could have evident knowledge "by reason or experience" that the intellective soul is the form of the human body.[53] As to the effort to demonstrate the existence of God, Ockham felt that our success depends on how God is initially defined. If God means "some thing more noble and more perfect than anything else besides Him, then it is impossible to demonstrate by natural reason that there is only one God, or even that God, in this sense, exists. On the other hand, if God be understood as "that than which nothing is more noble and more perfect," it may be possible to show that He exists but it is impossible to prove philosophically that He is unique.[54]

While he limited the power of human reason to prove philosophical conclusions, Ockham believed in the usual articles of Christian faith. He was particularly impressed by the omnipotence and freedom of God—and frequently appealed to these attributes in his reasoning about man's capacities and actions. Like Duns Scotus, Ockham identified moral action with volitional activity: "No act is virtuous or vicious unless it is voluntary and in the power of the will."[55] In discussing this, Ockham shows how he considers the will of God to be the ultimate source of morality. God may will that any action be good or bad, provided He does not become involved in contradiction. For instance, God could command a man not to love God for a certain time—and this would become a good action for that period.[56] Of course William still speaks of the need to be guided by right reason ("every right will is in conformity with right reason"), but this does not mean that reason rectifies the volitional act; rather, reason is right *because God has willed it* to be so.[57]

Thus begins in Christian thinking about morality the authoritarian teaching that God could rightly order man to do almost anything and, in view of the absolute omnipotence of God, the consequent actions would be good. Evidently, Ockham did not mean that, having established one set of moral rules, God is going to change them arbitrarily. But he did think that it is within the absolute power of God to alter most of the accepted precepts of morality. The consequences of this Ockhamistic doctrine are tremendous: moral law is reduced to positive divine law, obligation is contingent, and it is doubtful that a valid ethics can be constructed apart from theology.

Ockhamist ethics, then, is truly authoritarian. It is the clearest example in medieval Christian thought of a theological approbative theory. God is the boss and whatever He wills to be right is what is morally good. This became the standard teaching of this type of nominalistic Scholasticism. Gabriel Biel (1425–1495) continued this doctrine in the next century. His writings were studied by many of the early modern ethicians and influenced some of the prominent figures in the Reformation.

Natural law ethics contrasts with the positivist character of Ockhamism. There were some medieval writers who developed the notion of the "law of nature" within the context of jurisprudence. Henry de Bracton (d. 1268) exemplified this lawyer's approach to the right and the good in his book *On the Laws and Customs of England*. Two centuries later, Sir John Fortescue (ca. 1385–1476) continued the same natural law tradition in his work *On the Merits of the Laws of England.* Fortescue's views are close to the teaching of Aristotle. He quotes with approval the *Nicomachean Ethics:* "Natural law is that which has the same force among all men."[59] In fact, Fortescue's version of the right reason theory is very similar to what we saw in Thomas Aquinas.

At the end of the Middle Ages there were frequently three chairs of philosophy (and theology) in the great European universities. A student had a choice of Scotism, Ockhamism, or Thomism. To some extent the same divisiveness carried over into moral science and ethical theory. There were many commentators in each of the three schools but they showed little originality. Among the Thomist writers, Antoninus of Florence (1389–1459) was a bishop who expanded and updated Thomas' teaching on the moral problems of social life. He is considered a pioneer thinker on the moral aspects of economics. Antoninus' basic ethical position is Thomistic.

An oddity in the same period is the vernacular moralizing of the German priest Albrecht von Eyb (1420–1475). He was not interested in ethical theory: his two treatises contain long lists of virtues and pious maxims addressed to the common people rather than the world of scholarship. Von Eyb's forthright but simple teaching was not unlike that of Martin Luther in the next generation.

Two English writers bring to a close the history of right reason ethics in the Middle Ages. Reginald Pecock (ca. 1393–1460) was a Catholic bishop who became concerned about the effects of the Lollard movement within Christianity. In opposition to the view that simple faith and Bible reading offer adequate moral guidance for the good life, Pecock wrote a series of English treatises that stressed the primacy of reason. The natural function of reason, he argued, is to decide what ought to be done.[60] God accepts no good deed unless it be in accord with the judgment of reason ("the doom of resoun"). It is the natural function of man's will to do what right reason dictates. Bishop Pecock distinguished two branches of practical knowledge: moral philosophy and theology. At times he implied that ethics is the more important for salvation. As can be expected, he encountered much criticism both from his Catholic colleagues and from the Lollards. Toward the end of his life he wrote:

> I . . . confess and acknowledge that I here before time [was] presuming of mine own naturall witt, and preferring the judgment of naturall reason before the New and Old Testaments, and the authority and determination of our modern Holy Church.[61]

In point of fact, Pecock's ethical position was very close to that of Thomas Aquinas, although the bishop's optimism about the salvific role of moral philosophy in the life of the Christian no doubt exceeded that of St. Thomas.

Our last representative of this type of ethics, Richard Hooker (1553–1600), takes us well beyond the Middle Ages, but his version of right reason is well developed and very much in the tradition of the Middle Ages. He has been called the Anglican Aquinas. The first book of his *Laws of Ecclesiastical Polity* is an excellent summary of basic Thomistic ethics. Hooker taught that besides the supreme eternal law, which rests in "God's bosom," there is a second eternal law, which consists in the order of things in this universe. Man comes to understand this real order and its requirements from his natural experience and by the use of ordinary reasoning. He did not think that this view demands that one be a Platonist: "We are not of the opinion therefore, as some are, that nature in working hath before her certain exemplary draughts or patterns. . . ."[62] It is erroneous, he argues, to think that we need no reason besides God's will in order to do the good. His opposition to ethical voluntarism is evident in the following typical explanation:

> Where understanding therefore needeth, in those things reason is the director of man's Will by discovering in action what is good. For the Laws of well-doing are the dictates of right reason. . . . In the rest there is that light of Reason, whereby good may be known from evil, and which discovering the same rightly is termed right.[63]

Hooker's description of the law of reason in relation to other laws makes a fitting conclusion to this chapter on the ethics of right reason:

Now that law which, as it is laid up in the bosom of God, they call Eternal, receiveth according unto the different kinds of things which are subject unto it different and sundry kinds of names. That part of it which ordereth natural agents we call usually Nature's law; that which Angels do clearly behold and without any swerving observe is a law Celestial and heavenly; the law of Reason, that which bindeth creatures reasonable in this world, and with which by reason they may most plainly perceive themselves bound; that which bindeth them and is not known but by special revelation from God, Divine law; Human law, that which out of the law either of reason or of God men probably gathering to be expedient, they make it a law. All things therefore, which are as they ought to be, are conformed unto this second law eternal; and even those things which to this eternal law are not conformable are notwithstanding in some sort ordered by the first eternal law.[64]

Part Three

Early Modern Ethics:
1450–1750

Chapter VII
Humanist Ethics in the Renaissance

THE PRIMARY CHARACTERISTIC of ethical thinking in the Renaissance was its humanism. Man became the focal point of attention in the arts, in education, in philosophy, and eventually in religion. The view that man the microcosm epitomizes the whole of things was not unknown to the Middle Ages[1] but the fact remains that man was not the most fascinating object of investigation for the medieval scholar: God was, for both Christian and non-Christian. If we insist that Renaissance ethics was homocentric, that does not mean that the period was irreligious or atheistic. The good and right for man were still ultimately determined by reference to the law or will of God. The point is that even the more religious-minded ethicians at the dawn of modern philosophy focused their interest on the individual human person, his unlimited capacities, his freedom, his opportunities not only for future salvation but for terrestrial accomplishment.

In his *Oration on the Dignity of Man,* Giovanni Pico della Mirandola puts the following speech in the mouth of God. It is typical of this humanistic attitude.

> We have given you, O Adam . . . according to your desire and judgment, whatever place, whatever form, and whatever functions you shall desire. The nature of other creatures, which has been determined, is confined within the bounds prescribed by Us. You, who are confined by no limits, shall determine for yourself your own nature, in accordance with your own free will, in whose hand I have placed you. . . . You may fashion yourself in whatever form you shall prefer.[2]

No twentieth-century existentialist would criticize the thrust of this declaration of man's freedom to make of himself whatever he willed. However, the *Notebooks* of Leonardo da Vinci (1452–1519) show that all is not optimism in the Renaissance outlook on man. At one point Leonardo warns prophetically:

> Creatures shall be seen upon the earth who will always be fighting one with another, with very great losses and frequent deaths on either

side. These shall set no bounds to their mal-
ice; by their fierce limbs a great number of
the trees in the immense forests of the
world shall be laid level with the ground;
and when they have crammed themselves
with food it shall gratify their desire to deal
out death, affliction, labours, terrors and ban-
ishment to every living thing. And by reason
of their boundless pride they shall wish to rise
towards heaven. . . .[3]

Tied in with this humanism was Renaissance classi-
cism. Most of the Greek and Roman ethicians were
edited, printed for the first time, and avidly studied
in the fifteenth and sixteenth centuries. Plato, Aristotle, the Stoics and Epicureans, Seneca, Cicero, and
Plotinus were now re-examined. Nor were the classics
of Christian wisdom neglected: there was a renewed
interest in the Greek and Latin Fathers of the Church
and even in the teaching of Scholastics such as Thomas
Aquinas and Duns Scotus. Mankind became newly
conscious of the worth of its heritage from the past
at the same time that it looked forward to a greater
future on earth.

Platonic Ethics in Italy

One branch of this neoclassicism involved the revival
of Platonism. The Church Council of Florence

(1438–1445) was concerned with the project of reuniting the Greek and Latin branches of Christendom. Greek scholars (Gemistus Pletho, Georgios Scholarios, Teodoro Gaza, and Cardinal Bessarion) wrote on philosophical as well as religious topics. There was a tendency to downgrade Aristotle and to stress the thought of Plato and his school. Under Co-simo de' Medici a Florentine school of Platonic studies developed, partly as a courtly fad but also as a serious center of renewal in Christian education. Scarcely any formal writing or academic teaching of ethics was carried on in this school but its influence on other types of Renaissance ethics was profound. In this group we shall consider the thought of men like Nicholas of Cusa, Laurentius Valla, Marsilio Ficino, Giovanni Pico della Mirandola, Giordano Bruno, and Tommaso Campanella. All of them made some contribution to the growth of new philosophical attitudes in Italy.

Nicholas of Cusa was neither an Italian nor a simple Platonist but we will consider him here because he did much of his work in Italy and he incorporated a good deal of Platonism into his highly personal approach to ethics. His name was Nicholas Kryfts (Krebs) and he was born at Kues (Cusa) on the Moselle River, in 1401. His education at Deventer, Heidelberg, and Padua led to a doctorate in canon law and various services as an ecclesiastical diplomat. Raised to the cardinalate in 1448, Nicholas died at Todi (Italy) in 1464. In spite of his involvement in the external affairs of his

Church, he managed to write a good number of philosophical works. Of these, the treatise *On Learned Ignorance* (1440) and the work *On the Vision of God* (1453) deserve special mention. They combine several strains of Greek philosophy (Plato, Pythagoras, Plotinus) with various types of Christian thought (Augustine, Albert, Meister Eckhart) and even include a certain amount of dabbling in writers on magic and the mystery religions of the East. Some commentators see Nicholas as a continuator of the nominalism of William of Ockham.

Nicholas is critical of Aristotelian philosophy and its effects on theology and moral teaching. He sees the principle of contradiction as the keynote to the method of Aristotle. In his *On Learned Ignorance* (with a further development in the contemporary *De conjecturis)* he argues that contradiction may be overcome in infinity. In the absolute maximum of reality there is a *coincidentia oppositorum,* a fusion of contraries, which transcends the ordinary oppositions of syllogistic logic. This maximum is at once Creator and creature.[4] Human nature exists in the individual only but in the case of the human nature of Christ we find the absolute maximum, the unique instance of the microcosm which combines perfections of the lowest and highest order. The notion of "learned ignorance" goes back to Socrates, of course, but Nicholas sees this ignorance as the essence of wisdom. When he faces the infinite, man most requires the humility that consists in realizing his intellectual limitations.

Ethically, Nicholas is a teleological eudaimonist. Man's "intellect has a natural movement towards the most abstract truth as being the end of all its desires and its final and most delectable object."[5] This ultimate end of moral activity is God. To understand how to achieve final union with God one must start with faith. "In every science certain things must be accepted as first principles if the subject matter is to be understood; and these first postulates rest only upon faith."[6] There is, however, a natural desire in man's mind for the eternal. Thus the study of the good life for man (ethics) involves a combination of faith and natural understanding.

Very much interested in the eventual union of all men in one religion, Nicholas argued that there are a small number of initial moral rules known intuitively by all nations. These he takes to be roughly equivalent to the precepts of the Decalogue and the two Christian precepts of charity. All moral laws can be traced back to love as their source. His treatise *On the Peace of Faith* (1453) is a dialogue that develops this idea that men of all religions and all nationalities are in basic moral agreement on how to live well. Optimistically, Nicholas concludes this treatise: "Therefore, it was concluded from reason that in heaven a harmony is somehow permitted."[7] The influence of this remarkable thinker is found not only in his immediate successors of the Italian Renaissance but in much German mystical and moral speculation and even in the metaphysical edifices of Spinoza, Schelling, and Hegel.

One of the first Italian humanists to treat of ethical problems was Laurentius Valla (1406–1457). He was a blunt critic of Aristotelian philosophy and his *De voluptate* offers a defense of Epicurean ethics. Valla argued in the treatise *On Free Choice* that the relation of human freedom to divine omnipotence is such a great problem that philosophy cannot solve it. Like his contemporary, Nicholas of Cusa, Valla felt that faith was a necessary starting point for philosophy and that some problems can only be handled with the resources of Christian belief.

The two outstanding Platonists of this period in Italy were Marsilio Ficino and John Pico della Mirandola. Ficino (1433–1499) was the central figure in the Florentine academy and he made the first Latin translation of Plotinus' *Enneads*. He also translated and commented on several Platonic dialogues. The work in which his own somewhat eclectic ethical view is best seen is the *Platonic Theology* but he also developed his teaching in the *Book on Pleasure* and the treatise *On Divine Love*. Like Nicholas, Ficino exalted love as the ideal standard of moral living: the love that binds all men in one species as children of God is called *humanitas*. This ideal "humanity" is the source not only of the goodness and beauty in the life of the individual man; it is the standard of perfection in the arts and

all human endeavors. Ficino is a pioneer in the introduction of humanism into modern philosophy. Like
all followers of Plotinus, he taught that true happiness
requires a turning from the earthly to the transcendent: "Our soul by means of the intellect and will, as
by those twin Platonic wings, flies toward God."[9]

The same theme of "flight from the world" is evident
throughout the writing of Giovanni Pico della Mirandola (1463–1494). Echoing passages from the Old and
New Testaments in a text that is basically Platonic,
Pico says:

> Let us therefore fly from the world, which is
> confirmed in evil [cf. I John 5:19]; let us soar
> to the Father in whom are the peace that
> unifies, the true light, and the greatest hap-
> piness. But what will give us wings to soar
> [cf. Ps. 44:7]? The love of the things that are
> above [cf. Col. 3:1–3]. What will take them
> from us? The lust for the things below,
> to follow which is to lose unity, truth, and
> goodness.[10]

As we saw at the beginning of this chapter, Pico
epitomized the Renaissance optimism in regard to
the future of mankind in his *Oration on the Dignity of
Man* (1486). While he was eclectic in his ethics and
openly expressed his aspiration to combine the philosophies of Plato and Aristotle, Pico was actually the
funnel through which Platonic ideals poured into six-

teenth-century ethical writings. British Platonism is particularly indebted to him, as can be seen from Thomas Elyot's translation of Pico's *Rules of a Christian Lyfe* (1534), and from Thomas More's translation of the *Life of Pico della Mirandola* (1510), which was written by John Pico's nephew Gianfrancesco.

Even more influential was Giordano Bruno (1548–1600), who produced three ethical treatises: *The Expulsion of the Triumphant Beast* (1584), *The Cabal of the Horse Pegasus* (1585), and *The Heroic Frenzies* (1585). His speculative philosophy was much influenced by Neoplatonism and the theory of the *coincidentia oppositorum* of Nicholas of Cusa. The result in Bruno is something very close to a pantheism. Man as an individual is merely a modification of infinite substance. Yet man does live some sort of moral life by taking a personal stand in relation to the ongoing process of cosmic nature under the direction of divine necessity. It is clear that Stoicism lies in the background of Bruno's ethical theory and Spinozism in its foreground. One interpreter sums up Bruno's view of the ethical life as follows:

> When man, through wisdom, knows the eternal law and accepts it in his will, and he tends toward the goal assigned to the universe by God and in a social life regulated by the Law he represents the perfection of the world—he then becomes God's instrument

in the accomplishment of the ends of the Cosmos.[11]

The "heroic frenzy" in Bruno's poetic language means the agony that the human individual undergoes in trying to assert some degree of freedom and personality in a universe which is ruled by necessity and in which a man is but a bubble in the infinite.

Fragments of ethical theories of quite diverse origin appear disconcertingly in Bruno's writings. Thus in the work *On the Infinite, Universe and Worlds* he suggests that "there is in the spirit of everyone a certain natural holiness, which sits in the inmost shrine of the intellect, and distinguishes between good and evil."[12] This may simply be an echo of the Scholastic theory of synderesis. On the other hand, his notion that the heart is the center, or monad, from which radiate all the forces of human life and feeling, is frankly attributed by Bruno himself to Pythagoreanism.[13] So conceived, the "heart" becomes (with reason, concupiscence, and will) one of the four powers in which virtue may grow. Prudence in practical reason, fortitude in the heart, temperance in the concupiscible power—all three are subsumed under justice as a general virtue. This is, of course, very much like the teaching in the fourth book of Plato's *Republic*. Bruno's rather chaotic ethics may have influenced Leibniz and Spinoza; there is no question that he was popular with some of the German idealistic ethicians from Hegel onward.

With Tommaso Campanella (1568–1639) we are much removed from the simple Platonism of the early Florentine school. Yet his *City of the Sun* is a Utopian work which owes something to Plato's *Republic*. Although his theory of knowledge seems to reduce all human knowing to sense perception, Campanella speaks of the soul introspecting and finding that its three inner attributes are power *(posse)*, cognition *(nosse)*, and will *(velle)*. These are paralleled by the divine attributes: omnipotence, omniscience, and goodness. He even suggests that the ideal state will have three rulers corresponding to the foregoing: Power (in charge of war and peace), Wisdom (in charge of arts, sciences, and education), and Love (in charge of the procreation and upbringing of children). What is good for the individual citizen depends on the promotion of the welfare of society. In this teaching he may have anticipated in a vague way the later theory of social utilitarianism.

Platonic Ethics in England

A similar trend toward the philosophy of Plato is also found in England. Underlying all versions of Platonic ethics is the conviction that there are certain universal standards of goodness, rectitude, temperance, courage, equality, and so on. In Christian Platonism (which is what is found in the Renaissance) these ideals of virtue are considered to exist as exemplars in the mind of God. Such a view was very widespread in European centers of learning at the beginning of the modern era. Even thinkers like Bruno and Campanella who came to be regarded as heretics by ecclesiastical authorities did not challenge this teaching. Nor did the Protestant Reformation necessarily require the abandoning of the Platonic position in ethics, even though it became more and more difficult to maintain such a universalism in company with a nominalistic theory of knowledge and reality. The fact is that many personalities in the early Reformation movement did combine Platonism with their moral and religious views. Nowhere was this more evident than in early British humanism.

We have seen in the preceding chapter how Richard Hooker, in the last half of the sixteenth century, taught a kind of ethics that is in direct continuity with the *recta ratio* doctrine of Thomas Aquinas in the thirteenth century. To many readers at the end of the Renaissance (and to many today), Hooker would look like an ethical Platonist.[14] Much the same judgment could be made on that little-understood school of British philosophers called the "Cambridge Platonists." They, too, are Platonists in only a very special sense; we shall examine their ethical position in the next chapter. At present we are concerned with the rather direct influence of some of Plato's philosophy on English ethicians of the Renaissance. It would be possible to discuss many writers under this category, since nearly all English classical scholars of the period have some interest in Plato's moral dialogues, but our survey will be limited to three leading figures.

One of the most unusual humanists in Renaissance England was Thomas More (1478–1535). A Catholic layman, he became lord chancellor of England and was executed for refusing to acknowledge that Henry VIII was head of the Church in England. More's *Utopia* was written in Latin and published on the Continent forty-five years before its posthumous appearance in English from a London printer. The work is obviously influenced by Plato's *Republic.* It also appears to be a reaction to Machiavelli's *The Prince* (1513), but the fact is that More did not know the Italian treatise.[15]

The ethical position taken by More in his *Utopia* is deliberately marked off from Biblical and early Christian moralizing. After arguing that reason may develop certain principles of natural religion, More proceeds to a theory of psychological hedonism limited only by a reasonable concern for the welfare of society. Few secondary works seem to note this important statement of ethical egoism a whole century before Hobbes, and of the theory of natural religion a hundred years in anticipation of Herbert of Cherbury. Speaking of the Utopians, Thomas More writes:

> They define virtue thus, that it is a living according to Nature, and think that we are made

by God for that end; they believe that a man
follows the dictates of Nature when he pur-
sues or avoids things according to the direction of reason; they say that the first dictate
of reason is the kindling in us a love and rev-
erence for the Divine Majesty, to whom we
owe both all that we have and all that we can
hope for. In the next place, reason directs
us to keep our minds as free from passion
and as cheerful as we can, and that we should
consider ourselves as bound by the ties of
good-nature and humanity to use our utmost
endeavors to help forward the happiness of
all other persons. . . . [16]

Thus far, More's view does not differ from that of
many open-minded and socially conscious Christians.
However, he next draws his own inferences about the
value of seeking personal pleasure, in the immediately
following lines:

And from thence they infer, that if a man
ought to advance the welfare and comfort
of the rest of mankind, there being no virtue more proper and peculiar to our nature
than to ease the miseries of others, to free
from trouble and anxiety in furnishing them
with the comforts of life, in which pleasure
consists, Nature much more vigorously leads
him to do all this for himself. A life of pleasure is either a real evil, and in that case we

ought not to assist others in their pursuit of it . . . o r if it is a good thing, so that we not only may, but ought to help others to it, why then ought not a man to begin with himself? Since no man can be more bound to look after the good of another than after his own; for Nature cannot direct us to be good and kind to others, and yet at the same time to be unmerciful and cruel to ourselves. Thus, as they define virtue to be living according to Nature, so they imagine that Nature prompts all people on to seek after pleasure, as the end of all they do.[17]

Later More defines pleasure as "every motion or state, either of body or mind, in which Nature teaches us to delight." Within the next few pages he lists and examines in some detail what these mental and physical satisfactions are considered to be. Hobbes no doubt read all this and liked it.

If Thomas More's ethics is Platonic in a broad sense (as inspired by the *Republic* and a view that man's universal nature indicates the way of virtue to each person), then the outlook of Sir Thomas Elyot (ca. 1490–1546) is more strictly in the classic tradition of Plato. We have already noted that Elyot was associated with Italian Platonism by virtue of his translation of *The Rules of a Christian Life* written by Giovanni Pico della Mirandola (1534). Several years earlier Elyot had composed *The Boke Named the Gov-*

ernour, in continuation of the medieval literary tradition of the "Book for Princes." Elyot's ethical foundation for the education of a political ruler follows close upon the Greek doctrine of the great virtues. Prudence, justice, fortitude, and temperance are discussed with all their "parts" or associated virtues. The one non-classical virtue inserted by Elyot is that of faith.[18] Aristotle is much quoted throughout but Plato is "the most noble Philosopher." Perhaps the greatest contribution from Thomas Elyot to English ethical writing is his coining of many new vernacular terms to express the nuances of practical discourse. He, more than any other, may be regarded as the father of ethics written in English.[19]

Although a poet and not a moral philosopher, Edmund Spenser (ca. 1552–1599) probably did more than any philosophical writer of the period to transmit the Platonic outlook on the good and the beautiful to England. Compare him with a contemporary named William Baldwin who published in 1597 *A Treatise of Morall Philosophy, Wherein Is Contained the Worthy Sayings of Philosophers, Emperors, Kings, and Orators.* The contribution of Baldwin's work is minimal.[20] On the other hand, Spenser's *Foure Hymnes* publicized the doctrine that there are ideal standards of aesthetic and moral judgment which immutably and eternally regulate the proper expressions of human taste. Thus the *Hymne in Honour of Beautie* speaks of the "goodly Paterne" from which the Creator ("the great Workmaister") has formed all things on earth. It further suggests that the human soul is similarly informed from above with the "seede of vertue." Spenser's stress on the moral influence of high-minded love indicates the source of this poem: the treatise *De amore divino* of Marsilio Ficino. In point of fact, most British writing on Platonic ethics is tributary to Italian humanism.

Aristotelian Ethics in the Renaissance

The works of Aristotle that have survived are not elegant and attractive literary pieces. In the estimation of a period which valued aesthetic appeal, the *Nicomachean Ethics* ranked quite low. Yet one of the earliest of the Italian classicists, Leonardo Bruni, or Aretino (1369–1444), translated it along with the *Politics*. Even in his own *Introduction to Moral Instruction (Isagogicon Moralis Disciplinae)* Leonardo Bruni gives preference to the ethics of Aristotle, although he offers brief glimpses of the moral philosophies of the other Greek schools.[21]

In Renaissance Italy the great center of Aristotelian studies was Padua and many of the books written in this school were published by the printers of nearby Venice. The Paduan Aristotelians, unlike the majority of Renaissance scholars, were nonclerics. Medical doctors in north Italy took up the study of the scientific works of Aristotle and expanded their interests in the direction of the Averroistic interpretation of the peripatetic psychology and philosophy.[22] Their commentaries stressed the empirical and materialistic tendencies of the original works. In the area of practical philosophy, their Aristotelianism was somewhat deterministic and materialistic in orientation. The annotations of men like Alexander Achillini (1463–1512), Agostino Nifo (1473–1546), Marcantonio Zimara (d. 1532), and Giacomo Zabarella (1533–1589) were printed with the early Latin editions of Aristotle's works. They influenced even Scholastic writers of the period (such as Cardinal Tommaso de Vio, known as Cajetan, 1469–1534) so that they hesitated to offer philosophical arguments for the spirituality and immortality of the human soul and for the freedom of man and the noneternity of the world.

Pietro Pomponazzi (1462–1525) actually criticized the Averroist interpretation of Aristotle, in his treatise on the *Immortality of the Soul.* Yet he also argued that Aquinas had been too optimistic in thinking that he could establish the spirituality and immortality of the soul by using Aristotle's philosophy. Pomponazzi insisted that he *believed* these things but did not *know* them philosophically.[23] The thirteenth and fourteenth chapters of the *Immortality of the Soul* show that Pomponazzi viewed *eudaimonia* in terms of man's natural life on earth. The moral goal that is attainable by all men is a life in accord with the usual moral virtues. Man's oft-mentioned desire for immortality is not really different from the brute animal's natural desire to avoid death. Thus we have a version of Renaissance Aristotelian ethics which is completely naturalistic.

Pomponazzi always professed to believe in Christianity but one of his followers, Lucilio Vanini (1585–1619), pushed this position to its extreme in openly attacking the established religion in England. Vanini was eventually convicted as a libertine and atheist, at Toulouse. In contemporary Soviet scholarship, Vanini is regarded as an important predecessor of Diderot, Helvétius, and d'Holbach, as well as of dialectical materialism.[24]

A quite different school of Aristotelian ethics is found in Catholic Scholasticism. Its activities were centered in Spain and Portugal but extended somewhat into other countries of Europe. Typical of this movement was Francisco de Vitoria (1480–1546), a Dominican professor at the University of Salamanca. His *Commentary on the Second Part of the Summa Theologiae* is a well-informed study of the moral teaching of Thomas Aquinas. In his treatise *On the Law of War* (1532), however, Vitoria shows more of his personal ability as a practical thinker on problems of international relations. In the thirteenth century, Thomas had stated three conditions that would have to be satisfied before a country could be justified in waging war: (1) that it be waged by the authority of a sovereign state; (2) that it be waged for a just cause; and (3) that it be waged to promote some good or to avoid some evil.[25] Vitoria discusses each of these conditions very thoroughly. As to what is a good reason for going to war, he denies that difference of religion, extension of empire, or the glory of a prince are just causes for making war. He concludes: "There is a single and only just cause for commencing a war, namely, a wrong received. . . ."[26] The other two conditions are similarly clarified by Vitoria. More significant today, he adds a fourth condition of his own: the just war must be conducted in a reasonable and moderate manner. Thus he raises the important ethical question of the use of proper means. In particular, Vitoria emphasizes the point that the good results of a war should exceed the evil consequences: "If any war should be advantageous to one province or nation but injurious to the world or to Christendom, it is my belief that, for this very reason, that war is unjust."[27]

As a consequence of views such as the foregoing, Vitoria is regarded by many as the founder of the theory of international law. He lived at a time when national spirit and the theory of sovereignty reached their peak yet he strongly supported the project of one world state and of a law that would be truly international. This Vitoria viewed as not merely a matter of political expediency; his moral disapproval of refusal to cooperate with world regulation is frankly expressed. "It is clear," Vitoria wrote, "that they who violate these international rules, whether in peace or in war, commit a mortal sin." No Scholastic philosopher could be more forthright.

Besides the Dominican writers in the Iberian Peninsula the outstanding group of Aristotelian Scholastics was found in the Society of Jesus. Almost from the beginning the textbook for philosophical studies in the Jesuit course of studies was the *Opera Omnia* of Aristotle. A Renaissance Jesuit, Sylvester Maurus (1619–1687), provided the standard printing, with commentary, of Aristotle in Latin. In the textbook series published by the Jesuits of Coimbra (the famous *Cursus Conimbricensis)* the commentary on the *Nicomachean Ethics* went through many printings.[28] The Jesuit, Juan de Mariana (1536–1624), was very much in the tradition of Aristotle in his treatise on *The King and the Education of the King* (1599). In opposing the idea that whatever the ruler decreed was morally binding, Mariana was one of the originators of the theory of limited monarchy and of the origin of political power in the people.

The founder of the Jesuits, Ignatius of Loyola (ca. 1491–1556), had studied philosophy and theology at the University of Paris. He came away with a tremendous respect for Aristotle. The Jesuit concept of the education of the whole man owes a good deal to the ideals of classical humanism.[29] One of the early scholars who developed this ideal was Robert Bellarmine (1542–1621). It is possible that he was the Renaissance

Jesuit who best understood the practical philosophy of Thomas Aquinas, but his *Lectures on the Summa of Theology* have never been edited although they are preserved in the archives of the Gregorian University in Rome. We do know that on the thorny question of freedom of choice Bellarmine maintained that the act of human election is a joint function of intellect and will. Thus freedom is a function of the whole man and not merely of his will. In fact, the will "is free in electing, not because it is not necessarily determined by the last and practical judgment of reason, but because this ultimate and practical judgment is in the power of the will."[30]

Francisco Suárez (1548–1617) was the most important and influential ethician in the Renaissance. This Spanish Jesuit exerted a strong influence on many textbooks in ethics, in both the Catholic and Protestant traditions, well into the nineteenth century. Even today Suárez is important in the moral writings of Catholic thinkers in Spain and the Latin-American countries. Until a generation ago most ethics textbooks produced by British and United States scholastic ethicians were Suarezian in inspiration.

The works of Suárez that are of significance in the history of ethics are four. He taught a course *On the Soul* when he was a young man (possibly at Segovia, 1571), which he partly revised before his death; this is the *De Anima* published in 1621. It gives a good exposition of his early psychological views. Second, Suárez gave a series of lectures in moral theology (remotely based on Aquinas, *Summa Theologiae,* I–II) at the Roman College of the Jesuits, probably in 1580–1582. This course was posthumously published as a series of disputations entitled *On the Ultimate End, the Voluntary, and the Goodness of Human Acts (Opera Omnia,* Tome IV). Third, in his early twenties Suárez made a plan for a huge treatise in metaphysics; it was eventually finished and published in 1597 under the title *Metaphysical Disputations.* The tenth of the twenty "disputations" in this work treats of goodness in all its aspects, including the moral goodness of human acts. Fourth, his treatise *On Laws* was published in 1612; it is very important for his theory of obligation and of the relation of natural law to positive laws.[31]

Suárez continually cited almost two hundred authors from among his predecessors. He developed his own ethical position as a combination and rethinking of the views of Thomas Aquinas, Henry of Ghent, Duns Scotus, William of Ockham, and many others. He regarded himself as a Thomist but his philosophy, in the field of ethics especially, is not identical with that of Thomas Aquinas. Suarezian metaphysics deals with being as conceived almost univocally; the analogy of intrinsic attribution admitted in this theory is far removed from the Thomistic notion of analogy. Essence and *esse* are not radically distinguished by Suárez and his theory of matter and form grants a certain entity to matter that would not be admitted in Thomism.

But the two points in Suárez's speculative philosophy which have a most important bearing on his ethics are his diminution of the reality of the universal as a nature, and his depreciation of the role of final causality. He has been accused of nominalism (that is, the view that universal natures, such as humanity, are merely terms or signs) but his actual position seems somewhere between the terminism of Ockham and the moderate realism of Thomas. Suárez thought that a universal is a concept produced by the discursive action of the possible intellect moving from its initial conception of individual beings to a generalized meaning.[32] As a result of this diminished reality in the universality of human nature, Suárez is forced to adopt a teaching on ethical obligation that stresses the basing of this oughtness on God's will.

Of equal importance is the growth of the doctrine that the only important kind of causality is efficiency. In Aristotle, and in his commentators up to the fourteenth century, the final cause or end of an event was thought to be at least as important in the explanation of operations as was the efficient cause or agent. All the different kinds of things, trees and dogs and men, were thought to have natures with a finality (end-directedness) peculiar to each type of being. In such a metaphysics, the good actions of each species of being were those that promoted the development of this being as tending naturally toward its end. Ockham was one of the first thinkers to challenge this teaching on the finality of human nature. By the time that Francisco Suárez began to teach, it caused little or no stir when he bluntly called the causality of the end a metaphor.[83] This takes much of the force out of a teleological approach to ethical judgment. It is usually said that Francis Bacon threw final causes out of scientific explanation: they had already been thrown out in the fourteenth century.

The language of Suárez's ethics, then, is reminiscent of that of Thomas but the actual thinking is different. When the Spanish Jesuit says that human nature is the proximate standard of ethical judgment, he means what has come to be called in Suarezian textbooks *"natura humana adequate considerata"* that is, man viewed in all his essential relations. Internally, each man (the individual, not the universal) is composed of certain vegetal, sensory, and rational capacities; externally, each man is related to God, other men, and to subhuman things, in an order of rights and duties. This contextual view of the individual person is what a Suarezian means by human nature adequately considered.[34]

Suárez is a natural law ethician. He was a law student before becoming a Jesuit and he retained something of the mentality of the legal thinker. Natural law, for Suárez, is that part of the eternal law in which God freely decrees with His will the order to be observed in the free actions of intellectual creatures.[35] Moral law may be viewed in two ways: actively, as issuing from the divine will; passively, as received and accepted by men. Man's reason is the power in which natural law is known. We still have the language of "right reason" in Suárez's moral writings. This *recta ratio* is now "the capacity *(vis)* of distinguishing between actions that are suitable and those that are unsuitable to human nature."[36]

A contemporary Jesuit, Gabriel Vásquez (ca. 1551–1604), was teaching that natural moral law is identical with man's rational nature. Suárez disagreed, arguing that law *(lex)* has a more definite and limited meaning than nature. Natural law is equivalent, he thought, to the judgments of right reason.[37]

Suárez situates his own position between two extremes that he finds in earlier Scholasticism. Gregory of Rimini (d. 1358) is understood by Suárez as saying that natural law merely "indicates" to man what should or should not be done. As he reads Gregory, this natural law does not really command man but simply shows him the way to live well. In other words, Gregory recognized very little obligation in the constitution of natural law. On the other hand, Suárez takes William of Ockham as a rather thorough divine voluntarist: God's will is the sole source of all distinctions between moral good and evil. So understood, Ockhamism would be a pure extrinsicism: nothing in the nature of man or his actions would ground ethical judgments. Suárez tries to find a middle way: as he sees it, natural law has an obligatory force from the will of God but the fact that some actions are good for man is not the result of an arbitrary divine fiat; it is implied in a man's relations to his environment. Interpreters of the ethics of Suárez differ as to whether this is a moral voluntarism or an intellectualism.

In any event, three kinds of precepts make up the content of natural law, in Suárez. Primary precepts are rules known immediately and intuitively by all normal human beings: the standard example is, "Do good and avoid evil." Secondary precepts are more specific and limited; they require a certain amount of experience and thought so that their terms may be understood, but these are also self-evident principles. Examples are: "Do no injury to anyone" and "Live temperately." Suárez thought that these primary and secondary principles of ethical judgment do not change, except in the sense that new conditions or new knowledge may broaden the meaning of their component terms.[38] Lastly, there are tertiary precepts of moral law which require study and discursive reasoning to ground them. They are not self-evident but are derived from more basic rules. Precepts of this character are exemplified by: "Lying is always immoral" and "Usury is unjust."[39]

In his *De Anima* (4, 10, 9) the youthful Suárez had taught that moral conscience is not merely an act of practical judgment but that it is a habit of practical reason. In his later works, however, he described conscience as that judgment of practical understanding by which a man distinguishes between concrete good and evil *(bonum et malum)* and between what is commanded or prohibited *(praeceptum vel prohibitum)*. In this development he tended to agree with Thomas Aquinas.[40] So defined, conscience may be certain or doubtful. If certain, one must act in accord with conscience in order to do good. If doubtful, moral conscience is not an adequate guide; something should be done to remove the doubt, either by getting more information about facts or law, or by using "reflex principles." One such principle is the rule of tutiorism: when in doubt always do what is morally "safe." Another reflex principle is that of probabilism: when in doubt one may follow the guidance of any respected authority or expert, even if his judgment is not a majority opinion.[41] The application of these rules for the solution of problems of conscience is worked out in great detail. With other such reflex principles they have become part of the standard procedure used in that kind of applied moralizing which is called casuistry.

It would be difficult to overstate the scope of Suárez's influence in ethics. Many of the leading modern philosophers from Hobbes to Schopenhauer studied ethics in textbooks written from a partly Suarezian viewpoint. The seventeenth century saw the publication of dozens of manuals of moral philosophy written by both Catholic and Protestant ethicians. In most of these academic books the ethics of Suárez has some influence. Two examples of this sort of thing may be taken as typical. In Holland, Francis Burgersdijck (1590–1635) published a much-used textbook, *Idea philosophiae moralis* (Leiden, 1644). This book is a Protestant version of Suárez. It was the work that introduced John Stuart Mill to ethics.[42] Another Dutch Protestant ethician, Andriaan Heereboord (1614–1661), studied under Burgersdijck at the University of Leiden and eventually wrote his own textbook, *Philosophia rationalis, moralis et naturalis* (Leiden, 1654). Heereboord is often treated as a follower of Descartes; he was also an admirer of the ethics of Suárez.

Protestant Reform Ethics

This introduces the problem of the status of moral philosophy in the scholarship of the Reformed Churches. Philosophy, whether theoretical or practical, did not occupy a high place in the esteem of some of the initiators of the Protestant Reformation. As one historian puts it: "Luther and the early reformers were bitter in their attacks upon Scholasticism and the influence of Aristotle, 'the damned heathen' although later Protestants were not averse to explaining their theology by scholastic methods." Indeed, Martin Luther (1483–1546) had little use for philosophical ethics; he has been called "that most unphilosophical of characters."[43] Yet he did exert a great influence on later ethics and provided an excellent example of theological approbative ethics in a very pure form. A recent history sums up Luther's view: "The only true moral rules are the divine commandments; and the divine commandments are understood in an Occamist perspective—that is to say, they have no further rationale or justification than that they are the injunctions of God."[44] In *The Bondage of the Will* Luther wrote:

> But a man cannot be thoroughly humbled until he comes to know that his salvation is utterly beyond his own powers, counsel, endeavours, will, and works, and absolutely depending on the will, counsel, pleasure, and word of another, that is, of God only.[45]

The positive influence of Luther on modern ethics would seem to lie chiefly in his view of personal freedom. In spite of the fact that Luther wrote his *Bondage of the Will* to refute Erasmus' *Treatise on Free Choice (De libero arbitrio diatribe sive collatio,* 1524), it is clear that Luther placed the act of faith, or individual submission to the Will of God, in the "heart" or will. His denial of "free will" in man, at the conclusion of *The Bondage of the Will,* is simply a statement of the limitations under which human volition operates. Luther did a great deal to bring this problem of man's freedom under God to the forefront of attention in modern ethics. This emphasis on the individual man continued in the writings of Martin Bucer or Butzer (1491–1551), who was originally a Dominican friar and who preached on the importance of personal love of God as the keynote of the moral life, during his period at Strasbourg (1523–1549) and eventually at Cambridge University in England (1549–1551).

One of the most learned men among the early reformers was Philip Melanchthon (1497–1560). He did not share the general antipathy to Aristotle but lectured on the *Nicomachean Ethics* at Wittenberg and published his *Scholia* in 1542. Melanchthon also wrote a textbook in ethics *(Elementa philosophiae moralis).* His personal teaching in ethics was distinguished by a theory of innate ideas (which may have influenced Leibniz). He thought that every man is endowed with a natural light *(lumen naturale)* that enlightens him with the idea of God and with certain inborn ethical principles from which his moral conduct may be directed.

John Calvin (1509–1564) was another reformer who, though not a formal ethician, left his mark on practical philosophy. His teaching on original sin made men subject not only to the punishment for the sin of Adam but also with a nature vitiated by "the pollution to which the punishment is justly due."[46] Convinced of the utter depravity of all men, Calvin drew up a strict and harsh code of human conduct and then showed his opinion of academic ethics by saying: "Now let those who are of the opinion that the philosophers have the only just and orderly systems of moral philosophy show me, in any of their works, a more excellent economy than that which I have stated."[47] There is in Calvin's teaching on the absolute control of men by the divine will a view of moral law which is antithetic to the whole idea of natural law.[48]

Of course, there were some early Protestant scholars who wrote and taught ethics of a more conventional and academic sort. We have already noted how people like Burgersdijck and Heereboord carried on much of the Scholastic tradition. Erhard Weigel (1625–1699) produced in Germany a version of Aristotelian ethics in geometric style: *Analysis Aristotelica ex Euclide restituta* (1658). Leibniz was probably referring to this work when he mentioned an *Ethica Euclidea* that was a source for Pufendorf.[49] Another German textbook writer who was much in vogue on the Continent and in England was Bartholomaeus Keckermann (1571–1608). His *System of Ethics* (1607) is very critical of Aristotelian Scholasticism. Keckermann was associated with the attempt to supplant philosophy with rhetoric, in the movement founded by Pierre la Ramée (1515–1572) in French Calvinism.

Entirely apart from the academic tradition in ethics was the thought of the Silesian shoemaker Jakob Böhme or Behmen (1575–1624). He was a very unusual thinker, something of a mystic and something of a Protestant heretic. He saw God as a combination of good and evil (probably under the influence of some preacher who had read Nicholas of Cusa). At times Böhme seems to have adopted a dualistic theory of evil in which man's falling away from moral goodness is attributed to Satan, as a primordial cause of evil. An eschatological thinker, Böhme believed that all men would probably be brought back to goodness in the final days of creation. He took some of his teachings from another Protestant moralist, Valentine Weigel (1533–1588, not to be confused with Erhard Weigel in the seventeenth century). Valentine Weigel wrote both in Latin *(Libellus de beata vita,* Halle, 1609) and in German *(Erkenne dich selbst,* Neustadt, 1615). He was a devotee of the thought of Nicholas of Cusa. These men, especially Böhme, exerted a great influence on the ethical and religious thinking of the later German romantics.[50]

Neoclassical Ethics in the Renaissance

Platonism and Aristotelianism were by no means the only kinds of classical philosophy to be revived in this period. The three other schools that gave rise to some ethical speculation were skepticism, Epicureanism, and Stoicism. We shall examine each briefly.

Ethical skepticism might be defined as any point of view that denies that the moral philosopher has anything of value to teach. In this broad sense, Luther, Calvin, and many other religious teachers who are suspicious of ethics, would be skeptics. A Catholic layman,

Franz von Baader (1765–1841), expressed this attitude pungently: should the devil ever appear on earth, said von Baader, it would be in the garb of a professor of moral philosophy!

Besides this sort of thing there are several Renaissance examples of men who took the position that it is nonsense to try to distinguish moral good from evil. Niccolò Machiavelli (1469–1527) is one of the first names to come to mind. His treatise *The Prince* (1513) and his *Discourses on Livy* (1517) are now classic examples of the view that if you want something badly enough you may do almost anything to get it. He was fascinated by the problem of political power: his solution to this problem is frankly amoral, as these lines indicate:

> It is necessary for a prince, who wishes to maintain himself, to learn how not to be good, and to use this knowledge and not use it, according to the necessities of the case. . . . Some things which seem virtues would, if followed, lead to one's ruin, and some others which appear vices result in one's great security and wellbeing.[51]

This political cynicism seems to be based on a thoroughgoing ethical skepticism. Human actions are good or bad solely in terms of their technical competence as means to achieve a given end, in this case the preservation of political power. This may be viewed as an anticipation of utilitarianism of a peculiar sort: the standard is the advantage of the individual who happens to exercise civil power. This is not a formal species of ethics, perhaps, but it is an ethical position which has had many adherents.

More in the tradition of the Greek skeptics were some of the philosophers of sixteenth-century France. Michel de Montaigne (1533–1592) has had a minor role in the history of ethics. His *Essays* (first published in 1580, revised several times by Montaigne) show a mind which is very pessimistic about the value of any kind of natural science or wisdom. He felt that the teachings of Christianity are at least as believable as any of the deliverances of the philosophers. Montaigne adds, however:

> Should I examine, finally, whether it be in the power of man to find out that which he seeks, and if that quest wherein he has busied himself so many ages has enriched him with any new force or any solid truth: I believe he will confess, if he speaks from his conscience, that all he has got by so long an inquiry is only to have learned to know his own weakness. We have only by long study confirmed and verified the natural ignorance we were in before.[52]

As one historian has expressed it very well, Montaigne's best advice as a moralist reduces to this rule:

"Be content with your own human reality and learn to enjoy it moderately under its temporal, composite, and habit-forming conditions."[53] There is some resemblance between this "situationism" of Montaigne and the existential stance adopted by a thinker like Albert Camus. The great difference is that Montaigne felt that he could live a decent human life, whereas Camus was never quite sure of that.

Other examples of Gallic skepticism in Renaissance ethics are not hard to find. Pierre Charron (1541–1603) was a French priest who also based his moral philosophy on a special kind of skepticism. His work on *The Three Truths* (1593) was actually a defense of theistic belief and of Christian teachings. But his treatise *On Wisdom* (1601) criticized what he saw as the pretensions of philosophical wisdom. Theoretical philosophy had little appeal for Charron but he thought that there was a place for the practical wisdom of the ordinary man. Stoic ethics, with emphasis on a reasonable following of nature, is combined with a simple acceptance of God's providence.

A Portuguese physician, Franciscus Sanchez (ca. 1552–1632), became an instructor in medicine at Montpellier and Toulouse. He was impressed by the classic doubt of Pyrrho and also by an argument from Nicholas of Cusa.

To know any one thing well a person would have to know all things, and this is impossible. Sanchez's treatise *That Nothing Is Known* (1580) not only presents this negative conclusion; it suggests that empirical knowledge (as contrasted with syllogistically deduced systems) is possible. Because Sanchez stressed introspective experience of man's psychic functions, he was a contributing factor in turning the attention of philosophers and ethicians in the next generation, or so, to the study of personal consciousness.

Epicureanism, in the sense of an ethic of personal pleasure, had some devotees in Renaissance Italy. We have seen that Laurentius Valla wrote an essay on pleasure *(De Voluptate)* that combined Plato with Epicurus. The fifth dialogue in Giordano Bruno's *Concerning the Infinite* quotes at length from Lucretius' Epicurean poem *On the Nature of Things*. However, the primary example of ethical hedonism in the Renaissance is the French priest Pierre Gassendi (1592–1655). Chronologically, Gassendi is quite late to be considered as in this period (he is a contemporary of Descartes) but the ethical content of his writings is similar to that of many Renaissance writings, being merely a revival of the material on Epicurus and his teaching, as found in the tenth book of Diogenes Laërtius. Two points, however, are distinctive in Gassendi's version of the ethics of pleasure. First, unlike the original Epicureans, Gassendi believed that personal happiness is not attainable in this life but may be secured in the future life. His treatises *On the Life and Moral Teachings of Epicurus* (1647) and *Outlines of the Philosophy of Epicurus* (1658) offer a fusion of diluted Christian ethics with hedonism. Second, just as the Greek hedonists questioned the Stoic acceptance of the law of reason in nature, so Gassendi preceded Hobbes in attacking ethics based on the immutable and universal laws of nature. It is noteworthy that Ralph Cudworth treats Gassendi, along with Hobbes, as the prime opponent of the theory of natural justice.[54] On the Continent, then, Pierre Gassendi represents a transitional stage of ethical egoism.

Stoicism was much more popular than Epicureanism among ethical theorists of the Renaissance. In the Low Countries, Justus Lipsius, or Joest Lips (1547–1606), translated Seneca into the vernacular and wrote an *Introduction to Stoic Philosophy* which attempted to combine the practical wisdom of St. Augustine with the ethics of the Stoics.[55] Unlike the skeptics who were his contemporaries and who were all influenced by the ethics of Stoicism, Lipsius had a high regard for the theoretical part of Stoicism. He thought that their view of nature and reason does provide a sound basis for a system of ethics.[56]

Equally prominent as a Neo-Stoic ethician was Guillaume Du Vair (1556–1621). He, too, started as a translator, making one of the first vernacular versions of Epictetus' *Enchiridion*. His *Moral Philosophy of the Stoics* (1585) was soon translated into English, as was Lipsius' *Two Books of Constancy,* and these works helped to spread the doctrine of Stoicism in the formative period of British ethics. Besides the usual emphasis on practical wisdom that is characteristic of the Stoic, Du Vair developed his ethics in terms of other virtues held up as ideals: clemency, justice, charity, and constancy. He was one of the first to write on these ethical ideals in French.

Neo-Stoicism was never as influential in British ethics as it was on the Continent. Some of the English humanists were interested in classical Stoicism, of course, but they did not produce an ethics. It has been suggested that the famous translator of Homer, George Chapman (1559–1634), offered a "flamboyant" morality based on Stoicism in his plays.[57] It is hardly a theoretic ethics. One could argue that Herbert of Cherbury (1583–1648) was a British Stoic ethician. His treatises *On Truth* (1624) and *The Religion of the Gentiles* (1645) expound a theory of innate ideas *(notitiae communes)* that provides a foundation for both natural religion and ethics. The terminology is certainly Stoic, and so, possibly, is the inspiration. Lord Herbert's five innately known truths (as listed in his *De veritate)* are: (1) that God exists; (2) that God should be worshiped; (3) that a life of virtue is the best form of worship; (4) that sins are to be repented; and (5) that there are moral sanctions in the future life.[58] This is much more than Stoicism; it is a type of ethical a priori, long before Immanuel Kant.

In concluding this chapter on the ethics of the Renaissance, one should point out that few, if any, distinctive ethical theories originated at this time. That is the reason why the period is usually omitted from histories of ethics. Yet it should also be evident that the Renaissance marked an important transitional stage from the ethics of the classical and medieval thinkers to the better-known theories of the modern ethicians. In particular, it was in the Renaissance that a new and secular spirit came into ethical thinking. From this time onward, moral philosophy or ethics was no longer the exclusive domain of the cleric. It soon was recognized as a standard discipline in the liberal arts programs of the great university centers. In many, the teaching of philosophy bifurcated into the dual professorate of mental and moral philosophy. This was the real beginning of ethics in the academic institutions of the modern world.

Chapter VIII
British Egoism and Its Reactions

I**N THIS CHAPTER** we shall examine British ethics running through the seventeenth and into the first part of the next century. Most of our thinkers are clergymen in the Anglican or Presbyterian Church; a few are laymen. Many ethical treatises are still written in Latin but English is more and more the language of publication and controversy as the seventeenth century progresses. The central problem in ethics is seen as the explanation of the origin of man's notions of moral good and evil. Practically all these British thinkers assert that the divine will is the ultimate source of moral distinctions, but much diversity is found in their various explanations of how the individual man comes to know what God wills. Much of the ethics in this period consists of indignant rebuttal to Thomas Hobbes's assertion that the moral good is simply whatever pleasure may satisfy a man's desires. Few ethicians in his century accepted that answer, which has come to be called egoistic naturalism.

Something of a transition to the new ethics of the seventeenth century is found in the thought of Francis Bacon (1561–1626), who was actually a Renaissance man. His works still show the influence of medieval Scholasticism, neoclassicism, and empiricism. He wrote no treatise on formal ethics but there is a section in his famous *Advancement of Learning* (1605) where he gives a brief outline of his ethical thinking. The *Essays* (1597) contain much practical moralizing but little ethical theory. Bacon's *New Atlantis* is a utopian fragment that illustrates his interest in the use of knowledge to improve the material conditions of human life.

In the *Advancement of Learning* moral philosophy is described as "that knowledge which considereth of the Appetite and Will of Man."[1] It has two parts: one studies the exemplars of good, virtue, duty, and felicity; the other (the "Georgics of the mind") has to do with cultivating these seeds in the practical life of the individual man. Bacon feels that his predecessors have done rather well with the theory of the good life but earlier moralists have failed to show how these "exemplars" may be applied in practice. He criticizes

Seneca, Virgil, Zeno the Stoic, Epictetus, but especially Aristotle, on this score. Aristotle was wrong in taking the life of speculative contemplation as morally the best: the active life is better. Francis Bacon always treats Christian theology (Divinity) with great respect; he professes to approve its teaching that the highest felicity can only be attained in the future world. However, after making his bow to religion he proceeds to ignore it almost entirely. One gets the impression that what is important for Bacon is a good life on earth.[2]

Bacon distinguishes, in the same section of the *Advancement of Learning,* between the private good of the individual man and the common good of human society. The latter is the more important and it is most plainly treated in "Christian law." (This, of course, is but an echo of Scholastic moral teaching.) He gives very little information as to what the requirements of this law may be. There is throughout these chapters the suggestion that moral good and duty somehow are related to the welfare of human society. Bacon's utilitarianism is not obvious but it is there. It is in strong contrast with the egoistic attitude of his one-time secretary, Thomas Hobbes, which we will now consider in some detail.

Hobbes's Ethical Egoism

The moral theory that found somewhat random development in the various writings of Thomas

Hobbes (1588–1679) has been one of the most noted and most criticized in the history of the subject. Actually, Hobbes has three systems of ethics: one is a theological approbative theory in which the will of God is the immediate ground of good and evil; the second is a social utilitarianism in which right and wrong are determined by the sovereign power of the state; and the third is the view that has come to be called egoism, in which moral good and evil are equivalent to pleasure and pain for the individual man. It is the third position that is most important historically, for it elicited a great variety of critical responses in the readers of Hobbes.

Hobbes wrote both in Latin and in English. The first work of ethical significance was *The Elements of Law, Natural and Politic,* written in Paris about 1640, partly published in 1650, completely edited and published in 1889. Two parts of this were entitled *Human Nature* and *De corpore politico (On the Body Politic).* His *De cive (On the Citizen)* was written and first published in Paris (1642). Hobbes's most controversial work was published in 1651: *Leviathan, or the Matter, Form and Power of a Commonwealth, Ecclesiastical and Civil.* This was the book that most disturbed his contemporaries: its general message was that might is right. Some fifteen years later Hobbes finished and published *De corpore (On Body)* and *De homine (On Man);* these were published in London in 1655 and 1657.

The general philosophical position adopted by Hobbes may be summed up in two words: corporealism and sensism. All reality, he thought, was bodily; all events are of the nature of motion in place. As he describes it: "Motion is a continual relinquishing of one place, and acquiring of another." In men, motions are either *vital* (physiological functions) or *animal* (desire, aversion, and all functions of will). These two kinds of motion include all human activities. This is a thoroughgoing mechanism and it entails the teaching that the function of knowing is merely the motion of certain parts of the human body. "Sense, therefore, in the sentient, can be nothing else but motion in some of the internal parts of the sentient; and the parts so moved are parts of the organs of sense."[3] Understanding becomes simply a motion in the human brain; reasoning is the "addition and substraction" (sic) of sensory images. Will is merely the last act of desire or aversion in any process of deliberation.

Pleasure is that which "helps" vital or animal motion; pain hinders it. Good means whatever is the object of any man's appetite or desire; evil is the object of his aversion.[4] Thus, Hobbes's rule of egoism may be stated: "It is natural, and so reasonable, for each individual to aim solely at his own preservation or pleasure."[5] The distinction of good and evil, then, depends on the relation of the objects of appetite to the person who desires or hates them. In the context of civil society (the commonwealth), actions are good or evil depending on their relations to the laws of a given state. "For it was shown that the civil laws were the rules of *good* and *evil, just* and *unjust, honest* and *dishonest;* that therefore what the legislator commands, must be held for *good,* and what he forbids for *evil.*" And within the framework of the Kingdom of God, what God commands is good and what He forbids is evil.

Hobbes writes, of course, that the law of nature is the "dictate of right reason."[7] This should be understood in reference to his previously mentioned views on intellectual knowledge and its objects. There is no suggestion in Hobbes of a universal human nature that grounds such a law; humanity is merely a name that is conventionally given to some generalization that philosophers find useful in conversation.[8] Hence Hobbes bluntly states: "This *right reason,* which is the law, is no otherwise certainly right than by our making it so by our approbation of it and voluntary subjection to it."[9]

It is well known that Hobbes taught that man, in a state of nature before agreeing to form an organized society, is entirely selfish. This is the condition in which there is b*ellum omnium contra omnes* (war of everyone against everyone) and it gives rise, Hobbes says, to the first "law of nature": "that every man ought to endeavour peace, as far as he has hope of obtaining it; and when he cannot obtain it, that he may seek, and use, all helps, and advantages of war."[10]

The reason for asserting his first precept is that Hobbes was convinced that every man "has a right to every thing." Of course, men may agree to limit this egoistic claim to all things. This gives rise not only to Hobbes's theory of the conventional contract by which civil society is established but also to his second precept of the law of nature:

> that a man be willing, when others are so too, as far forth, as for peace, and defence of himself he shall think it necessary, to lay down this right to all things; and be contented with so much liberty against other men, as he would allow other men against himself.[11]

Hobbes has such a high opinion of this second precept that he calls it the "law of the Gospel" and the golden rule. Logically it is an odd law of nature, for it enjoins men to get away from the state of nature. If asked why men should obey this second precept, Hobbes would have to say: because it promotes the pleasure or preserves the life of each individual who submits to such a limitation of his "natural" appetites. It will be clear to any reader that Hobbes's notion of natural law is quite different from the traditional theory of Richard Hooker or of Thomas Aquinas.

To these two initial precepts of the law of nature Hobbes adds twelve more detailed rules: (1) "that men perform their covenants made"; (2) "that man who receives benefit from another of grace, endeavour that he which gives it, have not reasonable cause to repent of his good will"; (3) "that every man strive to accommodate himself to the rest"; (4) "that upon caution of future time, a man ought to pardon the offences past of them that repenting, desire it"; (5) "that in revenges . . . men look not at the greatness of the evil past, but the greatness of the good to follow"; (6) "that no man by deed, word, countenance, gesture, declare hatred, or contempt of another"; (7) "that every man acknowledge another for his equal by nature"; (8) "that at the entrance into conditions of peace, no man require to reserve to himself any right, which he is not content should be reserved to every one of the rest"; (9) "that such things as cannot be divided, be enjoyed in common, if it can be; and if the quantity of the thing permit, without stint; otherwise proportionably to the number of them that have right"; (10) "that the entire right; or else, making the use alternate, the first possession, be determined by lot"; (11) "that all men that mediate peace, be allowed safe conduct"; and (12) "that they that are at controversy, submit their right to the judgment of an arbitrator."[12] In case it is not possible for all men to remember all these excellent rules (from Scripture, Roman law, canon law, and classical and Scholastic ethics), Hobbes contracts them "into one easy sum," which is a negative formula of the golden rule: "Do not that to another, which thou wouldst not have done to thyself." These laws are immutable and eternal, according to Hobbes, "and the science of them is the true and only moral philosophy."

Often classified as an ethical naturalist, Hobbes would admit that there is a sense in which this is correct: at the lowest level he reduces the ground of ethical judgment to individual approval or disapproval. Yet Hobbes's ethics is also a crude version of the theological approbative theory: God's will or power (they are identical) is the source of the right of nature *(jus naturae)*. This does not mean that God has created men in a universe whose ontological structure requires certain types of human behavior (this would be the natural law theory of the thirteenth century); rather, Hobbes explains, these laws stem from His "irresistible power."[13] Or, as he puts it in the *Philosophical Rudiments:*

> The same law which is *natural* and *moral,* is also wont to be called *divine,* not undeservedly; as well because reason, which is the law of nature, is given by God to every man for the rule of his actions; as because the precepts of living which are thence derived, are the same with those which have been delivered from the divine Majesty for the *laws* of his heavenly kingdom, by our Lord Jesus Christ, and his holy prophets and apostles.[14]

Very few writers in his century were able to accept this pious declaration as genuine. Many wrote in rebuttal.

One of the first of these critics was John Bramhall, Anglican Archbishop of Armagh (ca. 1594–1663). He called the *Leviathan* a "horrendous monster." Bramhall's original objections to Hobbes had to do with the denial of free will in Hobbesian psychology.[15] In later essays Bramhall accused Hobbes of overturning all law with his teaching on the "irresistible power" of God.[16]

There are exceptions, of course, to the contemporary resentment of Hobbesian egoism. Sir Thomas Browne (1605–1682), the author of *Religio Medici* and *Christian Morals,* was quite undisturbed by Hobbes. Browne granted a certain autonomy to moral philosophy but felt that religion was a higher and surer guide. His advice was to "look beyond Antoninus, and terminate not thy morals in Seneca or Epictetus. . . . Be a moralist of the Mount, an Epictetus in the faith, and Christianize thy notions."[17]

One of the first extended criticisms of Hobbes was the treatise *Leviathan Drawn Out with a Hook* (1653) by Alexander Ross, which objected especially to the religious aspects of Hobbes's teaching. Sir James Tyrrell's *A Brief Disquisition of the Law of Nature* (1692) was another typical attack on the moral philosophy of Hobbes. In the second half of the seventeenth century, more than fifty such works appeared in opposition to the religious, political, and ethical views of Thomas Hobbes.[18]

Ethics in Cambridge Platonism

Among the reactions to Hobbes's moral philosophy some of the more important positive developments are found in the writers called the Cambridge Platonists. They were mostly scholars from Emmanuel College, Cambridge (a Puritan center), but their interest lay in the practical applications of Christianity to life. They were not "Platonists" in the sense of devotees of Plato's *Dialogues* but in the broader sense of being epistemological realists, of stressing the universality, immutability, and reality of the objects of human reason. Both natural and supernatural knowledges were understood by these men as manifestations of divine Reason. As Nathanael Culverwel (ca. 1615–1651) wrote: "God is the Spring and Head of reason."[19] The Cambridge Platonists were rationalists, not in the continental sense of logical system-builders but in the classic Greek sense of cultivators of the *logos* in all reality. We shall concentrate on the two men in this school who made significant contributions to ethics: Ralph Cudworth and Henry More.

It is not easy to decide where Ralph Cudworth (1617–1688) learned his philosophy: the tradition of Emmanuel College would hardly explain his grasp of the ethics of "right reason," which we examined in Chapter VI. The influence of Hooker is evident but hardly sufficient to explain the metaphysical and ethical philosophy of Cudworth. His *The True Intellectual System of the Universe* first appeared in 1678 and his *Treatise concerning Eterna and Immutable Morality* was finished within the next ten years but not published until fifty years later (London, 1731)·

The chief object of Cudworth's contempt is the theory that "arbitrary will" is the source of all distinction between good and evil. Plato, Aristotle, Protagoras, Polus, and Callicles are accused of this sort of voluntarism; so are Ockham, Pierre d'Ailly (1350–1420), and Andreas de Novo Castro. But his greatest scorn is reserved for the modern supporters of this view, Gassendi and Hobbes. Cudworth quotes from the *Leviathan* and points out that Hobbes makes "the Arbitrary Will and Pleasure of God" the first rule and measure of good and evil.[20] In his second chapter, Cudworth states his own understanding on the basis of ethical judgment:

> For though the will and power of God have an absolute, infinite, and unlimited command upon the existences of all created things to make them to be, or not to be at pleasure; yet when things exist, they are what they are, this or that, absolutely or relatively, not by will or arbitrary command, but by the necessity of their own nature. There is no such thing as an arbitrarious essence ... the natures of justice and injustice cannot be arbitrarious things, that may be applicable by will indifferently to

> any actions or dispositions whatsoever. . . .
> We must needs say that nothing is morally
> good or evil, just or unjust by mere will with-
> out nature, because every thing is what it is
> by nature, and not by will.[21]

Later in the *Treatise* Cudworth suggests that man has two kinds of knowledge, that which originates in sense perceptions and that which the activity of the mind produces within itself. From this second source come innate ideas of wisdom, prudence, vice, honesty, justice, injustice, plus notions of many relations (cause and effect, means and end, etc.). This is the origin of man's knowledge of the immutable principles of morality. These *noeta* are the proper objects of all sciences, the intelligible essences of things, and as necessary verities they "exist no where but in the Mind it self." Whether this is an anticipation of the a priori of Kant[23] is not clear; historically it is evident that Cudworth's view was never popular in British philosophy.

If he failed to convince Englishmen that morality and law do not depend on the will of the legislator, Cudworth did exert a strong influence with his qualified explanation of free will.[24] Cudworth's huge essay on this subject, A *Discourse of Liberty and Necessity,* is now partly edited and partly lost. In it Cudworth disagreed with both Hobbes and Bramhall concerning free will. It is obvious that he would object to Hobbes's physical determinism but he is just as much opposed to

Bramhall's "Scholastic" notion that will is a separate faculty. Cudworth takes will as the "whole soul redoubled upon itself,"[25] in much the same way that St. Augustine had understood *voluntas*. As will, the soul of man is not indifferent to good and evil; it is naturally inclined toward the good. Freedom of choice remains in those cases where the distinction of good from evil in action is not clearly evident. Free action is not rare. We know that we have free will because we experience it within us, we praise and blame free activity in other persons, we need freedom as the basis for moral life.

Cudworth rarely attempted to develop specific rules of ethical behavior, preferring to treat the theoretical ground of such judgments. His follower, Henry More (1614–1687), showed no such hesitation. More's *Enchiridion Ethicum* (1667) is an almost geometric exposition of the intellectual principles *(noemata)* that constitute "right reason." Speaking of the intellectual part of the soul, More says:

> I will take from this storehouse, therefore, certain principles which are immediately true and needing no proof, but into which almost all moral doctrine is plainly and easily resolved, even as mathematical demonstrations are resolved into their common axioms. Since these are the fruit of that faculty which is properly called *Nous,* I thought it not inappropriate to call them *Noemata.*

Astonishingly, More's first *Noema* states that a good is that which is pleasant, agreeable, and suited to the preservation of the recipient. This, of course, is Hobbes's definition of good! However, More proceeds to argue that one good may be superior to another in nature, duration, or both *(Noema* IV), that the superior good should be sought *(Noema* V), and that the cardinal virtues may be acquired by following these and similar *noemata*. Right reason, then, "is that which by certain and necessary consequences may be ultimately resolved into some Intellectual Principle that is immediately true" *(Noema* XXIII). This listing of many principles of moral reasoning by More anticipates the procedure of several later theorists: of the Deists and moral-sense ethicians, and of the Scotch common-sense thinkers. Richard Cumberland (1631–1718), for instance, represents a transitional stage between Platonist ethics and utilitarianism. His Latin treatise on the *Laws of Nature* (1672) insisted that "the nature of things in the universe ought first to be considered" before reasoning to an explanation of human faculties and human happiness.[27] This is combined with the further claim that "the common good of all is the supreme law." This leads into a utilitarian ethic, and we shall return to Cumberland in Chapter X, where British utility theories will be treated together.

Although he has a distinctive ethical position, John Locke (1632–1704) is not the great figure in the history of ethics that he is in epistemology. His thought has some relation to the kind of ethics that is found in Cambridge Platonism. Locke's early *Essays on the Law of Nature* (1660–1664) have only recently been published (1954). Presenting a theory of moral law, known naturally, these *Essays* are obviously much indebted to fourteenth-century Scholasticism. Here we find a completely voluntaristic explanation of moral law. The definition of natural law is: "an ordinance of the divine will knowable by the light of nature, showing what is in agreement or disagreement with rational nature and in that same act commanding or prohibiting it."[28] Like the Cambridge Platonists, Locke indicates that there are but three ways in which natural law could be known by man: by innate inscription, by hearsay, or by reasoning from sense perception. However, he is already much opposed to any suggestion of innate ideas and he criticizes this theory throughout one whole *Essay*. In regard to the second manner of learning about the principles of morality, Locke admits that we acquire a good deal from our parents and other such sources but this mode of knowing is from the dictates of men and not the *dictatum rationis*. It is by the third method, then, that we obtain our basic knowledge of natural law, that is, by reasoning from the data of sense experience.[30]

Longer and better-known than these recently discovered *Essays on the Law of Nature* are the sections of the famous *Essay concerning Understanding* (1690), which constitute Locke's most extended treatment of moral philosophy. Although his *Two Treatises of Civil Government* (1690) throw some light on his concept of the state of nature (in which men are less belligerent than in Hobbes's account), they have little to say about ethics. Locke has left other essays and fragmentary writings that deal with ethics; for instance, there are short essays entitled "Of Ethics in General" and "Thus I Think."

Another distinctive feature of the ethical position of John Locke stems from his epistemology. This is Locke's empiricism. The main message of the *Essay concerning Human Understanding* is the contention that all knowledge arises from experience, either sensation or reflection. Book I of the *Essay* is a thoroughly developed refutation of innatism. Whether it be the theory of Herbert of Cherbury, René Descartes, or the Cambridge Platonists, Locke cannot accept any suggestion that man is endowed with inborn notions. Neither speculative nor moral principles can be explained in this way. Reflection on the relations that we find among our acquired ideas (all objects of understanding are called "ideas") is our only way to reach primary rules of ethical judgment. Ethically, Locke is an empiricist.

The second point in the general philosophy of Locke that influences his ethics is his depreciation of the problem of free will. This is a pseudo-problem, Locke thinks, because "will" means a power to prefer or choose, whereas "liberty" is a different power, "to begin or forbear, continue or end several actions of our minds, and motions of our bodies."[31] It is the mind that exerts both these powers but they should not be confused by asking whether there is liberty of will: "Voluntary, then, is not opposed to necessary, but to involuntary." Desire is explained by Locke as a certain "uneasiness" at the absence of anything.

Good and evil are equated, then, with that which is apt to cause pleasure or pain; and happiness is desired by all men, for it is "the utmost pleasure we are capable of."[32] Not all pleasures necessarily move man's desire, only those which seem to be required for happiness. This is a remnant of classical eudaimonism but it is also not far removed, in its expression, from Hobbes's egoism.

Among the relations of ideas that become evident through inner reflection are those of moral relations: cases of "conformity or disagreement men's voluntary actions have to a rule. . . ."[33] There are three sorts of these moral rules or laws: divine, civil, and philosophical. God promulgates His laws "by the light of nature, or the voice of revelation." This is the only true touchstone of moral rectitude; so, Locke is fundamentally a theological approbative ethician. In the second place, there is civil law. It is enacted "by the commonwealth" to distinguish criminal from innocent actions. Thirdly, there is philosophical law, which distinguishes virtue from vice. It is also called the law of "opinion or reputation." Concerning this law, Locke adds:

Thus the measure of what is every where called and esteemed "virtue" and "vice," is this approbation or dislike, praise or blame, which by a secret and tacit consent establishes itself in the several societies, tribes, and clubs of men in the world, whereby several actions come to find credit or disgrace amongst them, according to the judgment, maxims, or fashions of that place. . . . By this approbation and dislike, they establish amongst themselves what they will call "virtue" and "vice."[34]

This form of the social approbative approach to ethics is Locke's most notable contribution to the subject.

In Book IV of the *Essay*, Locke returns to the description of the science of ethics, relating it to divinity in the following lines:

The idea of a Supreme Being, infinite in power, goodness, and wisdom, whose workmanship we are, and on whom we depend; and the idea of ourselves, as understanding rational beings, being such as are clear in us, would, I suppose, if duly considered and pursued, afford such foundations of our duty and rules of action, as might place morality among the sciences capable of demonstration: wherein I doubt not but from self-evident propositions, by necessary consequences, as incontestable as those in mathematics, the measures of right and wrong might be made out to any one, as he does to the other of these sciences.[35]

Later Locke repeats that "moral knowledge is as capable of real certainty as mathematics." There is a certain quality of idealistic intuitionism involved in this claim. Our moral ideas are "archetypes" like our mathematical ones; and our scientific certainty in ethics or mathematics is but "the perception of the agreement or disagreement of our ideas." So, in the end, Locke's empirical ethics is transmuted into an ethical intuitionism.

The influence of Locke is most obvious on Lord Shaftesbury (Anthony Ashley Cooper, 1671–1713). Most important are his *Inquiry concerning Virtue* (1699) and *The Moralists, a Rhapsody* (1709); both are reprinted with other pieces in the *Characteristics* (1711). The contemporary popularity of this three-volume work is amazing: it went through eleven editions in England before 1790; Diderot adapted it to French under the title *Essai sur le Mérite et la Vertu* (1745); and a complete German version was published at Leipzig in 1776–1779.

Shaftesbury was one of the first British thinkers to treat ethics independently of religion. In this he anticipated one of the features of Deism; indeed, he has been called the most important and plausible member of that amorphous school. At the beginning of the *Inquiry* he made it clear that Cudworth's ethics seemed to Shaftesbury to confuse theology with ethics. It was not that Shaftesbury denied the existence of a divine law which applies to human actions; rather, he insisted that men must first understand goodness, obligation, and virtue *in a natural way* before they can recognize and interpret the supreme requirements of God's law.

As the first prominent writer to speak of a moral sense, Lord Shaftesbury claimed that just as men have an aesthetic sense of the beautiful and the ugly, so do they have a moral sense of right and wrong.[86] Two things should be noted in his account of this moral sense. First, it is a function of man's understanding or reason; and second, it involves a feeling for what is decent and virtuous. Shaftesbury made a rather lengthy survey of the "affections" of man and came up with three conclusions about them. First, natural and kindly affections directed toward the public good are the source of our greatest personal joy. Second, too strong personal affections are the source of personal misery. Third, unnatural affections are neither in the public nor the private interest and they lead to misery in the highest degree.[37] In his discussion of the public good or interest, Shaftesbury several times uses the notion of the good of the species and speaks of the "common nature" of man. This is a Scotistic term, a way of looking at human nature as neutral in regard to both individuality and universality. It is impossible to establish the precise significance of Shaftesbury's usage of the term. He appears to have a somewhat more realistic notion of what constitutes the human species than either Hobbes or Locke. We shall see how his optimistic confidence in man's ability to reach a natural basis for moral judgment influences people like Bolingbroke and Alexander Pope in the Deist movement.

Shaftesbury's theory of the natural affections is an obvious reaction to Hobbes's view of man as naturally selfish. There were many more anti-Hobbes treatises at this time. Archbishop William King of Dublin (Established Church of Ireland, 1650–1729) published in 1702–1704 a Latin treatise *On the Origin of Evil;* it was put into English by Edmund Law and published in 1731, with dissertations by John Gay (1699–1745) *Concerning the Fundamental Principle of Virtue or Morality.* Gay surveyed the various attempts that have been made to find a criterion of virtue: "Some have placed it in acting agreeably to nature, or reason; others in the fitness of things; others in a conformity with truth; others in promoting the common good; others in the will of God, &c." He eventually argued that the will of God is the sole standard of virtue.[38]

A more fundamental attack on Hobbes is found in the work of Samuel Clarke (1675–1729), an Anglican clergyman. His *Discourse on Natural Religion* is actually a series of eight sermons or lectures, delivered in 1705 and printed in 1706. In rather forceful language, Clarke suggested that Hobbes had no basis for denying that the difference between good and evil is rooted in "the Nature of Things." He particularly objected to the idea "that all Obligation of Duty to God, arises merely from his absolute irresistible [sic] Power, and all Duty towards Men, merely from positive Compact."[39] Clarke's own position is that right reason discovers good and evil, and this is the law of nature.[40] Acknowledging his debt to Plato, Cicero, and especially to Cumberland, Clarke mentioned the Deists as "ranting" opponents of his theory. Oddly, a reply to the *Discourse on Natural Religion* was published in 1730 by a schoolmaster of Hull named John Clarke (not related, John lived from 1687 to 1734), under the title, *The Foundation of Morality in Theory and Practice*. This work claims that Dr. Samuel Clarke relies on the principle of benevolence and a universal moral sense to ground his ethics. John objected that even benevolence is reducible to private pleasure: "The main Use of the Moral Sense, and the Principal Intention of Nature therein, seems to be to put the Mind of Man upon the Hunt, to see if such actions as appear at first sight Beautiful, may not be attended with greater Pleasures. . . ."[41] It is evident that John Clarke came under the influence of Hobbes and that he thought that the impetus for moral sensism ("a very pretty ingenious Speculation") came from the teaching that all human actions spring from self-love.

Somewhat similar to the view of John Clarke is that of Bernard Mandeville (1670–1733), a Dutch physician who made his home in England. He first wrote *The Grumbling Hive: or, Knaves turned Honest* (1705); this was later revised into *The Fable of the Bees: or, Private Vices, Public Benefits* (1714). In the second edition of the *Fable* (1723) there appeared his *Enquiry into the Origin of Moral Virtue*. Mandeville directed his argument against Shaftesbury's notion that morally good actions are those directed to the public good. Instead, said Mandeville, it is obvious that "private vices" contribute most to the public welfare. By "vices" in the *Fable of the Bees* he means selfish tendencies; so, his point is that people who seek their own personal pleasures do more to advance the good of society than do the superficial altruists. A society of moral rigorists would be static in all ways, whereas a group of rugged individualists in search of material satisfactions would be a dynamic union. The public toleration of organized prostitution in Amsterdam was given as an example of vice contributing to the general good of a city. In his *Enquiry* Mandeville showed that he was more than a literary cynic. At one point he remarked: "It is impossible to judge of a man's performance, unless we are thoroughly acquainted with the principle and motive from which he acts."[42] He proceeded to discuss pity as a motivating passion and to argue that this altruistic feeling is the source of much immorality. In one sentence he anticipated much of Nietzsche. A few lines later, Mandeville mentioned the "love of goodness" as a motive and admitted that people so moved "have acquired more refined notions of virtue than those I have hitherto spoke of." This could have been said by Kant. In point of fact, much of Berkeley's *Alciphron* is a refutation of

Mandeville. Since the *Fable* maintains that "vicious" people are big, spenders, it is even possible that laissez-faire economics owes something to Mandeville.

Deistic Ethics

Our survey of this period in English thought requires a brief notice of the ethical views of those writers who have become known as Deists. Deism has been given a variety of meanings but we will use it here to name a point of view that developed in the seventeenth and early eighteenth centuries in England and France and that maintained that man can reason from his natural experience to the existence and some of the attributes of God, that revelation and the mysteries of faith may be unnecessary, and that the good life for man finds adequate guidance in philosophical ethics. It is the last feature that justifies mention of the movement in this history. Virtually all of the leading philosophers in these centuries (Hobbes, Locke, Descartes, Leibniz, Spinoza) have been called Deists. We shall briefly examine a group of less noted men who are nearer to the core of the movement.

We have noted at the end of Chapter VII how Herbert of Cherbury proposed a modified Stoic ethics that suggested to English readers that revealed religion might not be the sole source of moral guidance. Herbert was probably the founder of Deism in England. A hundred years later, William Wollaston (1659–1724) wrote the treatise which is, however, the best exposition of Deistic ethics: *The Religion of Nature Delineated* (1722). Its first section deals with religion. Truth is defined as "the conformity of those words or signs, by which are exprest, to the things themselves."[43] Wollaston never tires of saying that "every thing is what it is." Moreover, "if there is a supreme being," then this Deity is the author of nature, is truth itself, and his will is "revealed in the books of nature." Truth distinguishes right from wrong, and "moral good and evil are coincident with right and wrong."[44] The following passage shows that we have here a right reason theory:

> They who make right reason to be the law, by which our acts are to be judged, and according to their conformity to this or deflexion from it call them lawful or unlawful, good or bad, say something more particular and precise. And indeed it is true, that whatever will bear to be tried by right reason, is right; and that which is condemned by it, wrong. And moreover, if by right reason is meant that which is found by the right use of our rational faculties, this is the same with truth: and what is said by them, will be comprehended in what I have said.[45]

Wollaston's use of the hypothetical form in speaking of God does not mean that he doubted the divine existence: he thought that reason established the fact that God exists. It should be remembered that the first centuries of reformed Christianity generally distrusted philosophy and exalted personal belief, so Wollaston (whose views are not far removed from thirteenth-century Scholasticism) was given the reputation of an atheist, rationalist, and opponent of institutional religion. Actually, he insisted that the obvious distinction between moral good and evil necessarily implies the truth of religion, and that every intelligent being should act in accord with truth.[46] The second section of Wollaston's *Religion of Nature* treats of happiness. Like Hobbes, he starts with the claim that pain is a real evil and pleasure a real good. From this he proceeds to a detailed examination of pains and pleasures in the light of "truth." This is a sort of moral arithmetic that anticipates Bentham's moral calculus.

A similar argument that natural ethics justifies Christianity is found in the writings of a medical doctor, Thomas Morgan (1680–1743). His *Physico-Theology* was published in 1741, and his treatise *The Moral Philosopher* in 1738. We are now getting into an era in which this view of religion is more popular, at least among literary figures. It is well known that the *Essay on Man* (1734) by Alexander Pope (1688–1744) is a poetic summary of Deist psychology and ethics. Its famous last line ("One truth is clear, Whatever is, is right") is but an echo of Wollaston. Most of the poem repeats Shaftesbury almost verbatim. Pope was a friend of Henry St. John Bolingbroke (1678–1751), who is said to have supplied the philosophical base for Pope's *Essay.* A notorious rake, Bolingbroke did the cause of Deism no good in his personal mode of life. However, his writings *(Letters on the Study of History* and *On Authority in Matters of Religion,* both published shortly after Bolingbroke's death) had wide literary appeal for his contemporaries and influenced many serious writers. He was critical of organized Christianity and argued that moral obligations cannot be deduced from the revealed attributes of God.

Although this is a chapter on ethics in the British Isles, it should be noted that Deistic ethics extended to other countries. Shaftesbury is considered by some historians as instrumental in this transmission: we have seen how his writings were quickly translated into French and German. Voltaire (François Marie Arouet, 1694–1778) included entries on Deism in his *Philosophical Dictionary* (1765). Denis Diderot (1713–1784) moved from an early adherence to Deism to a later naturalistic pantheism. His *Philosophical Thoughts on the Sciences* (1746) presented a moral view partly inspired by Deism. The Abbé Étienne Bonnot de Condillac (1715–1780) pushed Locke's theory of knowledge to its extremity; in the *Traité des sensations* (1754) all knowing is reduced to the working of the sense of smell. Good means "whatever pleases our smell or our taste."[47] What there is of ethics in these French thinkers is closely associated with Deism.[48]

It is a commonplace to say that many of the founders of the United States of America were Deists. Of course they did not write treatises on ethics. However, the *Autobiography* of Benjamin Franklin shows his general acquaintance with Deistic ethics. He tells of compiling a little treatise on the virtues, for his own edification, and then he comments on it as follows: "Though my scheme was not wholly without religion, there was in it no mark of any of the distinguishing tenets of any particular sect."[49] It is probable that Franklin's Deism was closer to the French than the British variety.[50]

America also played a role in the career of another British thinker, Bishop George Berkeley (1685–1753) of Cloyne, Ireland. In 1729 he traveled to America in the interest of establishing an Anglican college in Bermuda but spent three years in residence at Newport, Rhode Island, and there wrote his *Alciphron, or the Minute Philosopher* (1732) in which he criticized freethinkers such as Shaftesbury and Bernard Mandeville. As a young man (before 1720) Berkeley had started to write a treatise on psychology and ethics but it was lost in an accident; he never took the trouble to rewrite it. The critique of Shaftesbury's moral sensism in the third dialogue of *Alciphron* is based on Berkeley's conviction that ethics requires Christian theology to ground it. There is a passage in his *Principles of Human Knowledge* (1710) where he says that there is little advantage in making abstract considerations of happiness or goodness and that such abstractions render morality difficult.[51] In the original edition of 1710 he had added this:

> One may make a great progress in *school ethics,* without ever being the wiser or better man for it, or knowing how to behave himself, in the affairs of life, more to the advantage of himself, or his neighbours, than he did before. This hint may suffice to let any one see that.[52]

This would suggest that Berkeley was a skeptic as far as the value of academic ethics is concerned. His own position in the early notes that constitute his *Philosophical Commentaries* (1707–1708) is surprisingly eclectic. At one point he says that sensual pleasure is the *summum bonum.* But on the same page he argues that such pleasure is good only when desired by a wise man, and he implies that those who are not motivated by a desire of heaven cannot perform good actions.

An essay by Berkeley on *Passive Obedience* (1712) has some sections (4–15, 28–34, 41, 42, 53) that outline a type of theological utilitarian ethics. As some people grow more mature, Berkeley tells us, they learn to look to the remote consequences of their actions, to see "what good may be hoped, or what evil feared . . . according to the wonted course of things."[54] At this same place he makes it plain that the real measure of good and bad actions is the will of

God. To the extent that he has an ethics, Berkeley always thinks in terms of such a theory as a derivative from divine law.

Much more important in the history of ethics was the teaching of another bishop in the Anglican Church, Joseph Butler (1692–1752). He presented his ethics in fifteen *Sermons* (1726) and in *A Dissertation upon the Nature of Virtue,* printed as an appendix to his *Analogy of Religion* (1736). Sermon I shows that Butler is concerned about the possible effects of Hobbes's egoism but that he is not convinced that men like Shaftesbury and Wollaston have all the truth on their side. There are three motivating principles in man's moral life, Butler suggests: a principle of benevolence, which inclines him to act for the good of other persons; a principle of self-love, which makes him tend toward his private good; and a principle of reflection (conscience), which enables man coolly to approve or disapprove of the motivations of the first two.[55]

The second and third sermons expand the meaning of conscience and relate it to human nature. It is a mistake to think that Butler takes human nature as something universal and common to all men. Like nearly all philosophers of this period, Butler is a nominalist. The nature of man is merely a set of tendencies that each man may discover within himself: thus self-love is natural, in the sense that I find myself instinctively disposed toward it. The compulsion of "duty" is similarly natural. Conscience is a sort of cool, disinterested, passionless viewing of the claims of these natural inclinations. As Butler explains:

> The whole argument ... may thus be summed up. ... The nature of man is adapted to some course of action or other. Upon comparing some actions with this nature, they appear suitable and correspondent to it: from comparison of other actions with the same nature, there arises to our view some unsuitableness or disproportion. The correspondence of actions of the nature of the agent renders them natural: their disproportion to it, unnatural. ... Reasonable self-love and conscience are the chief or superior principles in the nature of man: because an action may be suitable to this nature, though all other principles be violated; but becomes unsuitable, if either of those are.[56]

In the *Dissertation* conscience is described as the "approving and disapproving faculty" that each person experiences within himself. It reflects upon actions; it discerns that some require reward and others punishment; it "compares" these actions with the capacities of the agent; it involves a calm appraisal of one's own interest; and it recognizes the appeal of benevolence but does not regard it as the only mark of virtue.[57]

We must be cautious in classifying the ethical theory of Butler. It is an ethical intuitionism; one historian calls it "autonomic intuitionism."[58] Of course it is a deontological theory, for the awareness of duty is central to Butler's thought. It has been called a "sophisticated formalist theory" but it is not close to the sort of formalism that attempts to establish general rules of moral obligation. Rather, Butler's view resembled "act-utilitarianism" without the utilitarianism! That is to say, his conscience "compares" each proposed action or tendency to act, within the individual person, and comes up with a verdict of natural and suitable, or the opposite. This is the way that moral good and evil are distinguished in the concrete, by a personal intuition of certain inclinations within the agent.

Contemporary with Butler are two men with similar but less well-developed theories of ethics. Archibald Campbell (1691–1756) was a Scottish professor of church history at St. Andrews University who wrote *An Enquiry into the Original of Moral Virtue* (1728). Lord Kames (Henry Home, 1696–1782) published his *Essays on the Principles of Morality and Natural Religion* in 1751. The latter stresses the requirement that good action must conform to "the common nature of the species" and the power to perceive this suitability is moral sense.[59] Eventually, Kames identifies moral sense with "the voice of God within us."

The fullest treatment of the theory of moral sensism is given in the ten works produced by Francis Hutcheson (1694–1746). We shall examine but three of them: the

Inquiry into the Original of Our Ideas of Beauty and Virtue (1725), the *Essay on the Nature and Conduct of the Passions* (1728), and *A System of Moral Philosophy* (1755). The first sentence of the *Inquiry* states: "The Word Moral Goodness . . . denotes our Idea of some Quality apprehended in Actions, which procures Approbation, and Love toward the Actor, from those who receive no advantage by the Action."[60] Notice the use of "Quality" and also an intimation of the disinterested or impersonal spectator theory. Objects that excite personal or selfish pleasure seem to Hutcheson *naturally* good but those that are advantageous to other persons are *morally* good. The principle of benevolence is already foremost. God has given us an internal sense of the beautiful and harmonious; similarly "he has given us a MORAL SENSE, to direct our Actions, and to give us still nobler Pleasures; so that while we are only intending the Good of others, we 'undesignedly promote our own greatest private Good."[61] In the next section, Hutcheson dwells on this contention that moral good must be directed to the good of others (God or fellow men) by a love of benevolence.

Explaining the working of the moral sense, Hutcheson introduces into British ethical writing the notion of the good of the greatest number. He suggests:

> In comparing the moral Qualitys of
> Actions, in order to regulate our Election
> among various Actions propos'd, or to find

out which of them has the greatest moral
Excellency, we are led by our moral Sense of
Virtue to judge thus; that in equal Degrees
of Happiness, expected to proceed from the
Action, the Virtue is in proportion to the
Number of Persons to whom the Happiness shall extend; . . . so that, that Action
is best, which procures the greatest Happiness
for the greatest Numbers; and that, worst,
which, in like manner, occasions Misery.[62]

This anticipation of utilitarianism is modified, in
this same passage, by the suggestion that happiness or
pleasure varies in quality as well as in quantity.[63] Possibly under the influence of Wollaston, Hutcheson proceeds to a sort of moral arithmetic to be used by the
moral sense on "computing" the morality of actions.
Six axioms are proposed as guides in this computa-
tion: (1) "The moral Importance of any Agent, or the
Quantity of publick Good produc'd by him, is in a
compound Ratio of his Benevolence and Ability"; (2)
"the Moment of private Good, or Interest produc'd
by any Person to himself, is in a compound Ratio of
his Self-Love, and Abilitys"; (3) "when in comparing
the Virtue of two Actions, the Abilitys of the Agents
are equal; the moment of publick Good produc'd by
them in like Circumstances, is as the Benevolence";
(4) "when Benevolence in two Agents is equal, and
the other Circumstances alike; the Moment of publick Good is as the Abilitys"; (5) "the Virtue then of

Agents, or their Benevolence, is always directly as the Moment of Good produc'd in like Circumstances, and inversely as their Abilitys"; and (6) "the entire Motive to good Actions is not always Benevolence alone; ... we must look upon Self-Love as another Force, sometimes conspiring with Benevolence, . . . sometimes opposing Benevolence."[64] Hutcheson later suggests that the ideas of obligation and moral right may be "deduced" from the deliverances of moral sense.[65]

The *Essay on the Passions* appeared just before Hutcheson was appointed to the chair of moral philosophy at Glasgow, thus beginning a long line of distinguished ethicians in Scotland. (Hutcheson, himself, was born in Ireland.) This work, of course, develops a psychology of human feeling, but its contribution of an analysis of internal sensation is more important to ethical theory. He now has four internal senses: the aesthetic, public ("to be pleased with the Happiness of others, and to be uneasy at their Misery"), moral (to "perceive Virtue or Vice, in themselves, or others, as an Object"), and the sense of honor and shame.[66] The other noteworthy feature of this shorter work on the passions is a general tendency to criticize any use of final causality, such as Aristotle's notion that moral good depends on the directing of an action to an ultimate end. Hutcheson will have none of this; each affection is its own complete motive.

Hutcheson's *System of Moral Philosophy* is a very large work (two volumes) edited from his lectures at Glasgow and posthumously published.[67] The basic components of his teaching remain the same. In later life, Hutcheson read more of the classic Greek and Latin moralists and this interest shows in the *System.* The moral sense becomes something like the *hēgemonikon* of Hellenistic ethics: "This moral sense from its very nature appears to be designed for regulating and controlling all our powers."[68] The principle of benevolence is still dominant in the operation of the moral sense, "it makes the generous determination to public happiness the supreme one in the soul, with that commanding power which it is naturally destined to exercise." In the second book of the *System,* an effort is made to "deduce" various key concepts of morality (righteousness, obligation, moral right) from the moral sense. The theory is also extended into the discussion of special problems of morality and economics.

Hutcheson's writings in ethics influenced the whole later course of British moral philosophy. From this point onward, any attempt to discuss moral good in terms of an abstract relation, an ideal of goodness, will be unpopular in England. "Good" now means a certain perceived *quality* in a personal action or attitude. As we shall see in Chapter X, Richard Price will eventually try to reinstate the theory of an ideal human nature, but without great success.

In his *Foundation of Moral Goodness* (1728) John Balguy (1686–1748) claims that "Mr. Hutchinson" can demonstrate nothing about morality with his theory.[69] Balguy himself has a variant of the right reason teaching: "The Dictates and Directions of Right Reason are the very Rule which the Deity Himself inviolably observes, and which therefore must needs affect all intelligent Creatures."[70]

Another type of criticism directed against the moral sense theory of Hutcheson derived from the associationist psychology in the writings of David Hartley (1705–1757). Under the influence of John Locke, Hartley's *Enquiry into the Origin of the Human Appetites and Affections* (1747) suggested that all the "affections" of self-love, benevolence, and piety toward God originate in sense impressions. Certain elementary feelings of pleasure and pain are associated with other ideas to form more complex emotions of the aesthetic, moral, and religious types. Of itself the human mind is a *tabula rasa,* without any predispositions toward the beautiful or the good. If true, this associationist psychology kills the whole idea of a moral sense. However, Hartley proceeded in his *Observations on Man* (1749) to refurbish the principle of benevolence by explaining how psychological analysis explains the development of acquired dispositions to benevolence, piety, and moral sense.[71]

It was Abraham Tucker (1705–1774) who (in *The Light of Nature Pursued,* 1768) pointed out that Locke and Hartley had demolished innatism and that Hutcheson's moral sense involved some claim to innate moral dispositions. Tucker advocated a "translation" theory that relied on associationist psychology to explain how man's initially selfish and low-grade feelings may be transmuted into altruistic, moral, and high-grade attitudes. Comfortingly, Tucker assures us that there is a sort of bank or storehouse of happiness which is ever increasing under divine guidance; in the end, God will see to it that every man gets an equal share of happiness![72] His ethics is utilitarian, of course. In our tenth chapter, we shall take up the growth of the ethics of utility, in eighteenth-century and nineteenth-century England.

Chapter IX
Rationalistic Ethics on the Continent

EUROPEAN ETHICIANS IN the seventeenth and eighteenth centuries made moral philosophy an important and distinctive study. At this point ethics became a subject for university study but it was also cultivated by nonacademic writers in order to complete the practical dimensions of their philosophies, to provide a foundation for their theories of society and law, to explore the moral bearings of the new directions of religion. In general, these continental writers on ethics, from Grotius to Kant, are somewhat deductive in their approaches to the subject; they are inclined to fit ethics into the vaster framework of their entire philosophies. Moreover, these Euro-

pean ethicians are theists who retain a certain confidence in the ultimate character of the law of God,
even as they investigate the principles of goodness
and justice in the "light of natural reason." In the case
of those continental ethicians who are interested in
jurisprudence (and many are), their way of proceeding
is to start with some very general principles of law and
right, then to move by reasoning to more specific rules,
eventually to apply these broad regulations to individual cases. This contrasts with the tendency in British legal thinking to work from individual court cases,
taken as precedents, toward a growing body of laws which
accumulate as a living tradition. Continental thinking
in moral philosophy is not usually inductive, during
this period of the Enlightenment, even though there
is a general move toward empiricism in the field of
the sciences.

The Dutch Protestant jurisprudent Hugo Grotius
(1583–1645) is a good example of an ethician exhibiting
the foregoing characteristics. His treatise *On the Rights
of War and Peace* (1625), written in Latin, continues
much of the Scholastic tradition of right reason and
natural law. It is still recognized as a classic contribution to the theory of international law. He wrote
other things. The treatise *De imperio Summarum
Potestatum circa sacra* (1661) has not been translated
but it is his most philosophical treatment of natural law morality. Grotius' *Inleiding tot de Hollandsche
Rechts-Geleerdheid* (1631; *Introduction to the Jurispru-*

dence of Holland) is not only a source of legislation in the Netherlands; it is still used today in countries that have come under Dutch cultural influence, for instance, in the Union of South Africa.[1]

Reference works often suggest that Grotius abandoned the Scholastic and Catholic approach to natural law and adopted the lawyer's attitude that man's "social nature" and not metaphysics or theology constitutes the ground for legal judgment.[2] Nothing could be farther from the truth. This caricature of Grotius' teaching was drawn by his follower, Samuel von Pufendorf, for reasons of his own. The fact of the matter is that Grotius was very close to the right reason type of moral philosophy that we found in Thomas Aquinas.[3] Grotius did write that there would be a valid natural law, "even if it were granted that God does not exist," but this does not mean that he denied the ultimate foundation of natural law in the eternal law.[4] It was the recognized teaching of the Thomistic school of jurisprudence, particularly in Renaissance Spain, that once God had established certain laws for men and the universe He would not change them. Some eccentric Scholastics, such as Gregory of Valencia (1551–1603) and Rodrigo de Arriaga (whose *Cursus philosophiae* was published in Antwerp in 1632), taught that the dictate of right reason *(dictamen recta rationis)* would provide a basis for natural law, even if God did not exist.[5] It is in the light of this background, with which Grotius was very familiar, that we should read the following explanation of natural law.

Natural right (jus naturale) is the dictate of right reason, showing the moral turpitude or moral necessity of any act from its agreement or disagreement with a rational nature, and consequently that such an act is either forbidden or commanded by God, the author of nature. The actions, upon which such a dictate is given, are either binding or unlawful in themselves, and therefore necessarily understood to be commanded or forbidden by God. This mark distinguishes natural right, not only for human law, but from the law, which God himself has been pleased to reveal, called by some the voluntary divine right.[6]

Grotius is not a nominalist nor a voluntarist in his practical philosophy. The above quotation obviously continues the realistic theory of a rational moral order, as it is described by the Spanish Thomist, Gabriel Vasquez (ca. 1551–1604), in his *Commentary* on Thomas' *Summa Theologiae*. Even Grotius' emphasis on "socialitas" (the inclination of all men to combine in society) is not a break with the Scholastic teaching. All Scholastics had agreed with Aristotle that man is by nature a social animal. Grotius simply continued this emphasis on the "common good," or the welfare of the people *(salus populi),* in his *De imperio* (chap. 4, sect. 6) with his theory of right reason as the ground of ethical judgment. No less an authority than Leibniz says as much in one of his letters:

"In my judgment, Grotius rightly combined the Scholastic teaching on eternal law with the principle of sociality."[7]

The ethical views of Samuel von Pufendorf (1632–1694) tell quite a different story. He is the second noted Protestant advocate of natural law ethics, on the Continent. Pufendorf is in the tradition of William of Ockham, however, holding that all moral distinctions are imposed directly by God's will. Moral law is no longer "natural" in the sense of proclaiming what actions are suitable or unsuitable to the specific nature of a human being acting in the world of nature. For Pufendorf, an act is good because God willed it to be so: there is nothing else to it. As manifested through supernatural revelation, God's will is the divine law; as shown through the "light of natural reason," the same prescription of divine will is the natural law. In other words, we have here a theological approbative theory of natural law.

Pufendorf served as professor of natural and moral philosophy at Heidelberg from 1660 to 1668 and later taught jurisprudence at Lund, Sweden. Hence, he was probably the first occupant of a university chair of ethics in Germany. His huge work on *The Law of Nature and of Nations* (1672) had a tremendous influence. It was translated from the original Latin into most of the European vernaculars. He also wrote in Latin an *Elements of Jurisprudence* (1660), a study of the *Duties of Man and of the Citizen* (1673), and a reply to critics of his treatise on *The Law of Nature* under the title *Eris Scandica* (1686).

The first thing to notice about Pufendorf as an ethician is his almost pathological prejudice against the Scholastics. In one of the treatises in the *Eris Scandica* he names "Thomas, Papa Suaretz, Molina, Vasquetz, Valentia, the Conimbricenses and Sanchietz" and then intemperately castigates their teachings as nonsensical, empty, ornamented with frivolous subtleties, and so on. He frequently asserts that Scholastic philosophy was nothing but bad Aristotelianism. In reviving the moral teaching of the Stoics, plus the true message of Christian Moral Theology *(Theologia Moralis Christiana)*, Pufendorf's professed aim was to exterminate the "jejune ethics of Aristotle from the Protestant schools."[9]

From his teacher, Erhard Weigel, Pufendorf took the notion that ethics could be developed as a demonstrative science using the method of mathematics. He much resented Grotius' admission that there cannot be as much accuracy and certitude in moral reasoning as there is in mathematics.[10] Actually, Pufendorf's main contribution to the development of such an ethics was to pick up the notion of "sociality" from Grotius and suggest that it is the basis of natural ethics.[11] His own position is a combination of Grotius and Hobbes, resulting in a doctrine that uses the language of natural law to promote a voluntaristic and positivistic theory. As we shall see, Christian Thomasius, his most noted follower in Germany, became critical of Pufendorf as he grew more mature. Pufendorf's *Law of Nature* was highly regarded by John Locke, however, and was much read at Oxford in this period.[12]

In France, this sort of rationalistic ethics made its appearance in the early seventeenth century. René Descartes (1596–1650) is not as important in the history of ethics as he is in other parts of philosophy. However, he has said a few things that have influenced other ethicians. These are to be found chiefly in his *Discourse on Method* (1637), *Principles of Philosophy* (1644), *Passions of the Soul* (written about 1649), and in a few *Letters* to the exiled Princess Elizabeth of Bohemia. It is, of course, helpful to read his *Rules for the Direction of the Mind* (1628) and *Meditations* (1641) in order to understand his conception of the work of the philosopher. There is no treatise by Descartes that is devoted mainly to moral philosophy.

Dissatisfaction with the kind of philosophy that he had been taught at the Jesuit Collège Henri IV (it was a modified Suarezianism), plus a great admiration for the method and certitude of mathematics, led Descartes to attempt to begin philosophy all over again. He decided to doubt almost all the things that he had accepted as a youth, so that he might eventually see clearly what views would pass the test of rational examination. His criterion of truth was the clarity and distinctness of his ideas. He found that he could not doubt that he existed himself as a thinking thing *(res cogitans)* and he reasoned from his mental experience to the fact of the existence of God, and by considering that a good God would not permit him to be so continually persuaded of the reality of bodies he eventually concluded to the existence of the extra-mental world. He thought that his philosophy would logically culminate in a new moral philosophy but he never succeeded in reaching this goal.

The Preface to the *Principles of Philosophy* speaks of four degrees of pre-philosophical "wisdom" and suggests that there is the possibility of a fifth wisdom (philosophical) which would be a definitive moral philosophy growing out of the use of Descartes's method.[13] Descartes compares philosophy to a tree whose highest branches would be medicine, mechanics, and ethics. He had not reached these branches by 1644, and he never did. However, he says that this exalted ethics would be based on the principles presented in the *Principia Philosophiae,* because they are very clear and all other truths can be deduced from them.[14] He leaves no doubt, then, that his ethics would be the product of deduction. The character of his principles has been suggested in the preceding paragraph.

In the same Preface, we are reminded that there is "an imperfect ethic" sketched in the *Discourse on Method,* written some seven years earlier. This is the famous provisional code of morality found in Part III of the *Discourse.* There, after throwing many of his convictions into the hopper of methodic doubt, Descartes listed the practical maxims for living in this period of trial. They were: (1) to obey the laws of his country and to adhere to his Catholic faith; (2) to act firmly and decisively once a course of action has been adopted; and (3) to conquer self rather than externals or fortune. Concluding this "code of morals" was the resolution to study different ways of living, using the light of reason to distinguish truth from error, keeping in mind "that all that is necessary to right action is right judgment."[15] The impression that one gets is that the higher ethics which would be "perfect" in relation to the provisional morality is a demonstrative science in the practical order.

Descartes's *Passions of the Soul* was written in the late 1640s, in part as a response to questions about ethical matters asked in a series of letters exchanged with the exiled Princess Elizabeth of Bohemia. He submitted a version of the treatise to her before it was published. The work describes psychic "passions" as perceptions, feelings, or emotions in the soul caused by movement of the "spirits."[16] These animal spirits are something like physiological vapors coursing through the body and making contact with, and moving, the soul through the pineal gland. The appearance of a ferocious animal excites various changes in the bodily senses, stimulates the imagination to think of similar previous experiences that have been painful to the body, results in movements of the animal spirits and eventually terminates in certain disturbances in the soul. These emotions are classified by Descartes into major types of feelings. Such passions are all basically good by nature but they have a tendency to go to excess and to disturb the higher functions of willing and reasoning. So, they require to be controlled by the will.[17] This is effected by rational effort and also by cultivating certain helpful passions, of which the main example is generosity. It helps a person to feel his true relationship to things based on a wise estimate of himself. This reduces to the realization that one's will is the main thing that one can control. The ethical problem remains one of knowledge, however, for good desire results from true knowledge and bad desire springs from error.[18] This is not as intellectualistic as it first appears, since Descartes always thought that error is caused by a defective act of assent in the will.

In one letter to Princess Elizabeth, Descartes starts from Seneca's *De vita beata* to describe the happiness that is attainable on earth.[19] It is constituted of virtue and wisdom (which we can control) and of honors, wealth, and good health (not entirely under our control). To this modified Stoicism are now added three basic maxims of moral living which are very similar to the rules in the provisional code of morality. Another letter to the Princess[20] gives two requirements for sound moral judgment: to know the truth, and to form the habit of assenting to this knowledge. Included in the knowledge of the truth are four objects of practical cognition: (1) God, (2) the nature of the human soul,

(3) the vastness of the universe, and (4) the larger societal group of which man is part.

The strong intellectualist bent of Descartes's incomplete ethical view is obvious. This is somewhat balanced by the important role assigned to will in the governance of the passions. Like Socrates, Descartes felt that if you see the truth clearly you will do good actions.

A long line of thinkers in Europe attempted to follow in Descartes's footsteps and work out the higher wisdom of his ethics. One of these was a Belgian, Arnold Geulincx (1625–1669), who started as a Catholic professor of philosophy at Louvain but eventually became a Protestant and taught moral philosophy at Lyons and Leiden. He is chiefly known in histories of philosophy for his occasionalistic interpretation of Cartesian dualism. An example of the concomitance of human will and bodily motions as illustrated by two synchronized clocks was used by Geulincx long before Leibniz picked it up.[21] Actually, Geulincx wrote more in the field of ethics than in theory of knowledge or metaphysics. He produced an *Ethics,* in six treatises (1665–1709), which has only survived in part. He also wrote *Disputations on the Highest Good* and a series of *Ethical Disputations* (1664–1668).

His approach to ethics stresses the need for a metaphysical foundation for practical wisdom. In a set of *Notes,* he lays down the rule that "moral and ethical matters are based on natural and physical things."[22]

Influenced by Jansenism, Geulincx contrasts the radical imperfection of the *brutum* (which seems to mean the material universe) and the weakness and servitude of the natural man with the glorious power and liberty of man under the influence of God's grace. Like Descartes, he needed God in his philosophy and was fascinated by the concept of the omnipotence of God. Interestingly, he repudiated the "moral medicine" of the *Passions of the Soul* and would not accept it as part of the Cartesian ethics. Geulincx's *Ethica* is really a theory of virtue. Its six parts treat: I. Virtue in General; II. the Particular Virtues; III. The End of Virtue: the Good; IV. Passions; V. Reward for Virtue; VI. Prudence (unfinished). This position is restated in the *Ethical Disputations:*

> Ethics is concerned with virtue. Virtue is the unique love of right reason. In this I do not understand by "love" just any sort of passion, or a weak and mild affection... but a firm resolve *(firmum propositum),* an efficacious act of willing.[23]

As he works out the details of this ethics of virtue, it becomes evident that Geulincx stresses the voluntarism that is implicit in Cartesianism, falling back on God's will as the explanation of moral right and wrong.[24]

In 1692 some anonymous compiler put together a French summary of *Cartesian Ethics.* This was put into Latin, as the *Ethica Cartesiana,* and published in Germany in 1719. Its subtitle tells its story: "The art of living well and happily developed according to the clearest reasons and the ideas of a sound mind and the most solid principles of René Descartes."[25]

The Cartesian influence is also obvious in the thought of Benedict de Spinoza (1632–1677). He published a resume of the first two parts of Descartes's *Principles of Philosophy* (in 1663) but he was much more than a Cartesian. In spite of a certain vague and unfinished quality in his moral philosophy, Spinoza stands out as a key figure in modern ethics. There are many excellent studies of his treatise, named *Ethics,* but it is hard to find a coherent account of his moral philosophy, because most interpreters stress his metaphysics.

In 1658–1660 Spinoza wrote a *Tractatus brevis de Deo et homine ejuscque felicitate;* this has been lost but two Dutch versions of it were discovered in the middle of the nineteenth century and have been printed. This *Short Treatise* is an advance sketch of the *Ethics.* He insists in it that there can be but one substance and that it will have various attributes and accidents.[26] Even at this early date, he is vague in discussing personal immortality but quite certain about the "eternity of mind."[27]

Spinoza's great work, of course, is the *Ethics Demonstrated Geometrically.* The first draft dates from 1665; he revised it several times; it was published posthumously in 1677. As a Jew residing in Amsterdam, with unorthodox religious views, Spinoza was regarded with distrust by most people and he hesitated to publish his writings, even in that bastion of freedom which was seventeenth-century Holland. Two later treatises (*Tractatus Theologico-Politicus,* 1670, and *Tractatus Politicus,* about 1675) throw some light on the relation between Spinoza's moral and religious thought.

The *Ethics* as we now have it, is in five books: I. On God; II. Nature and Origin of Mind; III. Origin and Nature of the Emotions; IV. Strength of the Emotions; and V. Power of Understanding, or On Freedom. Each part begins with a set of definitions or with certain axioms and the argument progresses through numbered propositions, with corollaries and explanatory notes. Spinoza was quite serious about using the style of geometric demonstration. Much of the work is taken to present his monistic metaphysics but this is necessary to the exposition of his moral philosophy.

Substance exists in itself and is conceived through itself; it is consequently one, infinite, and identical with God.[28] Of substance there are infinite attributes (ways in which intellect may conceive the essence of substance) of which but two are known to us: thought and extension. The influence of Descartes's dualism of mind and matter is at work here. Nothing that exists or occurs in the universe is contingent; nor is there free will in the domain of mind.[29] Men are mistaken in attributing final causality to the universe;

there is no final end for all things. The only kind of teleology that is admissible is the conscious direction of human effort toward proximate goals. Modes are modifications of substance. They may be either infinite or finite. Like "accident" in Scholastic terminology, a Spinozistic mode exists in another and is conceived through another.

Body is God (or substance) existing determinately as an extended thing. Idea is the conception that is actively formed by mind. Will *(voluntas)* and understanding *(intellectus)* are identical and they are simply individual volitions and ideas. Each human mind is a limited aspect of the divine intellect—and is the idea of some thought-object *(ideatum)* that is actually existing.[30] The idea which is the human mind has as its object a certain mode of extension, which is the body. Man, for Spinoza, is constituted of a number of modes, some in the attribute of thought and others in the attribute of extension. Elsewhere, Spinoza calls man an "atom" in the eternal order of universal nature.[31] In another place, we are asked to imagine a worm existing in the blood stream and viewing the various particles about it as if they were individuals, and to compare this worm with a man living in the universe and thinking that he is surrounded by many individual things.[32] Each one of us is but a speck in the vast infinity of substance.

The second book of the *Ethics* also introduces us to Spinoza's three levels of knowledge (Proposition XL).

The lowest kind is called opinion or imaginative perception: it is the ordinary (one might even say "common sense") way of looking at man and nature. The second level of perception of knowing is that in which "we have notions common to all men, and adequate ideas of the properties of things." Spinoza calls this "reason" and sees it as operative in science. The highest kind of knowledge is "intuitive"; it "proceeds from an adequate idea of the absolute essence of certain attributes of God to the adequate knowledge of the essences of things."[33] What is important here is that Spinoza thinks that a true moral philosophy must be worked out on the third level, i.e. ethics must view human actions in terms of principles originating in mind and having a reference to the divine attributes. At the end of Book II of the *Ethics* there is a note that criticizes Descartes's *Passions de l'âme* as an inadequate theory of human feelings. The physiology of the pineal gland does not appeal to Spinoza.

At the start of the next book (III, prologue), Spinoza says: "I shall consider human actions and appetites just as if I were considering lines, planes, or bodies." His approach to the emotions is reminiscent of the naturalism of Hobbes but it is also very rationalistic. Spinoza defines "affects" as "modifications of body by which the power of acting of the body itself is increased, diminished, helped, or hindered, together with the ideas of these modifications."[34] Such affects involve both the attribute of extension and that of thought. Man is the inadequate cause of some of his affects, these are *passions;* he is the adequate cause of other affects, and they are *actions.* This is important to grasp, because his whole program in the remainder of his ethics consists in showing how man may, and should, convert his passions into actions. This is a gradual process of gaining self-control, or better mental initiative.

There is in each man what Spinoza calls the *conatus:* that basic and ongoing effort whereby everything tries to persist in its own being.[35] As "will" the *conatus* is mental; as "appetite" it belongs to both body and mind. The longer Cartesian list of passions of the soul, or emotions, are reduced by Spinoza to three primitive expressions of human feeling: desire *(cupiditas),* joy *(laetitia),* and sorrow *(tristitia).* The last two carry some connotation of bodily pleasure and pain, as well as the mental feelings corresponding thereto. Now, Spinoza does not think that the Stoics and Descartes were correct in simply saying that these feelings need to be curbed by reason or will, in the ethically developed person. At the beginning of the fourth part of the *Ethics,* the notion of "human bondage" to the emotions is introduced. Man must learn to be alert to the tendency of his passive feelings to take over his life; he must try to transmute his passive affects into dynamic actions. (One may see some similarity here between Spino-zism and existentialism.)

Good and evil name nothing positive in things; they are simply comparative notions that we form.

Good suggests an approach toward some idea of perfection, as described in these words:

> By "good," therefore, I understand in the following pages everything which we are certain is a means by which we may approach nearer and nearer to the model of human nature we set before us. By "evil," on the contrary, I understand everything which we are certain hinders us from reaching that model.[36]

The aim of Spinoza's ethics is to enable us to move toward a more intuitive, and philosophical, understanding of this process of self-perfection in man. This process is further described in a series of points (there are thirty-three) which constitute the Appendix to Book IV. In the main, they restate in orderly fashion most of the steps that we have followed above.

The last book of the *Ethics* shows how a man may develop himself by striving to detach disturbing affects from the thought of an external cause in order to connect it with inner thoughts. Further, man must come to realize that an affect loses its passivity as soon as he can form a clear and distinct idea of it; and this can be done for all affects that appear to arise from some modification of the body.[37] The import of this is that one becomes more perfect as a man in this effort to advance toward a personally developed understanding of initial mental disturbances. ("Peace of mind" books in present-day applied psychology owe something to

Spinoza.) Moreover, the mind may come to know that all things are necessary, and so connected with God, and so they should be consciously related to the idea of God. To know God is to love Him, and this is what man should do above all.[38] All of this is summed up in Proposition XXV, where he says that the highest mental endeavor and virtue is to understand things through the third level of knowledge. And his proof is as follows:

> The third kind of knowledge proceeds from an adequate idea of certain attributes of God to an adequate knowledge of the essences of things . . . in proportion as we understand things more in this way, we better understand God; therefore the highest virtue of the mind, that is, the power, or nature, or highest endeavor of the mind, is to understand things by the third kind of knowledge.[39]

Some years later, in the *Theological–Political Treatise*,[40] Spinoza set forth his views concerning man's duties to recognize and to obey God. These are not remarkable in their content but they are grounded entirely on natural reasoning and they have thus had a considerable influence on the later Deists. Spinoza's debt to Hobbes becomes more obvious in this treatise. There is no such thing as "natural" law or justice, since all events and tendencies in nature are equally natural. Before civil laws there is no difference between pious and impious: "wrong is conceivable only in an organized community."[41] The same rationalized naturalism is discernible in the *Political Treatise*. Natural right means the very laws or rules of nature. "Man, whether guided by reason or mere desire, does nothing save in accord with the laws and rules of nature." And later Spinoza adds: "I am altogether for calling a man so far free, as he is led by reason."[42] In the state of nature, wrongdoing is impossible, everything that you do is natural. In organized society, state law determines what is right and wrong. Frequently now, Spinoza mentions "utility" but this simply refers to the general human welfare and does not have the hedonistic connotation that is sometimes given the term in British writing.

It is impossible to fit Spinoza's ethics into the ordinary classifications of ethical theory. He is a naturalist only in the broadest sense: he did not think that the data or methods of the empirical sciences (his second-level knowledge) are directly applicable in moral philosophy. Yet he committed the "naturalistic fallacy" with complete abandon, by defining good in terms of several other features in his metaphysics, and so his ethics might be called a rationalistic naturalism.[43]

Descartes was a Catholic, Spinoza was originally of the Jewish faith, and our next rationalistic philosopher was an outstanding Protestant: Gottfried Wilhelm von Leibniz (1646–1716). A brilliant and learned scholar, Leibniz wrote in Latin, French, and even in his native German. He did not produce a treatise on ethics, as such. Most of his views on the subject are found in his works on jurisprudence and on miscellaneous subjects.[44] In the case of Leibniz, it is not essential to have a thorough knowledge of his theoretical philosophy in order to understand his ethical views. We might simply note that he was convinced that there is a reasonable explanation for everything that exists and happens, although he did not claim to know all these reasons. All reality is constituted of "monads," which are simple substances, indivisible and nonextended. These monads are like atomic force-centers which give rise to two kinds of activities: perceptions and desires. There is a very large number of created monads constituting the physical and mental universe. Monads do not interact (they have no windows) but each monad mirrors all the external universe in its internal perceptions. Monads with only *petites* (unconscious) *perceptions* cluster to form bodies. Monads with *grandes* (conscious) *perceptions* are souls which function as the entelechies (directive principles) of living bodies, including humans. God is the supreme Monad and does not have a body. Human soul monads have intelligence and free choice. The soul monads are destined for personal immortality.[45]

In 1693 Leibniz prepared and published an edition of documents dealing with the law of peoples (*Codex Juris Gentium Diplomaticus*) with a special Preface. Here, right *(jus)* is defined as "a kind of moral power, and obligation is a moral necessity." Moral means "something equivalent to natural for a good man." And a good man is "one who loves all men, so far as reason permits."[46] In the same place, wisdom is described as "nothing but the science of happiness itself." In a later commentary on this *Code of the Law of Peoples (Mantissa codicis juris gentium,* 1700) Leibniz singled out and stressed a definition of justice which he had given in the Preface. "Justice," he said, "is nothing but the charity of the wise man."[47] This leads to an explanation of the importance of the love of God but it does not mean that Leibniz is a voluntarist: the ultimate basis of ethical distinctions is not the will of God but divine wisdom or reason. He mentions an objection to his view: "It is more perfect so to submit to God that you are moved by his will alone and not by your own delight." To this anticipation of Kant's good-will theory, Leibniz replies that this objection "conflicts with the nature of things, for the impulse to action arises from a striving toward perfection, the sense of which is pleasure, and there is no action or will on any other basis." He adds that "even our evil purposes are moved by a certain perceived appearance of good or perfection."[48]

It is clear that Leibniz's ethics equates the good with an advance toward perfection. In a paper *On Wisdom,* written in German during the decade 1690–1700, he explained: "I call any elevation of being a perfection," and he adds that "perfection shows itself in great freedom and power of action."[49] As in Spinoza, the approach to personal perfection is a progress in understanding. Leibniz may be even more of an intellectualist than Spinoza, however. As he puts it in the same place, "Nothing serves our happiness better than the illumination of our understanding, and the exercise of our will to act always according to our understanding."

The view that moral obligation rests on the requirements of natural law as known through human reason, is strongly supported by Leibniz. About the year 1702 he wrote a French essay, *Reflections on the Common Concept of Justice.* It is very critical of the notion that law is simply a volitional command. Quoting the Latin dictum *"Stat pro ratione voluntas"* (Let my will stand for a reason), he insists that this is the motto of a tyrant:

> All our theologians, therefore, and most of those of the Roman Church, as well as the ancient Church Fathers and the wisest and most esteemed philosophers have favored the second view, which holds that goodness and justice have grounds independent of will and of force.[50]

As Leibniz sees it, Hobbes wrongly adopted the position of Thrasymachus that might is right, for he "fails to distinguish between right and fact. For what *can* be is one thing; what *ought* to be is another." The "formal reason" of justice, or what is right, must be common to God and man. To show this Leibniz uses the example of arithmetical numbers and relations: they must be the same in meaning for all intellects, even God's. So also, "the term or word *justice* will have some definition or intelligible meaning. And, by using the incontestable rules of logic, one can draw definite consequences from every definition."[51] Precisely as one can develop logic, metaphysics, and arithmetic by deductive demonstration from initial definitions, so can one produce the *science de droit* by reasoning.

This same point of view is evident in the *Nouveaux essais sur l'entendement humain* (written in 1704, not published until 1765). There, after reviewing Locke's theory that moral rules are established by human custom and convention, he mentions the suggestion that morality depends on the will of the divine lawgiver. Leibniz's spokesman in this dialogue (Theophilus) disagrees with this: "I prefer for myself to take as the measure of moral good and of virtue the invariable rule of reason which God is charged with maintaining."[52] Throughout this important twenty-eighth chapter Leibniz offers a theory of morality that reasons from an initial definition of goodness and the view that right action must conform to nature, to general rules of moral conduct.[53] This point of view is in complete accord with the *Reflections on Justice,* which we have been considering: in this work of the same period we read, "We may ask what is the true good. I reply that it is merely whatever serves the perfection of intelligent substances."[54]

About the year 1675, Leibniz visited Spinoza in Amsterdam and was shown a manuscript draft of the *Ethics* from which he made some notes. It is difficult to determine the extent of the impression which Spinozism made upon him. Leibniz is very much like Spinoza in his esteem for the "serenity of the spirit, finding pleasure in virtue."[55] Such high-minded Stoicism was very much in the air at this time. In a summary appended by Leibniz to his *Essais de Théodicée* (1710) he began an explanation of moral obligation by quoting Seneca, "*semel jussit, semper paret,*" which Leibniz took to mean that God commanded but once and then He obeys His own laws always. God's law imposes a type of necessity that is not physical but analogical.

This necessity is called moral, because, to the sage, *necessity* and *what ought to be* are equivalent things; and when it always has its effect, as it really has in the perfect sage, that is, in God, it may be said that it is a happy necessity. The nearer creatures approach to it, the nearer they approach to perfect happiness.[56]

It is in this passage that Leibniz enunciates his "principle of the best"—that God, or a perfect will, always chooses what is best. This is the source of his tremendous moral optimism and his confidence that God has made the best possible world.

The theme of the "love of God" runs through all of Leibniz's practical thinking. At the end of *Principes de la nature et de la Grâce* (1714) there is a beautiful and oft-quoted passage in which he speaks of this highest love which "makes us enjoy a foretaste of future felicity." Such love is disinterested, yet it gives us complete confidence in God as the guarantor of all our hopes and the assurer of happiness in a future life for those who live well.[57] He sees all men united under God as ruler of the "City of God" which is "a moral world within the natural world."[58] Supreme goodness is especially manifested in this most perfect state. In keeping with these views, Leibniz was a most tolerant man religiously and worked assiduously for the reunion of Christendom.

While Leibniz wrote no treatise on ethics, a Leibnizian manual of moral philosophy was produced by one of his followers, Christian von Wolff (1679–1754). He was the original "Herr Professor" of German philosophy and, indeed, has been called the schoolmaster of Europe. Wolff wrote very systematic, and very rationalistic, textbooks for all the traditional divisions of philosophy. In fact, though Aristotle had done a rather exact job of naming the parts of philosophy, Wolff added more divisions and names and we are still using them.[59] In 1738–1739 he published his two-volume textbook *Universal Practical Philosophy,* in an academic Latin that has been blamed on the Scholastics. A good deal is told about Wolff's character by the dedications: the first volume is addressed to Cardinal Melchior de Polignac, the second to Frederick Wilhelm, king of Prussia! This "practical philosophy" is intended to provide the principles for ethical, domestic, and political philosophy. These principles are the precepts of natural law *(lex naturalis)* which "makes known the sufficient reason *(rationem sufficientem)* within the essence and nature of man and of things."[60] His expansion of this teaching is based on Grotius and Leibniz. Everything is simple for Wolff; he solves the problem of a ground for moral obligation in a few words. "Granted, then, the essence and nature of man and things, obligation is granted, and it comes from the law of nature."[61] At times, Wolff's simplistic rationalism is but a caricature of Leibniz.

The great textbook is, of course, Wolff's *Moral Philosophy, or Ethics Treated by the Scientific Method* (1750–1753). Its five volumes are also well dedicated; one is to Charles, the Duke of Brunswick, another is to Andrzej Zaluski, Bishop of Cracow! Their subjects are: I. On the Intellect and Its Faculties and on the Intellectual Virtues; II. On Willing and Not-Willing *(De voluntate et noluntate)*; III. On the Virtues and Moral Duties in regard to God; IV. On the Virtues and Moral Duties in regard to Ourselves; V. On the Virtues and Moral Duties in regard to Other People. This takes care of almost everything. The opening sentence of Volume I, page 1, reads: "Moral philosophy or ethics is a practical science, teaching the way in which man may perform his free actions in accord with the law of nature." All the rest of his ethics follows from this with Leibnizian rigor.

Christian Wolff's textbooks have had a tremendous influence. Their teaching is in the background of Kant

and much of German idealistic ethics. In another tradition, Wolffian teaching has been accommodated
to Catholic Scholastic ethics and was thought, until
recently, to be the authentic doctrine of Thomas
Aquinas. Not a few textbooks in "Christian Ethics,"
written for use in modern Protestant schools, owe a
great debt to Wolff.

Another version of natural law ethics was developed by the German Protestant philosopher of law,
Christian Thomasius (1655–1728). As a young writer
he followed the views of Pufendorf and produced a
number of books on jurisprudence and on the life of
virtue, written in Latin or German. Thomasius helped
to adapt the German vernacular to the use of practical
philosophers. His emphasis was on the general utilitarian aspects of Pufendorf's theory of morality.

At the beginning of the eighteenth century in
France, the leading practical philosopher was Charles
Louis de Secondat, baron de Montesquieu (1689–
1755). His *Spirit of the Laws* (1748) carried on the tradition of Cartesian rationalism but with good sense and
moderation. Laws, according to Montesquieu, "are the
necessary relations arising from the nature of things."[62]
All law is an expression of an original reason in God that
establishes relations between it and other beings and
among all other beings. In itself, this rational order
is natural law. Human laws are "positive" in the sense
that they are established on particular occasions by
men or societies in order to regulate human intercourse

and to curb excessive force. The relations among all things under God all together constitute the "Spirit of Law." The main thing that Montesquieu brings to ethics in France is a growing awareness of the possibility of an empirical study of right and justice as realized in human customs and society.

Another French writer of this period was Jean Jacques Rousseau (1712–1778), who was born in Switzerland but lived in Paris for many years. His *Discourse on the Arts and Sciences* (1749–1750) introduces one of the basic themes in his practical philosophy: that man existed originally in an innocent state of nature, unregulated by laws but naturally good and unspoiled by "civilization." Right at the beginning of Part II of this *Discourse,* Rousseau shows that he even regarded the usual learned disciplines, including ethics, with suspicion: "Astronomy was born of superstition, eloquence of ambition, hatred, falsehood, and flattery; geometry of avarice; physics of an idle curiosity; and even moral philosophy of human pride."[63] In another work, the *Discourse on the Inequality of Men* (1754–1755), Rousseau further treats man in the state of nature and his passage into the artificial conditions of societal life. Unlike Hobbes, Rousseau does not see the "natural" man as warlike and quarrelsome. His happy savage only gets into difficulties with his fellows when he thinks of claiming exclusive title to a piece of land: from this point onward, laws must be devised and they are artificial and not natural. In a sense the possibility of evil, in the way of illegal activity, is attendant upon man's fabrication of positive laws. Rousseau also wrote novels that helped to popularize the importance of "naturalness" in moral and social living, and in education.

The famous *Social Contract* (1762) is Rousseau's most serious effort to explain how human society and its laws come into being. In it he describes two principles in man's nature that are prior to reason and that incline him toward his personal good and toward the good of others. These a priori factors were taken over later by Kant. Here is what Rousseau says of them:

Meditating on the first and simplest operations of the human soul, I think that I perceive two principles prior to reason, one of which makes us intensely concerned about our well-being and personal self-preservation, and the other inspires us with a natural repugnance to seeing any other being that is capable of feeling, and especially those of our own species, die or suffer.[64]

It is the suggestion that man has some innate endowments in the moral order and prior to experience that will interest Kant, but there is still another teaching in the *Social Contract* which influenced later ethicians and especially Kant. This is the theory of the "general will" *(la volonté générale)*. In a well-organized society, as Rousseau understands it, the judgment of the people on moral and social questions is the general or popular will. It is usually expressed by the vote of the majority but it is, for Rousseau, no ordinary counting of opinions. There is something mystical and almost divine about the general will. It is infallibly right and pure; it requires obedience from all citizens. It is the social expression of what is right and moral.[65] Rousseau did not develop this "general will" into a theory of ethics but it is an important antecedent to Kant's doctrine of the autonomous will.[66]

Critical of Rousseau's "moral naturalism" and of John Locke's empiricism was Cardinal Sigismond Gerdil (1718–1802), an Italian by birth and long residence in Rome but French in culture. His fundamentally Augustinian philosophy is now little known (partly because he taught a theory condemned later by the Catholic Church, his *ontologism,* which held that all things are known by men on earth through seeing them in the divine essence). His dependence on the Christian spiritualism of Malebranche (whom we shall treat in Chapter XII) is generally recognized. Gerdil's main writing in ethics is the *Metaphysical Principles of Christian Morality* (published posthumously in 1806). In this work, Gerdil presents a "natural law" ethics which asserts that man knows the principles of morality and justice by seeing them in the wisdom of God.[67] His teaching is a simple and forthright theological approbatism. In effect, he denies all difference between revealed and ordinary knowledge, and between supernatural and natural wisdom. Despite official ecclesiastical disapproval of his views, Cardinal Gerdil was read by many Catholics who saw his brand of Christian spiritualism as a bulwark against the novelties of Locke and the French "philosophes."

Germany in the early eighteenth century witnessed the growth of an academic ethics that was under the influence of the Leibniz-Wolffian approach to the subject; that is, it started with a very general theory of practical reasoning, plus certain initial definitions, and then reasoned deductively[1] to various derivative ethical judgments and to an applied ethics that treated typical moral problems. Martin Knutzen (1713–1751), who was Immanuel Kant's teacher at Königsberg, belonged to this school of thought. He wrote a *Philosophical Proof of the Truth of the Christian Religion* (1740). More important as a writer in the field of ethics was a contemporary professor at Frankfurt, Alexander Gottlieb Baumgarten (1714–1762), who usually appears in histories of philosophy as the founder of German aesthetics. Actually, Baumgarten produced the textbooks in metaphysics and ethics that were used by Kant as a young teacher. Specifically, Kant taught his first courses in ethics from two Latin books by Baumgarten, *Philosophical Ethics* (1740) and the *Elements of First Practical Philosophy* (1760). These texts were followed closely in Kant's teaching between 1775 and 1781.[68]

Wolff's philosophy was not unopposed, of course. Professors like Joachim Lange (1670–1744) at Halle and Johann Andreas Rüdiger (1673–1731) at Leipzig criticized his rationalism and mathematicism. Particularly in the area of ethics, one of Wolff's out-standing German critics was Christian A. Crusius (1715–1775). He is mentioned by Kant as teaching that the will of God is the objective ground of moral-ity and was called a "theological moralist."[69] In another work, Kant reports that Crusius rejected the Leibniz-Wolffian principle of sufficient reason but substituted his own, equally fundamental, principle: "That which I cannot think except as true is true."[70] This does not meet with Kant's approval but, in general, Kant had a high regard for Crusius.

The most important ethician in this whole rational-ist school was Immanuel Kant (1724–1804) and many experts think that he was the greatest moral philoso-pher in modern times. In his teaching and writing at Königsberg, Kant began a revolution in ethics which is still important in the twentieth century. It is usual to divide his thought into the precritical and critical peri-ods. His first *Critique (of Pure Reason)* was printed in its first edition in 1781. During the decade preceding this publication he had been turning away from Wolf-fian philosophy toward a more personal way of think-ing. His *Inquiry into the Distinctness of the Principles of Natural Theology and of Morals* (1764) is the main ethical work of the precritical period. It deals with the question of whether strict geometrical demonstration is possible in ethics and philosophical theology.[71] The *Lectures on Ethics* were edited from students' notes taken in his classes at Königsberg during the years 1775 to 1781. As we have seen, they show a professor dealing wittily and often eloquently with the systematic outlines of Baumgarten's ethics. At this point, Kant is in transition toward his own critical ethics. The *Foundations of the Metaphysic of Morals* (1785) is one of his important contributions to ethics. The other is the *Critique of Practical Reason,* published in 1788 after the appearance of the second edition (B) of the *Critique of Pure Reason.* Much of the same subject matter is treated in the *Foundations* and in the *Critique of Practical Reason* but the order of the arguments is different and the style of the former is more popular in comparison with the rigorous and systematic procedure of the second *Critique.* In 1797 Kant published his *Metaphysics of Morals* which carried his ethics into the philosophy of law (Part I) and the theory of special duties and virtues (Part II). In the last decade or so of his life Kant produced a good many notes and miscellaneous essays which contain some material on his later ethical views.[72] Among other things, the *Opus Postumum* shows that the elderly Kant is ready to grant a more immediate and real role to God as a moral legislator.[73]

Just how much of Kant's speculative philosophy one needs to know in order to understand his ethics is problematical. Certainly one would have to study the *Critique of Pure Reason* before attempting any thorough study of the practical philosophy.[74] Kant distinguished three cognitive faculties in man. Sensibility is man's receptivity to sensory data under the subjective forms of space and time. Understanding *(Verstand)* is the faculty of synthesizing sense data so that they may be thought in terms of the categories of human knowledge. Reason *(Vernunft)* is the faculty that transcends the conditions of experience and spontaneously gives rise to certain ways of relating the objects of understanding among themselves and to some higher principle. It is by reason that our knowledge of objects is ordered into systems. What reason contributes apart from the data of experience is a priori, from within the very constitution of man's consciousness. The phenomenal objects which are constructed in the imagination out of the presentations of sense experience as formed by the categories of sensibility and understanding are not things-in-themselves. These latter are by definition unknown, for, if they were known they would be in consciousness and not in themselves. When Kant investigates "pure" reason, he is endeavoring to discover what is characteristic of the mind and its functioning, quite apart from the empirical or received elements of thought.

The part of the *Critique of Pure Reason* devoted to the "Transcendental Dialectic" has a section that deals with the antinomy of natural causality and human freedom.[75] One may argue that another sort of causality, that of freedom, is necessary; and one may also argue that freedom has no place in the explanation of the phenomenal world. In attempting to resolve this conflict of reasonings, Kant suggests, in the following passage, that morality is a domain to which pure reason may be extended:

The legislation of human reason has two objects, nature and freedom, and therefore contains not only the law of nature, but also the moral law, presenting them at first in two distinct systems, but ultimately in one single philosophical system. The philosophy of nature deals with all that *is*, the philosophy of morals with that which *ought to be*.

This provides an important transition to Kantian ethics: in effect, a complete theory of pure reason would have to extend into the sphere of practical reason.

The *Foundations of the Metaphysic of Morals* is easier than the *Critique of Practical Reason* to digest; so, we will use its argument as the main part of our consideration of Kant's ethics. What he is attempting in this work is a general account of what is needed to reason out a theory of ethics. Kant proposes to explain the formal basis of moral judgment. A complete ethics would include material received from experience (practical anthropology) interpreted in the light of certain laws or principles provided prior to experience from the resources of reason itself. More particularly, in discussing these "foundations" or fundamental principles, Kant is dealing with the preconditions to a general philosophy (metaphysics) of ethical judgment. (He wrote the "metaphysics" of ethics in the treatise published in 1797, *Metaphysik der Sitten*.) The first section of the

Foundations shows how we move from common rational knowledge of morals to a philosophical knowledge. It is here at the start that Kant introduces one of his most famous ethical doctrines: the only unqualified good is a good will. Moreover, he insists that it is the function of practical reason to give rise to such a volition.[77]

This leads to the enunciation of three propositions of morality: (1) to have moral worth an action must be done from duty; (2) the action does not derive its moral worth from its results but from the maxim which produces it; and (3) duty is the necessity in an action performed out of respect for law. Already at this point there is also the suggestion that the rule, or maxim, from which moral activity springs must be capable of becoming a universal law.

Section two of the *Foundations* considers the process from popular moral philosophy to a metaphysics of morals. All moral concepts have their seat in reason prior to all data of experience. Natural (or physical) events always occur according to laws; only rational beings, however, act according to *conceptions* of laws. This implies a peculiar and distinctive ability in men. "This capacity is will. Since reason is required for the derivation of actions from laws, will is nothing else than practical reason."[78] The formula of any command of reason is an imperative, of which there are two kinds: hypothetical (if you wish this, then do that) and categorical (commanding an action that is of itself objectively necessary). Thus we are introduced to the name and notion of a "categorical imperative." In the ensuing few pages,[79] three formulations of this absolute kind of command are given by Kant. The first is: "Act only according to that maxim by which you can at the same time will that it should become a universal law." A few paragraphs later is the second: "Act as though the maxim of your action were by your will to become a universal law of nature." The third formula is given later: "Act so that you treat humanity, whether in your own person or in that of another, always as an end and never as a means only." What we have here is an attempt by Kant to show the most basic formal pattern that would regulate the expression of more specific ethical or moral judgments.

The categorical imperative is "formal" in the sense of containing no definite subject matter but providing a principle of all moral commands. (It has given rise to various other formulations of the principle of universalization or generalization, in more recent ethics.) Implied in Kant's discussion of these formulas is the notion of the "autonomy of will"—suggesting that practical reason (which is "will" as legislative) has here something of the force of Rousseau's general will.[80] Furthermore, the idea of a "realm of ends" is brought out here. In fact, the principle of autonomy is stated in such a way as to be equivalent to another formula for the categorical imperative: "Never choose except in such a way that the maxims of the choice are comprehended in the same volitions as universal law."[81] As opposed to autonomy of will, Kant speaks of heteronomy of will (choosing for motives apart from the maxim implied in the categorical imperative) as the source of all spurious principles of morality. Explicitly, the concept of perfection and the notion of a most perfect divine will are regarded as heteronomous principles.

The third section of the *Foundations* is devoted to the process from the metaphysics of morals to pure practical reason. Here, freedom becomes the most important presupposition of the autonomy of will. A rational being may consider himself as belonging to the world of sense and nature, or as part of the intelligible world under laws that derive from reason. It is the idea of freedom that makes one a member of the intelligible world. Freedom makes the categorical imperative possible.[82] At the end of the *Foundations,* Kant admits that we do not fully understand the unconditional necessity of the categorical imperative but argues that we do grasp its incomprehensibility.

In the *Critique of Practical Reason,* Kant covers much the same ground but more thoroughly and in reverse order. We saw that the *Foundations* begins with moral law and freedom and analyzes them to find their grounds. The second *Critique* is synthetic in its method, starting with experience and moving toward a more general organization of the data of morality. Perhaps the chief conclusion which the practical *Critique* adds to the *Foundations* is the demonstration of the great unity between practical and theoretical reason. Still another formulation of the categorical imperative is offered in the *Critique of Practical Reason:* "So act that the maxim of your will could always hold at the same time as a principle establishing universal law."[83] This is probably the best-known statement of the categorical imperative. It is again intimately related to the autonomy of will as practical reason.

In the *Critique of Practical Reason* the famous postulates of ethics are clearly presented.[84] Kant had shown in the first *Critique* that it is impossible, in the context of his principles, to demonstrate the existence of God, the freedom of the human agent, and the immortality of the human soul. Now, in the light of the demands of practical reason, he argues that freedom must be granted in order that moral action be possible, that God is needed to guarantee man's independence from the world of sense, and that immortality is required to provide a duration adequate to the fulfillment of moral law.

Kant's ethics is a deontology. In the last resort the basis for doing good and avoiding evil is one's personal awareness of duty. There is a much quoted passage in the *Critique of Practical Reason* where he hails duty as that which requires obedience without threatening, which moves without enticing, and which provides a law that is unconditionally binding.[85] Obedience to moral duty cannot be motivated by fear of punishment or the desire for happiness, although practical reason suggests that happiness will follow upon action that is motivated by good will. This is an idealistic and high-minded ethics. It demands a degree of intellectual integrity and sophistication which is rare even among men of learning.

Much German ethics in the nineteenth century consists of controversies between the followers and the critics of Immanuel Kant. Many thinkers accept part of his teaching but attempt to modify other elements. Typical is Salomon Maimon (1753–1800), who agreed that the supreme law in ethics is an a priori datum of consciousness.[86] Yet Maimon could not agree that the desire for happiness should be excluded from the motivation for good action. He also felt that Kant had neglected the impact of moral feelings on the human agent: high-minded pleasure seemed to Maimon to be a most valuable incentive to good behavior.[87] We shall see in Chapter XI how Kantian ethics continued to play a central role in later German thinking.

Notes

Chapter I

Early Greek Eudaimonism

1. The Greek fragments of these earliest philosophers are printed in H. Diels and W. Kranz, *Die Fragmente der Vorsokratiker* (Berlin: Weidmann, 1956); there is a complete English translation in Kathleen Freeman, *Ancilla to the Pre-Socratic Philosophers* (Oxford: Blackwell, 1948).

2. Freeman, op. cit., pp. 76–77 (Philolaus, frag. 14 and 22).

3. Aristotle, *Nicomachean Ethics*, II, 6; 1106ai4–1107a25.

4. Freeman, op. cit., p. 75 (Philolaus, frag. 11).

5. Freeman, op. cit., p. 80 (frag. 3).

6. See fragments 1, 2, 45, 50, 72, and 115, in Freeman, op. cit., pp. 24–32.

7. Joseph Owens, *A History of Ancient Western Philoso-*

phy (New York: Appleton-Century-Crofts, 1960), pp. 160–66, and C. Mazzantini, *Eraclito* (Torino: Vita e Pensiero, 1945), p. 24, speak of Heraclitus as the first Greek moralist.

8. Cf. Frederick Copleston, *History of Philosophy* (Garden City, N.Y.: Doubleday, 1962), Vol. 1, Pt. I, pp. 146–47.

9. Freeman, op. cit., pp. 107–09 (frags. 170, 171, 187).

10. The translation of Democritus' fragment 31 is from Owens, op. cit., p. 141.

11. Freeman, op. cit., pp. 84–85 (frag. 12; cf. frags. 11, 13, and 14).

12. Aristotle, *Metaphysics*, I, 3–4; 984b18–985a20; compare Plato, *Phaedo*, 97C–98D.

13. Aristotle, *Sophistic Elenchi*, 1; 165a21.

14. Plato, *Sophistes*, 231D.

15. Diogenes Laërtius, *Lives and Opinions of Eminent Philosophers*, trans. R. D. Hicks (Cambridge: Harvard University Press, 1950), IX, 51.

16. Plato, *Protagoras*, 361A-D.

17. Milton C. Nahm, *Selections from Early Greek Philosophy*, 3rd. ed. (New York: Appleton-Century-Crofts, 1947, p. 239); cf. Plato, Theaetetus, 152A.

18. Plato, *Protagoras*, 318.

19. Nahm, op. cit., citing *Pyrrhonenses Hypotyposes*, I, 216.

20. Aristotle, *Metaphysics*, IV, 5; 1008a35–1009a14.

21. Plato, *Republic*, 338C; the English is from F. M. Cornford, *The Republic of Plato* (New York: Oxford University Press, 1956), p. 18.

22. Plato, *Laws*, X, 889D–890A; trans. B. Jowett (New York: Random House, 1937), II, 631.

23. Plato, *Gorgias*, 482E–484B.

24. Cf. Eduard Zeller, *Outlines of the History of Greek Philosophy*, trans. L. R. Palmer (New York: Humanities Press, 1931), p. 103.

25. Miles Dawson, *The Ethics of Socrates* (New York: Putnam, 1924).

26. Xenophon, *Memorabilia*, trans. E. C. Marchant (Cambridge: Harvard University Press, 1938), III, 7, 1–9, 1; cf. Hilda D. Oakeley, *Greek Ethical Thought from Homer to the Stoics* (New York: Dutton, 1925), p. 50.

27. On the personality of Socrates, see the Platonic dialogues: *Charmides*, 164D; *Phaedrus*, 230A; and *Philebus*, 45E.

28. *Nicomachean Ethics*, VI, 12; 1144b 18–20.

29. Xenophon, *Memorabilia*, III, 9, 14; Plato, *Republic*, X, 621D.

30. Sören Kierkegaard, *Concluding Unscientific Postscript*, trans. D. F. Swenson and Walter Lowrie (Princeton, N.J.: Princeton University Press, 1944), p. 28.

31. Cf. R. Marcel, "'Saint' Socrate," *Revue Internationale de Philosophie*, V (1951), 135–43.

32. Diogenes Laërtius, *Lives*, II, 106; Seneca, *Epistulae*, IX, 1; on the teachings of the Megarics, see Copleston, *History*, 1, I, 138.

33. Augustine, *City of God*, XIV, 20; cf. Diogenes Laërtius, *Lives*, VI, 69, and Cicero, *De Offciis*, I, 41.

34. Aristotle, *Metaphysics*, III, 2; 996a33.

35. Xenophon, *Memorabilia*, II, 1.

36. Cf. Zeller, *Outlines*, p. 132.

37. Alexander of Aphrodisias, in *Aristotelis Metaphysicam*, ed. M. Hayduck (Berlin, 1891), 55, 20–57, 2.

38. Cf. R. N. Nettleship, *Lectures on the Republic of Plato*

(London: Macmillan, 1922; reprinted New York: St. Martin's Press, 1962), chapter VII, especially p. 160.

39. Comford, *The Republic*, p. 222.

40. The English terms for these four levels of cognition vary in different translations. Cornford's terminology (p. 222) is used here.

41. Cf. Nettleship, Lectures, pp. 212–37; Paul Shorey, "The Idea of Good in Plato's *Republic*," *Studies in Classical Philology* (Chicago, 1895), Vol. I. Kevin Doherty, "God and the Good in Plato," *New Scholasticism*, XXX (1956), 441–60.

42. See Basil Willey, *The English Moralists* (New York: Norton, 1964), pp. 41–53.

43. For an interpretation of the intellectualism of Plato's ethics, couched in value terminology, see R. C. Lodge, *Plato's Theory of Ethics* (London: Routledge, 1928, reprinted 1950).

44. On these stories see J. A. Stewart, *The Myths of Plato* (London: Oxford University Press, 1905).

45. Cornford, *The Republic*, p. 356.

Chapter II

Teleological Eudaimonism: Aristotle

1. Cf. M. Moraux, "From the Protrepticus to the Dialogue On Justice," in *Aristotle and Plato*, ed. I. Düring and G. E. L. Owen (Göteborg: Almqvist & Wiksell, 1960), pp. 113–29; see also A. H. Chroust, "Aristotle's 'On Justice' a Lost Dialogue," *The Modern Schoolman*, XLIII (1966) 249–63.

2. See W. D. Ross, *Aristotle* (London: Methuen, 1923), pp. 14–16; more up-to-date information is found in the Introduction to *L'Ethique à Nicomaque, ed. R. A. Gauthier* (Paris: Nauwelaerts, 1958), I, l*–90*.

3. *Nicomachean Ethics* (henceforth cited as *NE*), 1102a5; *Eudemian Ethics* (henceforth *EE*), l219a32; cf. Jean Vanier, *Le Bonheur principe et fin de la morale aristotélicienne* (Paris: Desclée de Brouwer, 1965).

4. Rhetoric, 1360b14–28; cf. Vanier, p. 186.

5. *NE*, 1177b25; the translation is from W. D. Ross's version, Oxford Translation, Vol. VIII.

6. Gauthier, op.cit., p. 569, notes that duty, in various verbal forms, occurs 170 times in the Greek text of *NE*.

7. *NE*, 1105b20–1106a11; *EE*, l220b11.

8. See Vanier, p. 53, with his criticism of J. D. Monan, *The Doctrine of Moral Knowledge in Aristotle's Proptrepticus, Eudemian and Nicomachean Ethics* (Louvain: Nauwelaerts, 1959).

9. *NE*, l096a20–1097b15; cf. Enrico Berti, *L'Unità del Sapere in Aristotele* (Padova: Cedam, 1965).

10. See *NE*, 1107b1–1108b10; *EE*, l220b25–1222b15.

11. *NE*, 1130b30–1131a9.

12. For the discussion of voluntariness, see *NE*, 1109b30–1111b3; on the contemporary value of this theory, consult P. H. Nowell-Smith, *Ethics* (Baltimore: Penguin, 1954), p. 292.

13. *NE*, 1139b15–1141a19; for the moral dimensions of practical wisdom (*phronesis*) see 1141a20–1144a35.

14. *NE*, 1144b9–10; see Pierre Aubenque, *La Prudence chez Aristote* (Paris: Presses Universitaires, 1963).

15. On pleasure, *NE*, 1174b15–1175a20; for a hedonistic interpretation of Aristotle (which is not generally accepted) see J. Léonard, *Le Bonheur chez Aristote* (Bruxelles: Palais des Académies, 1948).

16. *NE*, 1177b26–28.

17. *EE*, 1249b15–24.

18. See Benjamin Farrington, Greek Science (Baltimore: Penguin, 1949), II, 17–27.

19. Cf. R. Walzer, *Greek into Arabic: Essays on Islamic Philosophy* (Cambridge: Harvard University Press, 1962), Essay 9: "New Light on Galen's Moral Philosophy."

20. See Odon Lottin, *Psychologie et Morale* (Gembloux: Duculot, 1942), I, 278–80; Daniel Callus, "The Date of Grosseteste's Translations," *Recherches de Théologie Ancienne et Médiévale*, XIV (1947) 200–208; F. Van Steenberghen, *Aristotle in the West* (Louvain: Nauwelaerts, 1955).

Chapter III

Hellenistic Ethics: Stoic, Epicurean, and Neoplatonic

1. Zeno is sometimes credited with introducing a technical term for duty (to kathekon) into Greek; it is found earlier in Plato's *Statesman*, 295B.

2. See Benson Mates, *Stoic Logic* (Berkeley: University of California Press, 1953); and H. Ritter et L. Preller, *Historia Philosophiae Graecae* (Gotha: Perthes, 1913), p. 411.

3. Trans. T. W. Rolleston, in *The Teaching of Epictetus* (London: Walter Scott, 1888), pp. 1–2.

4. See Copleston, *History of Philosophy*, 1, II, 139.

5. Cicero, *De natura deorum*, II, 11, 30–33, reports this teaching.

6. For this sophisticated Stoic psychology, see G. Verbeke, *L'Evolution de la doctrine du pneuma* (Louvain-Paris: Desclée, 1945), pp. 90–142.

7. Cf. A. P. Wagener, "Reflections of Personal Experience in Cicero's Ethical Doctrine," *Classical Journal*, XXXI (1935–36) 359–70; Milton Valente, *L'Ethique Stoicienne chez Cicéron* (Paris: Saint-Paul, 1956).

8. See W. C. Korfmacher, "Stoic apatheia and Seneca's De clementia," *Transactions American Philological Assoc.* LXXVII (1946), 44–52; K. D. Nothdurft, *Studien zum Einfluss Senecas auf die Philosophie und Theologie des zwoelften Jahrhunderts* (Leiden: Brill, 1963).

9. Epictetus, *Enchiridion*, trans. George Long (Philadelphia: Altemus, 1908), p. 56.

10. Epictetus, *Moral Discourses*, trans. W. A. Oldfather (Cambridge: Harvard University Press, 1928), p. 97.

11. Marcus Aurelius, *Meditations*, ed. and trans. C. R. Haines (Cambridge: Harvard University Press, 1930), V, 27, and XII, 1.

12. Ibid., XI, 1.

13. Cf. W. W. Tarn, *Hellenistic Civilization* (New York: Longmans, 1927), pp. 266–81.

14. Diogenes Laërtius, *Lives*, X, 30–34, is our chief source of information on this aspect of Epicurus' thought.

15. See the letter from Epicurus to Menoeceus in Epicurus, *The Extant Remains*, ed. Cyril Bailey (Oxford: Clarendon Press, 1926); cf. A. J. Festugière, *Epicurus and His Gods*, trans. W. Chilton (Cambridge: Harvard University Press, 1956).

16. Cf. John Ferguson, *Moral Values in the Ancient World* (London: Methuen, 1958; New York: Barnes & Noble, 1959), p. 149; the quotation is from the Letter to Menoeceus.

17. Epicurus, *The Letters, Principal Doctrines, and Vatican Sayings*, trans. R. M. Geer (Indianapolis: Library of the Liberal Arts, 1964), pp. 27–28.

18. Lucretius, *De rerum natura: On the Nature of Things*, trans. W. H. D. Rouse (Cambridge: Harvard University Press, 1959); see the opening lines of Bks. I, III, and V.

19. Ibid., Ill, 1. 1081.

20. Ibid., V, 1. 1019.

21. See Hans Lewy, *Three Jewish Philosophers* (New York: Harper, 1960), pp. 109–10, for a detailed list of the writings of Philo Judaeus.

22. Philo Judaeus, *De opificio mundi*, I, 69–71, and IV, 16; in Philo, ed. F. H. Colson and G. H. Whitaker (Cambridge: Harvard University Press, 1929), Vol. I; compare Lewy, op. cit., pp. 54–55.

23. Philo Judaeus, *On the Migration of Abraham*, 9–11; in Lewy, p. 72.

24. H. A. Wolfson, in *Philo*, 2 vols. (Cambridge: Harvard University Press, 1948), possibly exaggerates Philo's influence on the Middle Ages.

25. Plutarch, *Moralia: Morals*, 14 vols., ed. and trans. F. C. Babbitt et al. (Cambridge: Harvard University Press, 1927–58); in spite of the vast scope and promising title of this work, it contains little evidence of original thinking in ethics.

26. See G. H. Clark, *Selections from Hellenistic Philosophy* (New York: Appleton-Century-Crofts, 1940), pp. 211–16.

27. On this *Metaphysics* consult A. H. Armstrong, *The Architecture of the Intelligible Universe in the Philosophy of Plotinus* (London: Cambridge University Press, 1940).

28. Cf. Plotinus, *The Ethical Treatises*, trans. Stephen MacKenna (London: Medici Society, 1926).

29. See Emile Bréhier's comment in *Ennéades* (Paris: Les Belles Lettres, 1924–38), especially I, 94.

30. Ennead, IV, 8, 1; my English version is adapted from Bréhier's French, IV, 216.

31. See H. van Lieshout, *La Théorie plotinienne de la vertu* (Paderborn: Schöningh, 1926).

32. Ennead, VI, 9, 11; cf. Bréhier, *Ennéades*, VI, 188.

33. See Ferguson, *Moral Values in the Ancient World*, pp. 99–100; and Copleston, History of Philosophy, 1, II, 221–24.

Chapter IV

Patristic and Early Medieval Ethics

1. For general information on the Fathers of the Church, see Johannes Quasten, *Patrology*, 4 vols. Westminster, Md.: Newman Press, 1950–66).

2. See R. B. Brandt, "The Use of Authority in Ethics," in *Ethical Theory* (Englewood Cliffs, N.J.: Prentice-Hall, 1959), pp. 56–82; for the contrary view, that Christian ethics is the only adequate ethics, see Jacques Maritain, *Science and Wisdom*, trans. Bernard Wall (New York: Scribner's, 1940); and R. C. Mortimer, *Christian Ethics* (London: Hutchinson University Library, 1950).

3. Emil Brunner, *The Divine Imperative* (Philadelphia: Westminster Press, 1947), p. 83.

4. This terminology is used in T. E. Hill, *Contemporary Ethical Theories* (New York: Macmillan, 1950), pp. 97–113, to describe similar types of twentieth-century ethics.

5. Matt. 5:17; Confraternity trans. (1941), p. 14.

6. See Bardaisan of Edessa, *The Book of the Laws of Countries* (Syriac text plus English version), by H. J. W. Drijvers (Assen, Netherlands: Van Gorcum, 1965); and the same scholar's biographical and doctrinal study, Bardaisan of Edessa, id., 1966.

7. On Hippolytus, see Etienne Gilson, *History of Christian Philosophy in the Middle Ages* (New York: Ran-

dom House, 1954), pp. 24–26, 563–65.

8. See Gilson, op. cit., pp. 33–35, 565–69.

9. On *First Principles*, III, 1, 13, and I, 8; see the trans, by G. W. Butterworth (London: Society for the Promotion of Christian Knowledge, 1936; reprinted, New York: Harper Torchbooks, 1966), pp. 181 and 67; cf. Jean Daniélou, *Origen*, trans. W. Mitchell (New York: Sheed & Ward, 1955), pp. 73–98.

10. On *First Principles*, III, 1–6; trans. Butterworth, pp. 161–249.

11. Gregory of Nyssa's *De hominis opificio* and *De vita Moysis* are now being critically edited under the direction of Werner Jaeger et al.; see Gilson, op. cit., p. 583.

12. The immediate source for the Pseudo-Dionysius seems to be Proclus' *De subsistentia mali*.

13. On the Divine Names, chap. 4, sec. 24; trans. C. E. Rolt (London: Society for the Promotion of Christian Knowledge, 1920), p. 123.

14. Ibid., sect. 9; trans. Rolt, pp. 98–99.

15. Ibid., sect. 30; Rolt's trans, (p. 126) is modified here to conform to the Greek.

16. Thomas Aquinas (In librum *De divinis nominibus*, lectio 22, n. 572; ed. C. Pera, p. 213) will later make extensive use of this teaching.

17. See Gilson, op. cit., p. 88.

18. My translation is made from *De fide orthodoxa*, MS Paris, Bibliothèque Nationale, 14557, fol. 204vb–205va, as transcribed by O. Lottin, Revue Thomiste, XXXVI (1931), 631.

19. For *bulesis* and *thelesis* in Thomas Aquinas, see *Summa Theologiae*, I, 83, 4, ad primum; and III, 18, 3c.

20. See O. Lottin, *Psychologie et Morale*, I, 393–424; and

Vernon J. Bourke, Will in Western Thought (New York: Sheed & Ward, 1964), pp. 55–76.

21. For a discussion of the meaning of this notorious statement from *The Flesh of Christ* (chap. 5), see Gilson, op. cit., p. 45.

22. Adversus Praxean, 12–18; trans, in *Writings of Tertullian* (Edinburgh: Clark, 1870), XV, 357–72.

23. Pierre de Labriolle, *Histoire de la littérature latine chrétienne* (Paris: Les Belles Lettres, 1947), I, 124.

24. Cf. de Labriolle, op. cit., pp. 299–300.

25. Ambrose, *De officiis ministrorum*, is analyzed in N. E. Nelson, Cicero's *De officiis in Christian Thought* (Ann Arbor: University of Michigan Press, 1933); cf. R. Thamin, *Saint Ambroise et la morale chrétienne au IVe siècle* (Paris: Masson, 1895).

26. For the evidences of Plotinian influence in Ambrose's *De Isaac et anima*, VII, 60–79, see Pierre Courcelle, *Recherches sur les Confessions de saint Augustin* (Paris: De Boccard, 1950), pp. 106–38.

27. See, for instance, Joseph Fletcher, *Situation Ethics* (Philadelphia: Westminster Press, 1966), p. 81.

28. Brief texts on ethical questions are found in *The Essential Augustine*, ed. V. J. Bourke (New York: Mentor, 1964), chap. VII; for longer Latin selections, see G. Armas, *La Moral de San Agustin* (Madrid: Difusora del Libro, 1954).

29. Sermon 150, in Quincy Howe, Jr., *Selected Sermons of St. Augustine* (New York: Holt, Rinehart and Winston, 1966), pp. 89–110.

30. *De beata vita*, trans. as *The Happy Life*, by L. Schopp (New York: Fathers of the Church, Inc., 1948), I, 43–84.

31. Cf. Michael Schmaus, *Die psychologische Trinitätslehre des hl. Augustinus* (Münster: Aschendorff, 1927).

32. See *The Essential Augustine*, pp. 48–57.

33. *De libero arbitrio*, II, 19, 52; Sermo 341, 6, 8; cf. E. Gilson, *The Christian Philosophy of St. Augustine* (New York: Random House, 1960), Pt. I, chap. 5, for the theory of divine illumination.

34. *De Genesi ad litteram*, XII, 31, 59; trans. J. H. Taylor, in *The Essential Augustine*, p. 97.

35. For Augustine's views on law and morality, see *Confessions*, III, 7, 13; Letter 157, 15; *De libero arbitrio*, I, 6, 15; and Gustave Combès, *La doctrine politique de s. Augustin* (Paris: Plon, 1927); and Alois Schubert, *Augustins Lex-aeterna-Lehre nach Inhalt und Quellen* (Münster: Aschendorff, 1924).

36. In Joannis *Epistolam ad Parthos*, 4, 7, 8.

37. Enarrationes in *Psalmos*, 118, *Sermo*, X, 5.

38. *City of God*, VIII, 8; trans. G. Walsh et al. (New York: Doubleday Image Book, 1958), p. 155.

39. The best secondary work is Joseph Mausbach, *Die Ethik des hl. Augustinus* (Freiburg im Breisgau: Herder, 1909). ·

40. In *Isagogen Porphyrii*, ed. prima, I, 3 (*Corpus Scriptorum Ecclesiasticorum Latinorum*, XLVIII, 8–9); *De Trinitate*, ed. and trans. H. Stewart and E. K. Rand (Cambridge: Harvard University Press, 1918), pp. 8–12; cf. Thomas Aquinas, *The Division and Methods of the Sciences*, trans. A. Maurer (Toronto: Pontifical Institute of Mediaeval Studies, 1953).

41. See Stewart and Rand, op. cit., pp. 40–42.

42. Cf. J. Mariétan, *Le Problème de la classification des sciences d'Aristote à saint Thomas* (Paris: Alcan, 1901).

43. Stewart and Rand, op. cit., p. 50; cf. Charles Fay, "Boethius' Theory of Goodness and Being," in *Readings in Ancient and Medieval Philosophy*, ed. James Collins (Westminster, Md.: Newman Press, 1960), pp. 164–72.

44. "Confitendum est summum deum summi perfectique boni esse plenissimum," Boethius, *De consolatione philosophiae*, III, 10, prosa; in Stewart and Rand, op. cit., p. 268.

45. This is the view of Alois Dempf, *Ethik des Mittelalters* (München-Berlin: Oldenbourg, 1927), p. 56.

46. *On the Division of Nature*, I, 1, trans. in Herman Shapiro, *Medieval Philosophy* (New York: Random House, 1964), pp. 85–103.

47. *On the Division of Nature*, IV, 7; trans, in R. P. McKeon, Selections from *Medieval Philosophers* (New York: Scribner's, 1929), I, 117.

48. Cf. Gilson, *History of Christian Philosophy*, pp. 125–27.

49. Aimé Forest, *Le Mouvement doctrinal du IXe au XIVe siècle* (Paris: Bloud et Gay, 1951), p. 63.

50. Liber de voluntate, in *Patrologia Latina*, CLVIII, 487–90; *De concordia*, PL 158, 538–40; cf. J. Sheets, "Justice in the Moral Thought of St. Anselm," *The Modern Schoolman*, XXV (1948), 132–39.

51. De veritate, chap. 11; trans. McKeon, op. cit., I, 172.

52. "Rectitudo voluntatis propter se servata," ibid., chap. 12; in McKeon, I, 173–79.

53. "Potestas servandi rectitudinem voluntatis propter ipsam rectitudinem," *De libero arbitrio*, III; PL 158, 494.

54. *Ethica*, chap. 3; trans, by J. R. McCallum as Abailard's

Ethics (Oxford: Blackwell, 1935); sixteen chapters are reprinted in Shapiro, op. cit.; see especially Shapiro, pp. 137, 141.

55. Ibid., 12; in Shapiro, p. 162.

56. See Richard Thompson, "The Role of Dialectical Reason in the Ethics and Theology of Abelard," *Proceedings of the American Catholic Philosophical Association*, XII (1936), 141–48, who traces the theory of evil consent back to Augustine, *De continentia*, I, 23.

57. *De gratia et libero arbitrio*; see the English analysis in G. B. Burch, Early Medieval Philosophy (New York: King's Crown Press, 1951), pp. 90–93.

58. *On the Necessity of Loving God*, chap. 13; trans. in A. C. Pegis, *The Wisdom of Catholicism* (New York: Random House, 1949), p. 263.

59. Twelfth-century moral philosophy has not yet been fully studied; some idea of the possibilities may be gleaned from Philippe Delhaye's research articles; see, for example, "L'Enseignement de la philosophic morale au XIIe siècle," Mediaeval Studies, XI (1949), 77–99.

60. Cf. Steven Runciman, *The Medieval Manichee* (Cambridge, Eng.: University Press, 1947); and P. Alphandéry, *Les idées morales des hétérodoxes latins au debut du XIIIe siècle* (Paris: Leroux, 1903).

61. Joachim Abbatis, *Liber contra Lombardum*, ed. C. Ottaviano (Roma: Reale Accademia d'Italia, 1934); cf. H. Bett, *Joachim of Flora* (London: Cambridge Univ. Press, 1931); and M. W. Bloomfield and Marjorie E. Reeves, "The Penetration of Joachism into Northern Europe," *Speculum*, XXIX (1954), 772–93.

Chapter V

Medieval Jewish and Moslem Ethics

1. Wisdom 11:21 and 8:1.

2. Exodus 20:3–17; the translation is from *The Jerusalem Bible*, ed. Alexander Jones (Garden City, N.Y.: Doubleday, 1966), p. 102.Another listing of these precepts is found in Deut. 5:6–21.

3. Levit. 24:17–21.

4. For other formulations of the golden rule in various religious documents, see Dagobert Runes, *Pictorial History of Philosophy* (New York: Philosophical Library, 1955), p. vii.

5. See Maimonides, *The Guide of the Perplexed*, trans. Shlomo Pines (Chicago: University of Chicago Press, 1963), p. 509; also W. S. Sahakian, *Systems of Ethics and Value Theory* (Paterson, N.J.: Littlefield, Adams, 1964), p. 176.

6. Cf. Israel I. Efros, *Ancient Jewish Philosophy: A Study in Metaphysics and Ethics* (Detroit: Wayne State University Press, 1964), p. 179, note 22; on *kadosh* and *kavod*, see pp. 7–10.

7. For the sake of uniformity dates are given in the Christian Era.

8. Saadia ben Josef, *Kitab al-'Amanat wa'l-'I'tikadat* (Arabic original written in 933), ed. S. Landauer (Leiden, 1880); trans, by Alexander Altmann as *Book of Doctrines and Beliefs*, in *Three Jewish Philosophers* (Philadelphia: Jewish Publication Society, 1945; reprinted New York: Harper Torchbooks, 1965); see Altmann, "Prolegomena," pp. 26–31.

9. Ibid., chap. 3, sect. 2; Altmann, p. 94.

10. Ibid., p. 97; Altmann adds that Saadia's use of the Ara-

bic term (*'akl*) for "reason" indicates the influence of Mu'tazilite, and more remotely, Stoic teachings here.

11. Ibid., pp. 99–100, 111–15.

12. *Avencebrolis Fons Vitae, ex arabico in latinum translatus ab Johanne Hispano et Dominico Gundissalino*, ed. C. Baeumker (BGPM I, 2–4) (Münster: Aschendorff, 1892–95); see III, sects. 24–32, pp. 136–155.

13. Cf. Julius R. Weinberg, *A Short History of Medieval Philosophy* (Princeton, N.J.: Princeton University Press, 1964), pp. 148–49.

14. Jehuda Halevi, *Book of Kuzari*, trans. Hartwig Hirschfeld (New York: Pardes Publishers, 1946); abbreviated version by Isaak Heinemann, in *Three Jewish Philosophers*, see pp. 86–90.

15. Ibid., Bk. II, sects. 48–50, pp. 76–78.

16. Ibid., Bk. V, sect. 27, p. 128.

17. Bahya ibn-Pakuda, *Hovot Halevavot*, trans. by Moses Hyamson as *Duties of the Heart*, 5 vols. (New York: Bloch, 1925–47); the quotation is from V, 27.

18. Cf. Leon Roth, *The Guide for the Perplexed: Moses Maimonides* (London: Hutchinson's Library, 1950), p. 58.   (This is a doctrinal study, not a translation.) The best English version of the *Guide* is that by Shlomo Pines, cited above in note 5.

19. The influence of this view on Thomas Aquinas has often been noted; see Gilson, *History of Christian Philosophy*, p. 650.

20. *Guide for the Perplexed*, I, 72, and III, 27; see Pines, pp. 190 and 511.

21. J. S. Minkin, *The World of Moses Maimonides, with Selections from His Writings* (New York: Yoseloff, 1957), pp. 243–44, citing Maimonides, *Repentance*, V.

22. *Guide*, III, 54; *Pines*, p. 630; cf. Roth, op. cit., p. 119, citing Maimonides, *Eight Chapters*, V.

23. Cf. Roth, op. cit., p. 119; and Minkin, p. 188, where the passage from *Fundamental Principles* is quoted.

24. Maimonides, *Ethical Conduct*, Deot I, in Minkin, pp. 394–95.

25. *Guide*, II, 40; and III, 34.

26. *Guide*, III, 27; trans, from *Pines*, p. 511.

27. *Guide*, II, 36; this quotation is from the version in R. Lerner and M. Mahdi, *Medieval Political Philosophy: a Sourcebook* (New York: Free Press, 1963), p. 202.

28. See the text of this Letter, in Minkin, pp. 28–29.

29. Maimonides, *Eight Chapters*, VIII, in Minkin, p. 245; see also the *Letter on Astrology*, in Lerner and Mahdi, pp. 227–36.

30. *Deot* III, trans, in Roth, p. 107.

31. *Guide*, III, 26, in Pines, pp. 506–10.

32. On these three thinkers, see Isaac Husik, *A History of Medieval Jewish Philosophy* (Philadelphia: Jewish Publication Society, 1941), pp. 323–27, 329–61, and 388–405.

33. Joseph Albo, *Book of Principles*, V; the quotation is from Husik's version, reprinted in Lerner and Mahdi, p. 240.

34. In the *Tahdhib al-Akhlaq of Miskawaihi*, for instance; cf. M. M. Sharif, ed., *A History of Muslim Philosophy*, 2 vols. (Wiesbaden: Harrassowitz, 1963), see I, 475.

35. See D. M. Donaldson, *Studies in Muslim Ethics* (London: Society for the Promotion of Christian Knowledge, 1953), pp. 118–20.

36. Donaldson, op. cit., pp. 136–37.

37. See Ezio Franceschini, Il "Liber philosophorum mora-

lium antiquorum" (Roma: Bardi, 1930).

38. Brief summaries of the moral teaching of the Koran are given in Donaldson, op. cit., pp. 14–59, and in Sharif, op. cit., pp. 136–55.

39. Cf. A. Badawi, "Muhammad ibn Zakariya Al-Razi, Moral Philosophy," in Sharif, I, 434–49.

40. For the extensive literature on al-Farabi, see Nicholas Rescher, *Al-Farabi: An Annotated Bibliography* (Pittsburgh: University of Pittsburgh Press, 1962); of original works of al-Farabi we have in English, *The Fusul al-Madani of al-Farabi* (*Aphorisms of the Statesman*), ed. and trans, by D. M. Dunlop (London: Cambridge University Press, 1961); and *The Philosophy of Plato and Aristotle*, trans. Muhsin Mahdi (New York: Free Press, 1962).

41. *Enumeration of the Sciences*, chap. 5; in Lerner and Mahdi, op. cit., pp. 24–30.

42. Donaldson, op. cit., studies this theory in detail, pp. 148–55.

43. *The Political Regime*, trans. F. M. Najjar, in Lerner and Mahdi, p. 34; cf. p. 61.

44. Al-Ameri, *As-Saʿadah Waʾı-Isʿad*, facsimile of copy by Mojtaba Minovi (Teheran University) (Wiesbaden: Steiner Verlag, 1957–58).

45. Donaldson, op. cit., p. 125.

46. Badawi, A., "Miskawaihi, Ahma ibn-Muhammad," in *Sharif*, op. cit., I, 474, citing the Cairo, 1928, edition of *Tahdhib*, pp. 15–19.

47. Badawi, op. cit., p. 476.

48. For a transcription of the Latin version, see *Avicenna De Anima*, ed. G. P. Klubertanz (St. Louis, Mo.: the Modern Schoolman, 1949); the corresponding por-

tion of the Najat is printed as *Avicenna's Psychology*, Arabic text and trans. F. Rahman (New York: Macmillan, 1952); chaps. 10–15.

49. Cf. G. P. Klubertanz, *The Discursive Power* (St. Louis, Mo.: The Modern Schoolman, 1952), pp. 89–105.

50. See H. Corbin, *Avicenna and the Visionary Recital*, trans. W.P. Trask (New York: Pantheon Books, 1960).

51. A. M. Goichon, *Le récit de Hayy ibn-Yaqzan, commenté par textes d'Avicenne* (Paris: Desclée, 1959).

52. The version by Corbin and Trask includes a Commentary by an unidentified Persian contemporary, indicating the popularity of the story of Hayy.

53. Avicenna, *On the Divisions of the Rational Sciences*, in Lemer and Mahdi, p. 97.

54. Al-Ghazzali, *Deliverance from Error*, trans. W. M. Watt, in The Faith and Practice of al-Ghazzali (London: Allen and Unwin, 1953), pp. 19–86.

55. Cf. Donaldson, op. cit., p. 134.

56. Ibid., p. 135.

57. Cf. Abdul Khaliq, "Al-Ghazzali, Ethics," in Sharif, op. cit., I, 624–25.

58. Al-Ghazzali, *Ihya*, III, 48–50; trans, in Donaldson, op. cit., pp. 142–43.

59. For detailed references, see Donaldson, op. cit., p. 137.

60. *The Romance of the Rubaiyat*, ed. by A. J. Arberry, of Edward FitzGerald's First Edition reprinted with Introd. and Notes (London: Macmillan: 1959).

61. Ibn Hazm, Kitab al-Akhlaq Wa-l-Siyar, *Epitre morale, texte et traduction par Nada Tomiche* (Beyrouth: Commission Internationale pour la Traduction des Chefs-d'Oeuvre, 1961).

62. Ibn Bajja, *Governance of the Solitary*, trans. L. Berman, in Lerner and Mahdi, pp. 131–32.

63. See M. S. H. Al-Ma'sumi, "Ibn Bajjah, Ethics," in Sharif, op. cit., I, 523–24.

64. See also the *Letter of Farewell*, in Salomon Munk, *Mélanges de philosophie juive et arabe* (Paris: Franck, 1859), pp. 383–418.

65. Ibn Tufail, *Hayy, the Son of Yaqzan*, trans. G. N. Atiyeh, in Lerner and Mahdi, op. cit., p. 160.

66. B. H. Siddiqi, "Ibn Tufail," in Sharif, op. cit., I, 537.

67. See *Encyclopaedia Britannica*, 14th ed., IX, 849.

68. Weinberg, op. cit., p. 131; and Luis Alonso, *Teologia de Averroes* (Madrid: Institute) "Miguel Asin," 1947), p. 121.

69. Averroës, *Decisive Treatise*, trans. G. Hourani, in Lerner and Mahdi, pp. 171, 172, and 178.

70. Ibid., p. 169.

71. Cf. Klubertanz, *The Discursive Power*, pp. 110–22, with the references to Harry Wolfson's research studies.

72. *Decisive Treatise*, pp. 175–76; cf. Weinberg, op. cit., p. 139.

73. Ahmed F. El-Ehwany, "Ibn Rushd," in Sharif, op. cit., I, 364.

74. *The Nasirean Ethics*, trans, from the Persian by G. M. Wickens (London: Allen and Unwin, 1964); see the Introduction, p. 10.

75. Ibid.; in his note 141 Wickens gives these alternatives as suggested by George Hourani.

76. Ibid., p. 49.

77. See the section on purity, ibid., pp. 66–68.

78. Ibid., p. 86.

79. Ibid., pp. 140–41; cf. Donaldson, op. cit., pp. 169–82.

80. See Wickens, "Introduction," p. 12.

81. On modem Islamic ethics, consult Donaldson, op. cit., pp. 247–61.

Chapter VI

Right Reason Theories

1. Crane Brinton, *A History of Western Morals* (New York: Harcourt, Brace, 1959), p. 185.

2. For Bishop Tempier's condemned propositions, see Lerner and Mahdi, op. cit., pp. 335–56.

3. Brand Blanshard, *Reason and Goodness* (New York: Macmillan, 1961), p. 61.

4. Commentary on the *Nicomachean Ethics*, Bk. II, lectio 3; trans. C. I. Litzinger (Chicago: Regnery, 1964), I, 126.

5. In *Ezekialem*, I, 1; PL 25, 22B.

6. Cf. O. Lottin, *Psychologie et Morale* (Gembloux: Duculot, 1948), Tome II, 103–350.

7. See Walter Burleigh, *Commentaria in Ethicam Aristotelis* (Venetiis, 1521); cf. S. Harrison Thomson, "The 'Notule' of Grosseteste on the *Nicomachean Ethics*," *Proceedings of the British Academy*, XIX (1933).

8. Cf. A. C. Crombie, *Robert Grosseteste and the Origins of Experimental Science* (Oxford: Clarendon Press, 1953).

9. Robert Grosseteste, *On Truth*, trans. in McKeon, Selections from Medieval Philosophers, I, 273.

10. See D. E. Sharp, *Franciscan Philosophy at Oxford in the Thirteenth Century* (London: Oxford University Press, 1930), p. 116.

11. This is translated as *Moral Philosophy*, by R. P. McKeon et al., in Lerner and Mahdi, op. cit., pp. 355–90.

12. Ibid., p. 359.

13. Cf. Ignatius Brady, "Law in the Summa Fratris Alexandri," *Proceedings of the American Catholic Philosophical Association*, XXIV (1950), 133–46.

14. Joanni de Rupella, *Summa de Anima*, ed. crit, Ignatius Brady (Quaracchi: Collegio San Bonaventura, 1967).

15. Cf. O. Lottin, op. cit., Tome III, seconde partie (1949), pp. 393–424.

16. Bonaventure, In *Il Sententiarum*, d. 39, 2, 1; Opera Omnia, II, 910.

17. Ibid., d. 30, 1, 1, concl.; II, 899.

18. Bonaventure, *Retracing the Arts to Theology*, trans. Sister E. T. Healy, reprinted in Shapiro, *Medieval Philosophy*, p. 382.

19. For more information on Albert's writings, see Gilson, History of Christian Philosophy, pp. 666–68.

20. Translated from a section of Albert's *Lectura* transcribed from the Stuttgart MS by O. Lottin, op. cit., III, seconde partie (1949), p. 544.

21. Albert, *Summa de creaturis*, II, De homme; ed. Borgnet, XXXV, 599.

22. *Summa de bono*, transcribed from MS Bruxelles Bibl. Royale 603, fol. 84 rb, in Lottin, op. cit., p. 544.

23. Cf. Lottin, Le droit naturel (Bruges: Beyaert, 1931), p. 117.

24. Albert, *Commentaria in libros Ethicorum*, I, 5, 1; ed. Borgnet, VII, 57; *Summa de creaturis*, II, q. 65, 2, 3; ed. Borgnet, XXXV, 552.

25. On the relation of Thomas' ethics to the thought of his predecessors, one of the most useful studies is Michael Wittmann, *Die Ethik des hl. Thomas von Aquin* (München: Hueber, 1933).

26. See, for instance, T. E. Hill, *Contemporary Ethical Theories*, p. 246; W. T. Jones et al., *Approaches to Ethics* (New York: McGraw-Hill, 1962), p. xviii.

27. *Summa Theologiae*, I–II, 90, 4, c.

28. Sahakian, *Systems of Ethics*, pp. 220–27, views Thomistic ethics in terms of self-realization.

29. Thomas Aquinas, *The Virtues*, trans. J. P. Reid (Providence, R.I.: Providence College Press, 1951), pp. 22–51; see also *Summa Theologiae*, I–II, pp. 49–56.

30. *Expositio in Job*, 11, lectio 1; see a partial translation in Vernon J. Bourke, *Ethics in Crisis* (Milwaukee: Bruce, 1966), p. 125.

31. *Summa contra Gentiles*, III, 122; trans. in A. C. Pegis et al., *On the Truth of the Catholic Faith* (Garden City, N.Y.: Doubleday, 1955–57), Bk. III, Pt. 2, p. 143, n. 2.

32. Boethius of Dacia, *De summo bono*, in M. Grabmann, *Mittelalterliches Geistesleben* (München: Hueber, 1936), Bde. I, 200–204.

33. See Tempier's propositions numbered 1, 170, 171, and 172, in Lerner and Mahdi, op. cit., pp. 338 and 351.

34. Cf. R. A. Gauthier, "Trois commentaires 'averroistes' sur l'Ethique à Nicomaque," *Archives d'histoire doctrinale et littéraire*, XVI (1947–48), 187–336.

35. This letter is edited by G. Bruni in *New Scholasticism*, VI (1932), 5–12.

36. Giles of Rome, *De potestate ecclesiastica*, II, 6; see the English in Lerner and Mahdi, op. cit., p. 399.

37. Cf. E. Bettoni, "La libertà come fondamento dei valori umani nel pensiero di Pier di Giovanni Olivi," *Atti del XII Congresso Internazionale de Filosofia* (Venezia, 1958), XI, 45.

38. See A. San Cristobal-Sebastian, *Controversias acerca de la voluntad desde 1270–1300* (Madrid: Editorial y Libreria Co. Cul., 1958).

39. Henry of Ghent, *Quodlibeta*, I, q. 14; ed. Venetiis (1613), fol. 17D.

40. For details, see Gilson, *History of Christian Philosophy*, p. 352.

41. Ramón Lull, *Blanquerna*, trans. E. A. Peers (London: Jarrold, 1926), pp. 478–79.

42. Armand Maurer, *Medieval Philosophy* (New York: Random House, 1962), p. 301.

43. Eckhart, *Talks of Instruction*, trans. R. B. Blakney; reprinted in Jones, *Approaches to Ethics*, pp. 162–63.

44. Dante, *Convivio*, II, 1; and III, 15.

45. Cf. Efrem Bettoni, *Duns Scotus: The Basic Principles of His Philosophy*, trans. B. Bonansea (Washington: Catholic University Press, 1961), pp. 27–46, 81–86.

46. Duns Scotus, *Ordinatio*, I, d. 17, par. 1, qq. 1–2, n. 62; *editio Vaticana*, V (1959), 163–164; trans. Bourke.

47. Duns Scotus, *Quaestiones Quodlibetales*, q. 18, n. 3; ed. Wadding, XII, 475.

48. *Ordinatio*, prologo, pars. 5, qq. 1–2; ed. Vaticana, I, 156–58.

49. Duns Scotus, *Opus Oxoniense*, II, d. 39, qq. 1–2; this portion of the Ordinatio is not yet available in the Vatican edition.

50. Ibid., II, d. 39, n. 926.

51. For data on William of Ockham's writings, see Philotheus Boehner, Introduction, to *Philosophical Writings* (Edinburgh: Nelson, 1957).

52. See ibid., pp. xxviii–xxix.

53. *Quodlibet*, I, .q. 10; in Boehner, *Philosophical Writings*,

p. 158.

54. Ibid., q. 1; Boehner, pp. 139–40.

55. *Quodlibet*, III, q. 13; Boehner, p. 161.

56. Ibid., pp. 162–63.

57. As Óckham puts it: "Eo ipso quod voluntas divina hoc vult, recta ratio dictat quod est volendum." In I *Sententiarum*, d. 41, q. 1, k; cf. In III Sent., d. 12, NN.

58. Henry de Bracton, *De legibus et consuetudinibus Angliae*, ed. G. E. Woodbine, 4 vols. (New Haven: Yale University Press, 1915–42).

59. Sir John Fortescue, *De laudibus legum Angliae*, chap. 16; see the trans, by S. B. Chrimes, in Lerner and Mahdi, op. cit., p. 523.

60. Reginald Pecock, *The Reule of Crysten Religioun*, ed. W. C. Greet (London: Oxford University Press, 1927), pp. 24 and 227.

61. Reginald Pecock, *Book of Faith*, ed. J. L. Morison (Glasgow, 1909), p. 23.

62. Richard Hooker, *Of the Laws of Ecclesiastical Polity*, ed. J. Keble (Oxford: Clarendon Press, 1839), I, 208.

63. Ibid., I, 222.

64. Ibid., I, 205.

Chapter VII

Humanist Ethics in the Renaissance

1. Cf. Rudolf Allers, "Microcosmus," in *The Philosophical Work of Rudolf Allers* (Washington, D.C.: Georgetown University Press, 1965), pp. 123–91.

2. Oratio de dignitate hominis, trans. M. McLaughlin, in *Portable Renaissance Reader* (New York: Viking Press, 1953), p. 478.

3. Leonardo da Vinci, *Notebooks*, trans. Edward MacCurdy

(London: Cape, 1928); reprinted in G. de Santillana, *The Age of Adventure* (New York: Mentor, 1956), p. 87.

4. *On Learned Ignorance*, III, 2.

5. Ibid., chap. 10; trans. G. Heron, in *Unity and Reform*, ed. J. P. Dolan (Notre Dame, Ind.: Notre Dame University Press), 1962, p. 85.

6. Ibid., p. 87.

7. *De pace fidei*, trans. J. P. Dolan, op. cit., p. 236.

8. Cf. A. Maurer, *Medieval Philosophy*, p. 336.

9. Marsilio Ficino, *Platonic Theology*, trans. J. L. Burroughs, in *Portable Renaissance Reader*, p. 391.

10. Pico della Mirandola, *Of Being and Unity*, trans. V. M. Hamm (Milwaukee: Marquette University Press, 1943), pp. 33–34.

11. From J. R. Charbonnel, *L'Ethique de Giordano Bruno et le deuxième dialogue du Spaccio* (Paris: Champion, 1919), p. 210, trans. Bourke.

12. Bruno, *On the Infinite*, trans. Agapito Rey, in D. S. Robinson, *Anthology of Modern Philosophy* (New York: Crowell, 1931), p. 50.

13. Bruno, *De Monade numero et figura*, 2; trans. J. H. Pitman, in Robinson, pp. 56–57.

14. For a similar meaning of "Platonism" in contemporary philosophy, see the discussion in Morton White, *Toward Reunion in Philosophy* (Cambridge: Harvard University Press, 1956).

15. Cf. Copleston, *History of Philosophy*, 3, II, 134.

16. *Utopia*, trans. Ralph Robinson (New York: Lupton, 1890), p. 65.

17. Ibid., pp. 65–66.

18. Elyot, *The Governour*, ed. F. Watson (New York: Dut-

ton, 1907), p. 191.

19. Ibid., pp. 298–308, for a lengthy Glossary.

20. Cf. Herschel Baker, *The Image of Man* (New York: Harper, 1961), p. 271.

21. See Felice Tocco, "L'Isagogicon Moralis Disciplinae di Leonardi Bruni Aretino," A*rchiv für Geschichte der Philosophie*, VI (1892), 157–69.

22. The outstanding study is Bruno Nardi, *Studi sull'aristotelismo Padovano* (Firenze: Sansoni, 1958).

23. Cf. Maurer, op. cit., p. 339.

24. See M. A. Dynnik, "Vanini et l'aristotélisme de Padoue," *Atti del XII Congresso di Filosofia* (Firenze: Sansoni, 1960), IX, 81–89.

25. Thomas Aquinas, *S.T.*, II–II, 40, 1, c.

26. Vitoria, *De jure belli*, see *Portable Renaissance Reader*, p.367.

27. Ibid., p. 371.

28. *Commentarii collegii conimbricensis, societatis Iesu . . . ethica Aristotelis* (Lugduni: Pillenotte, 1616), is but one example.

29. Cf. G. M. Ganss, *St. Ignatius: Idea of a Jesuit University* (Milwaukee: Marquette University Press, 1954).

30. Bellarmine, *De gratia et libero arbitrio*, 9; see Davitt, The Nature of Law, p. 200.

31. Selections are available in Suárez, *On the Laws*, trans. G. L. Williams et al., in *The Classics of International Law*, ed. J. B. Scott (Oxford: Clarendon Press, 1944), Vol. II.

32. Suárez, *Disputationes Metaphysicae*, VI, 2, 14; the best secondary study is J. M. Alejandro, *La gnoseologia del Doctor Eximio y la acusación nominalistica* (Comillas, Spain: Universidad Pontificia, 1948).

33. Suárez, *De Anima*, V, 3, 8.

34. For a typical explanation: Timothy Brosnahan, *Prolegomena to Ethics* (New York: Fordham University Press, 1941), p. 183; the teaching is based on Disputation X, in the *Disputationes Metaphysicae*.

35. Suárez, *De Legibus*, II, 5, 6–14.

36. Ibid., sec. 9.

37. For an expanded report on this point, see Copleston, *History of Philosophy*, 3, II, 206.

38. Suárez, *De Legibus*, II, 13, 1–8.

39. Ibid., II, 7, 5.

40. *De fine ultimo*, tract. III, d. XII, 1, 5, 6; in *Opera Omnia*, ed. Berton, Tome V, 438.

41. Ibid., sects. 3–5; Tome V, 442–53.

42. Cf. Ueberweg et al., *Die Philosophie der Neuzeit* (Berlin: Mittler, 1924), p. 275.

43. Giorgio de Santillana, op. cit., p. 143.

44. Alasdair MacIntyre, *Short History of Ethics* (New York: Macmillan, 1966), p. 162.

45. Luther, *The Bondage of the Will*, trans. Henry Cole (Grand Rapids, Mich.: Zondervan, 1931); reprinted in *Santillana*, op. cit., p. 148.

46. For a selection of ethical significance from Calvin's *Institutes*, see M. Mothersill, *Ethics* (New York: Macmillan, 1965), pp. 29–34.

47. Ibid., p. 31.

48. Cf. L. G. Crocker, *Nature and Culture: Ethical Thought in the French Enlightenment* (Baltimore: Johns Hopkins Press, 1963), p. 148.

49. Leibniz, Letter to J. Thomasius, Sept. 2, 1663; in G. W. Leibniz, *Sämtliche Schriften und Briefe*, hrsg. von der Preussischen Academie der Wissenschaften, Darm-

stadt: Reichl, 1926, Zweite Reihe, Bde. I, p. 3.

50. On this influence, see James Collins, *Modern European Philosophy* (Milwaukee: Bruce, 1954), p. 572.

51. *The Prince*, trans. L. Ricci and C. E. Detmold (New York: Random House, 1940); reprinted in Jones, *Approaches to Ethics*, pp. 171–72.

52. Montaigne, *Essays*, 12, 2; in Santillana, op. cit., pp. 177–78.

53. James Collins, *The Lure of Wisdom* (Milwaukee: Marquette University Press, 1962), pp. 25–26.

54. See Ralph Cudworth, *A Treatise concerning Eternal and Immutable Morality* (London, 1731), p. 6.

55. Cf. Collins, *Lure of Wisdom*, pp. 13–19.

56. Léontine Zanta, *La Renaissance du stoicisme au XVIe siècle*, (Paris: Champion 1914), pp. 225–36.

57. See R. W. Battenhouse, "Chapman on the Nature of Man," *English Literary History*, XII (1945), 89–92.

58. See the further analysis in Copleston, *History of Philosophy*, 5, I, 63.

Chapter VIII

British Egoism and Its Reactions

1. *Advancement of Learning*, II, 20–21; see Bacon Selections, ed. M. T. McClure (New York: Scribner's, 1928), pp. 197–99.

2. This view of Francis Bacon is shared by Basil Willey, *The English Moralists* (New York: Norton, 1964), p. 125.

3. Hobbes, *De corpore*, 8, 10, and 25, 2; see *Hobbes Selections*, ed. F. J. E. Woodbridge (New York: Scribner's, 1930), pp. 83, 106.

4. *Leviathan*, I, 6; in Woodbridge, p. 188.

5. Henry Sidgwick, *Outlines of the History of Ethics* (London: Macmillan, 1886; revised ed. of 1931, reprinted Boston: Beacon, 1964), p. 169.

6. Philosophical Rudiments, that is, the English version of *De Cive*; in *English Works*, ed. W. Molesworth (London: Bohn and Longmans, 1839–45), II, 196.

7. Ibid., cf. Woodbridge, p. 284.

8. *Elements of Philosophy*, on Body, 2, 4; Human Nature, 5; see Woodbridge, pp. 15–24.

9. *Questions concerning Liberty*, in English Works, V, 192.

10. Leviathan, chap. 16; in Woodbridge, p. 270.

11. Ibid.

12. Leviathan, chaps. 14–15; in Woodbridge, p. 309.

13. Ibid., chap. 31; in Woodbridge, p. 384.

14. *Philosophical Rudiments,* in *English Works*, II, 50; cf. Decorpore politico, in Opera Philosophica, ed. Molesworth, IV, 224.

15. John Bramhall, *A Defence of True Liberty . . . Answer to a Late Book of Mr. Thomas Hobbes* (London, 1655).

16. Cf. J. K. Ryan, "St. Thomas Aquinas and English Protestant Thinkers" *New Scholasticism*, XXII (1948), 146–58, for an account of Bramhall's argument.

17. Browne, *Christian Morals*, III, 21; cited in Willey, *The English Moralists*, p. 193.

18. For extensive discussion of these reactions to Hobbes, see John Bowie, *Hobbes and His Critics* (New York: Oxford University Press, 1952); and S. I. Mintz, *The Hunting of Leviathan* (Cambridge, Eng.: University Press, 1962).

19. Culverwel, *An Elegant and Learned Discourse of the Light of Nature*, 1652; in the ed. of Edinburgh, 1857,

p. 162.

20. Cudworth, *Treatise concerning Eternal and Immutable Morality* (London, 1731), pp. 6–9.

21. Treatise, p. 17; or see B. Rand, *Classical Moralists* (Oxford: Clarendon Press, 1897), pp. 230–31.

22. Treatise, Bk. IV, 2, p. 148.

23. Willey, *The English Moralists*, p. 176, sees Cudworth as a pre-Kantian.

24. See Mintz, op. cit., chap. VI: "The Free-Will Controversy: Bramhall and Cudworth," pp. 126–33, especially.

25. Mintz, p. 131, gives MS citations from the unedited portions of Cudworth's *A Discourse of Liberty and Necessity*; the printed sections are in *A Treatise of Free-Will*, ed. John Allen (London, 1838).

26. More, *Enchiridion Ethicum*, 3, 2; trans. E. K. Rand, in B. Rand, *Classical Moralists*, p. 242.

27. Richard Cumberland, *A Treatise of the Laws of Nature*, trans. J. Maxwell (London, 1727); in Rand, *Classical Moralists*, p. 248.

28. Locke, *Essays on the Law of Nature* (1660–1664), ed. Latina, W. von Leyden (New York: Oxford University Press, 1954), p. 110.

29. Ibid., III, pp. 136–45.

30. Ibid., pp. 146–59; cf. M. B. Crowe, "Intellect and Will in John Locke's Conception of Natural Law," *Atti del XII Congresso Internazionale di Filosofia* (Firenze, 1960), XII, 132–33.

31. Essay concerning *Human Understanding*, II, 21, 7; see L. A. Selby-Bigge, *British Moralists* (Oxford: Clarendon Press, 1897), II, 334.

32. Ibid., 20, 2–21, 42.

33. Ibid., 28, 4; in Selby-Bigge, p. 343.

34. Ibid., 28, 10; in Selby-Bigge, p. 346.

35. Ibid., IV, 3, 18.

36. Shaftesbury, *Inquiry concerning Virtue*, 1, 2, 3; and I, 3, 1; see the text in Selby-Bigge, I, 11–21.

37. Ibid., II, 2, 3; in Selby-Bigge, I, 33.

38. John Gay, *Concerning the Fundamental Principle of Virtue or Morality*, sect. 3; in Selby-Bigge, II, 273.

39. Samuel Clarke, *Discourse on Natural Religion*, 1; in Selby-Bigge, II, 6.

40. Ibid., 5; in Selby-Bigge, II, 29.

41. John Clarke, *The Foundation of Morality*; in Selby-Bigge, II, 242.

42. See Bernard Mandeville, *The Fable of the Bees*, ed. Douglas Garman (London: Wishart, 1934), pp. 82–85; the lines quoted are from Mandeville, *Enquiry into the Origin of Moral Virtue*, in Selby-Bigge, II, 354–55.

43. William Wollaston, *The Religion of Nature Delineated*, 1; in Selby-Bigge, II, 362–65.

44. Ibid., 8; in Selby-Bigge, II, 370.

45. Ibid., 9; in Selby-Bigge, II, 372.

46. Ibid., 10–11; in Selby-Bigge, II, 381–82.

47. Condillac, *Treatise on Sensations*, III, 1; the passage is translated in L. M. Marsak, *French Philosophers* (New York: Meridian, 1961), p. 196.

48. For well-chosen selections illustrating this point: L. W. Beck, *18th-Century Philosophy* (New York: Free Press, 1966), pp. 164–91.

49. Franklin, *Autobiography*, ed. Herbert Schneider (New York: Liberal Arts Press, 1952), p. 90.

50. Cf. L. G. Crocker, *Nature and Culture: Ethical Thought in the French Enlightenment* (Baltimore: Johns Hop-

kins Press, 1963), p. 212.

51. Berkeley, *Principles of Human Knowledge*, 100; ed. A. C. Fraser, (Oxford: Clarendon Press, 1901); II, 84.

52. This passage from the 1710 edition of *Berkeley's Principles* is reprinted in G. Berkeley, *A New Theory of Vision and Other Writings* (New York: Dutton, 1925), p. 163, note 1.

53. Berkeley, *Philosophical Commentaries*, in Works, ed. A. A. Luce and T. E. Jessop (London: Nelson, 1948), I, 93.

54. Berkeley, *Passive Obedience*, in Works, VI, 19.

55. Butler, *Sermons*, I; in Selby-Bigge, I, 197–202.

56. *Sermons*, III: in Selby-Bigge, I, 224–25.

57. Butler, *A Dissertation upon the Nature of Virtue*, in Selby-Bigge, I, 246–53.

58. R. A. P. Rogers, *Short History of Ethics* (New York: Macmillan, 1911), p. 167.

59. Lord Kames, *Essays on the Principles of Morality*, II, 1–5; in Selby-Bigge, II, 300–13.

60. Francis Hutcheson, *Inquiry into the Original of Our Ideas of Beauty and Virtue*, Introduction; in Selby-Bigge, I, 69.

61. Ibid., I, 8; in Selby-Bigge, I, 83.

62. Ibid., III, 8; in Selby-Bigge, I, 106–07.

63. Cf. James Bonar, *The Moral Sense* (Oxford: Clarendon Press, 1930), p. 77.

64. Hutcheson, *Inquiry*, III, 8; in Selby-Bigge, I, 110–11.

65. Ibid., VII; in Selby-Bigge, I, 153–54.

66. Hutcheson, *Essay on the Nature and Conduct of the Passions*, 1; in Selby-Bigge, I, 393–94.

67. An excellent analysis of the *System of Moral Philosophy* is provided in Bonar, *The Moral Sense*, pp. 95–99.

68. Hutcheson, *System*, I, 6; in Selby-Bigge, I, 420; cf. Bonar, p. 98.

69. Balguy, *Foundation of Moral Goodness*, art. 21; in Selby-Bigge, II, 195.

70. Ibid., II, art. 4; in Selby-Bigge, II, 188.

71. Cf. Henry Sidgwick, *History of Ethics*, pp. 218–22.

72. For the general philosophical position of Abraham Tucker, see Copleston, *History of Philosophy*, 5, I, 205.

Chapter IX

Rationalistic Ethics on the Continent

1. See Hans Thieme, *Das Naturrecht und die Europäische Privatrechtsgeschichte* (Basel: Helbing, 1954).

2. See, for instance, *An Encyclopedia of Religion*, ed. Vergilius Ferm (New York: Philosophical Library, 1945), p. 316.

3. In a Letter to Benjamin Maurer (Epistola 154), Grotius formally commends Thomas' treatment of lex and jus.

4. Grotius, *De jure belli et pacis*, Proleg., 11.

5. For these writers, see the summary in F. Suárez, *De Legibus*, II, 6, 2.

6. Grotius, *The Rights of War and Peace*, I, 1, 10; trans, in B. Rand, *Classical Moralists*, pp. 208–09.

7. Leibniz, *Epistolae ad Diversos*, Leipzig, 1734–42, Vol. IV, n. 22.

8. Pufendorf, *Spicilegium Controversiarum, printed in Jus Naturae et Gentium* (Frankfurt, 1744), p. 174.

9. *Jus Naturae*, introd., p. 102.

10. Ibid., I, 2, 9–10.

11. Ibid., II, 3, 15.

12. See Sidgwick's severe comment on Pufendorf's lack of clarity on the golden rule, *History of Ethics*, p. 167; see also p. 270.

13. For an extended analysis, see Collins, *The Lure of Wisdom*, pp. 63–108.

14. Descartes, *Principles of Philosophy*, Preface; trans. J Veitch (New York: Dutton, 1924), p. 153.

15. Descartes, *Discourse on Method*, in Veitch, p. 23.

10. Descartes, *Passions de l'âme*, I, 27; in Charles Adam et Paul Tannery, eds., *Descartes's Oeuvres*, XI, 349.

17. Ibid., I, 45; XI, 363.

18. Ibid., II, 144; XI, 436–37.

19. Descartes, Lettre 397; 4 août, 1645; in *Adam et Tannery*, IV, 263–68.

20. Lettre 403, 15 septembre, 1645; *Adam et Tannery*, IV, 290–96.

21. See Leibniz, *Monadology*, ed. R. Latta (London: Oxford University Press, 1925), p. 330, for an English version of the Geulincx text.

22. Geulincx, *Annotata ad Ethicam*, in Opera (The Hague: Nijhoff, 1891–93), III, 168.

23. Geulincx, *Disputationes Ethicae*, id., III, 275.

24. Cf. Eugène Terraillon, *La morale de Geulincx dans ses rapports avec la philosophie de Descartes* (Paris: Alcan, 1912), pp. 173–74.

25. See F. Ueberweg et al., *Die Philosophie der Neuzeit*, p. 247.

26. Spinoza, *Short Treatise*, I, 1, 9; see the text in H. Wolfson, *The Philosophy of Spinoza* (Cambridge: Harvard University Press, 1934), I, 71.

27. *Short Treatise*, II, 22, and App. 2; trans. in J. Wild, *Spinoza Selections* (New York: Scribner's, 1930), pp.

84–93.

28. Spinoza, *Ethics*, Pt. I, def. 3, and propositions 1–10.

29. *Ethics*, Pt. II, prop. 48.

30. Ibid., prop. 11.

31. *Political Treatise*, 2, 8; trans, in *Chief Works*, by R. H. M. Elwes (London: Bell, 1883), I, 295.

32. Spinoza, Letter to H. Oldenburg, XXXII, 20 November 1665.

33. See Wolfson, op. cit., II, 131–63, for a study of these three sorts of knowledge.

34. *Ethics*, Pt. III, def. 3.

35. Ibid., props. 6–11.

36. *Ethics*, Pt. IV, preface; text cited from a modified trans, in Jones, *Approaches to Ethics*, p. 203.

37. *Ethics*, Pt. V, props. 2–4.

38. Ibid., props. 14–16.

39. Ibid., prop. 25.

40. Spinoza, *Theological-Political Treatise*, p. 14; trans. Elwes, I, 182–87.

41. Ibid., I, pp. 207–08, 246–47; cf. Crocker, *Nature and Culture*, pp. 195–96.

42. *Theological-Political Treatise*, pp. 18–19.

43. It is so classified in Rogers, *Short History of Ethics*, pp. 143–46.

44. These works are conveniently excerpted in the *Philosophical Papers and Letters*, ed. L. E. Loemker (Chicago: University of Chicago Press, 1956).

45. This general theory is well outlined in N. Rescher, *The Philosophy of Leibniz* (New York: Prentice-Hall, 1967).

46. Leibniz, *Codex Juris Gentium*, praefatio, in Loemker,

II, 690.

47. Loemker, II, 693.

48. Ibid., II, 698.

49. Ibid., II, 699–700.

50. Ibid., II, 912–13.

51. Ibid., II, 915–16.

52. Leibniz, *New Essays concerning Human Understanding*, trans. A. G. Langley (La Salle, Ill.: Open Court, 1916), II, 28, 5.

53. Rescher, op. cit., pp. 137–39, attributes this "legalism" to the influence of mathematics and of Catholic theology on Leibniz.

54. See Loemker, II, 917.

55. Ibid., II, 926–27.

56. Leibniz, *Philosophical Works*, trans. G. M. Duncan (New Haven: Yale University Press, 1890), pp. 231–32.

57. Leibniz, *Principles of Nature and of Grace*, 18; in Duncan, p. 217.

58. Leibniz, *Monadology*, nn. 85–86.

59. Wolff, *Preliminary Discourse on Philosophy in General*, trans. R. J. Blackwell (New York: Library of Liberal Arts, 1963), gives a good sampling of these terms.

60. Wolff, *Philosophia Practica*, I, 117.

61. Ibid., I, 120.

62. Montesquieu, *Spirit of the Laws*, I, 1; trans. Thomas Nugent, reprinted in L. M. Marsak, *French Philosophers from Descartes to Sartre* (New York: Meridian, 1961), pp. 133–34.

63. Rousseau, *Discourse on the Arts and Sciences*, in *The Social Contract, and Other Works*, trans. G. D. H. Cole (New York: Dutton, 1926), p. 140.

64. Rousseau, *Contrat social*, in *Oeuvres*, ed. M. Raymond (Paris: La Pléiade, 1959), IV, 206.

65. See especially *Social Contract*, IV, 1, and the companion *Discourse on Political Economy*.

66. Cf. Bourke, *Will in Western Thought*, pp. 154–58.

67. Gerdil, *Principes métaphysiques de la morale chrétienne*, III, 2–7; in Opere (Rome: Poggioli, 1806–21), II, 48–70.

68. See Kant, *Lectures on Ethics*, trans. L. Infield (New York: Harper, 1963).

69. Kant, *Critique of Practical Reason*, trans. Beck (1949), p. 151.

70. Kant, *Natural Theology and Morals*, trans. Beck (1949), pp. 278–79.

71. See P. A. Schilpp, *Kant's Pre-Critical Ethics* (Evanston, Ill.: Northwestern University Press, 1938), on these early works.

72. These are in *Opus Postumum*, ed. Erich Adickes (Berlin: Reuter u. Reichard, 1920).

73. T. M. Greene, ed., *Kant Selections* (New York: Scribner's, 1929), pp. 371–74, gives some passages translated from Adickes' edition.

74. On the relation between the *Critique of Pure Reason* and Kant's ethics, see Graham Bird, *Kant's Theory of Knowledge* (New York: Humanities Press, 1962), especially pp. 189–204.

75. See this section of Bk. II, sect. 2, in Greene, pp. 195–97, 219–33.

76. Kant, *Critique of Pure Reason*, trans. N. Kemp Smith (London: Macmillan, 1933), A840–B868.

77. See *Critique of Practical Reason and Other Writings*, trans. L. W. Beck (Chicago: University of Chicago

Press, 1949), pp. 53–64.

78. Ibid., p. 72.

79. Ibid., pp. 73–87.

80. For the important distinction between Wille and Willkür in Kant, see L. W. Beck, *Commentary on Kant's Critique of Practical Reason* (Chicago: University of Chicago Press, 1964), p. 91.

81. Beck, *Critique of Practical Reason and Other Writings*, p. 97.

82. Ibid., pp. 107–15.

83. *Critique of Practical Reason*, I, 1, 7; trans. Beck (New York: Liberal Arts Press, 1956), p. 30.

84. Ibid., II, 2, 3; Beck (1956), pp. 124–39.

85. Ibid., I, 1, 3; Beck (1956), p. 89.

86. See Maimon, "Ueber die ersten Gründe des Naturrechts," in *Fichte-Niethammers Philosophisches Journal*, I (1795), 142.

87. Cf. David Baumgardt, "The Ethics of Salomon Maimon," *Journal of the History of Ideas*, I (1963), 199–210.

Bibliography

Note

THE LAST FULL-SCALE history of ethics in English is almost one hundred years old. Henry Sidgwick's *Outlines of the History of Ethics* was written before 1886. In the sixth edition (1931), Alban G. Widgery added a chapter on ethics in the first quarter of the twentieth century. Despite its obvious lacunae, Sidgwick's work has remained a standard source of information in this field. It is very weak on the ethics of the Middle Ages and on non-British modern and contemporary ethics. Of course, a great deal has happened in twentieth-century ethics since the last revision of Sidgwick. The *Short History of Ethics* written by R. A. P. Rogers in 1911 is briefer and less informative than Sidgwick. After most of the research and writing on the present book was completed, Alasdair MacIntyre's A *Short History of Ethics* (1966) was published. He has chosen to concentrate on the ethical views of about thirty main thinkers, from the Sophists to Sartre, and to ignore lesser figures in the field. My effort has been to treat a much larger number of ethicians.

Of histories of ethics in other languages, Ottmar Dittrich's four-volume *Geschichte der Ethik* (1923–1932) is the most complete work. However, it includes a great deal of material that is not central to ethics, and it does not cover recent ethics, of course. The most helpful French history of the subject is found in René Le Senne's *Traité de morale générale* (1942), but it is not (and was not intended to be) a complete history of ethics. Excellent surveys of the history of ethical thinking are now available for most of the distinct periods of philosophy. The only era that is not well covered by such special studies is the medieval; we are just beginning to learn the history of medieval philosophy. Alois Dempf's work *Die Ethik des Mittelalters* (1927) is extremely brief and its coverage is inadequate. There is much more information on the ethics of the Middle Ages in a general work such as F. C. Copleston's *History of Philosophy*. Most general histories of philosophy, however, give little space to ethical theory.

The bibliographical lists offered herein are more complete than in most other histories. Data on origi-

nal writings in ethics, chief translations and collections
of texts, plus the most helpful secondary studies make
up the bibliographies appended to each chapter. In the
case of Greek, Arabic, and Russian works, the original titles and terms have been transliterated or given in
translation. The difficulties of printing in non-Roman
alphabets probably outweigh the value of having these
data in the original. It is hoped that the information
included on the literature of ethics will help to make
up for the brevity and defects of the doctrinal expositions in this history.

General Works

Brinton, Crane. *A History of Western Morals.* New York:
Harcourt, Brace, 1959.

Brunschivicq, Léon. *Le progrès de la conscience dans la
philosophie occidentale.* 2 vols. Paris: Alcan, 1927.

Copleston, F. C. *A History of Philosophy.* 8 vols. Westminster, Md.: Newman Press, 1946–66; reprinted
New York: Doubleday Image Books, 1962–65.

Dittrich, Ottmar. *Geschichte der Ethik.* 4 Bde. Leipzig:
Meiner, 1923–32.

Ferm, Vergilius (ed.). *Encyclopedia of Morals.* New York:
Philosophical Library, 1956.

Hastings, James (ed.). *Encyclopaedia of Religion and Ethics.* 12 vols. Edinburgh: Clark, 1908–21. 7 vols. New
York: Scribner's, 1924–27.

Hobhouse, L. T. *Morals in Evolution. A Study in Comparative Ethics.* London: Chapman & Hall, 1906; New York: Macmillan, 1951.

Janet, Paul. *Histoire de la philosophie morale et politique dans l'antiquité et les temps modernes.* 2 vols. Paris: Delagrave, 1852.

Jodl, Friedrich. *Geschichte der Ethik als philosophischer Wissenschaft.* 2 Bde. Stuttgart: Cotta, 1906, 1912.

Kropotkin, P. A. *Ethics, Origin and Development.* Trans. L. S. Friedland and J. R. Piroshnikoff. New York: Dial Press, 1924; reprinted 1947.

Lecky, W. E. H. *History of European Morals from Augustus to Charlemagne.* 2 vols. New York: Appleton, 1869; reprinted in 1 vol., New York: Braziller, 1955.

Leclercq, Jacques. *Les grandes lignes de la philosophie morale.* Louvain-Paris: Vrin, 1946; 2me éd., 1964.

Le Senne, René. *Traité de morale générale,* Paris: Presses Universitaires, 1942.

MacIntyre, Alasdair. *A Short History of Ethics.* New York: Macmillan, 1966.

Maritain, Jacques. *Moral Philosophy.* Trans. Marshall Suther *et al.* New York: Scribner's, 1964.

Martineau, James. *Types of Ethical Theory.* 2 vols. Oxford: Clarendon, 1866; New York: Macmillan, 1886.

Meyer, Hans. *Abendländische Weltanschauung.* 5 Bde. Paderborn: Schöningh, 1949–53.

Rogers, R. A. P. *A Short History of Ethics, Greek and Modern.* London: Macmillan, 1911; reprinted 1964.

Schweitzer, Albert. *Civilization and Ethics.* New York: Macmillan, 1923.

Sidgwick, Henry. *Outlines of the History of Ethics.* London: Macmillan, 1886; revised ed. of 1931, reprinted Boston: Beacon, 1964.

Wentscher, M. *Geschichte der Ethik.* Berlin: De Gruyter, 1931.

Werkmeister, W. H. *Theories of Ethics.* Lincoln, Neb.: Johnsen, 1961.

Westermarck, E. A. *The Origin and Development of Moral Ideas.* London: Macmillan, 1926.

Chapter I

Adkins, A. W. H. *Merit and Responsibility (Homer to Aristotle).* Oxford: Clarendon Press, 1960.

Aristophanes. *The Clouds,* ed. Cyril Bailey. London: Oxford University Press, 1921.

Boas, George. *Rationalism in Greek Philosophy.* Baltimore: Johns Hopkins Press, 1961.

Chroust, A. H. *Socrates, Man and Myth: The Two Socratic Apologies.* Notre Dame, Ind.: University of Notre Dame Press, 1958.

Dawson, M. M. *The Ethics of Socrates.* New York: Putnam, 1924.

Dickinson, G. L. *The Greek View of Life.* Garden City, N.Y.: Doubleday, Doran, 1925.

Diels, H., and Kranz, W. *Die Fragmente der Vorsokratiker.* Aufl. 8. Berlin: Weidmann, 1956.

Diogenes Laërtius. *Lives and Opinions of Eminent Philosophers.* Trans. R. D. Hicks. Cambridge: Harvard University Press, 1925, 1950.

Dittrich, Ottmar. *Geschichte der Ethik*. Bde. 1: *Vom Altertum bis zum Hellenismus*. Leipzig: Meiner, 1923.

Doherty, Kevin. "God and the Good in Plato," *New Scholasticism*, XXX (1956), 441–60.

Dudley, D. R. A *History of Cynicism, from Diogenes to the Sixth Century*. London: Methuen, 1937.

Ferguson, John. *Moral Values in the Ancient World*. London: Methuen, 1958; New York: Barnes & Noble, 1959.

Freeman, Kathleen. *Ancilla to the Pre-Socratic Philosophers*. Oxford: Blackwell; Cambridge: Harvard University Press, 1948.

Gould, John. *The Development of Plato's Ethics*. New York: Cambridge University Press, 1955.

Hackforth, R. *Plato's Examination of Pleasure (Philebus)*. New York: Liberal Arts Press, 1957.

Helsel, P. R. "Early Greek Moralists," in *History of Philosophical Systems,* ed. V. Ferm. New York: Philosophical Library, 1950, pp. 82–92.

Jaeger, Werner. *Paideia. The Ideals of Greek Culture*. 3 vols. Trans. G. Highet. New York: Oxford University Press, 1939–45.

Kirk, G. S., and Raven, J. E. *The Presocratic Philosophers*. New York: Cambridge University Press, 1960.

Lachièze-Rey, P. *Les Idées morales, sociales et politiques de Platon*. Paris: Vrin, 1951.

Lodge, R. C. *Plato's Theory of Ethics*. London: Routledge, 1928, 1950.

Mazzantini, C. *Eraclito*. Torino: Vita e Pensiero, 1945.

Mondolfo, Rodolfo. *Moralisti Greci. La Coscienza morale da Omero a Epicuro.* Napoli: Ricciardi, 1960.

Nahm, Milton C. *Selections from Early Greek Philosophy.* New York: Appleton-Century-Crofts, 1947.

Nettleship, R. N. *Lectures on the Republic of Plato.* London: Macmillan, 1922; reprinted New York: St. Martins Press, 1962.

Oakeley, Hilda D. *Greek Ethical Thought from Homer to the Stoics.* London: Dent; New York: Dutton, 1925; Boston: Beacon Press, 1950.

Owens, Joseph. A *History of Ancient Western Philosophy.* New York: Appleton-Century-Crofts, 1960.

Pearson, Lionel. *Popular Ethics in Ancient Greece.* Stanford, Calif.: State University Press, 1962.

Plato. *Opera,* ed. John Burnet. Oxford: Clarendon Press, 1910.

———. *The Dialogues.* Trans. R. G. Bury *et al.* 12 vols. Cambridge: Harvard University Press, 1914–36.

———. *The Dialogues.* Trans. B. Jowett, 2 vols. London: Macmillan, 1892. Revised in 4 vols., by D. J. Allan and H. E. Dale. London: Macmillan, 1953.

———. *The Republic of Plato.* Trans, with notes by F. M. Cornford. Oxford: Clarendon Press, 1941.

Robin, Léon. *La morale antique.* Paris: Alcan, 1939.

Sauvage, Micheline. *Socrates and the Human Conscience.* New York: Harper Torchbooks, 1960.

Schwartz, Eduard. *Ethik der Griechen,* hrsg. Will Richter. Stuttgart: Koehler, 1951.

Shorey, Paul. "The Idea of Good in Plato"s *Republic."* *(Studies in Classical Philology,* Vol. I.) Chicago, 1895.

Snell, Bruno. *The Discovery of Mind. The Greek Origins of European Thought.* Cambridge: Harvard University Press, 1953; New York: Harper Torchbooks, 1964. (Chap. VIII: The Call to Virtue.)

Taylor, A. E. *Socrates.* New York: Nelson, 1939.

Tenkku, J. *The Evaluation of Pleasure in Plato's Ethics.* Helsinki: Societas Philosophica, 1956.

Untersteiner, M. *The Sophists.* Trans. K. Freeman. New York: Philosophical Library, 1953.

Versenyi, Lazlo. *Socratic Humanism.* New Haven: Yale University Press, 1963.

Vlastos, Gregory. "Ethics and Physics in Democritus," *Philosophical Review,* LIV (1945), 578–92; LV (1946), 53–64.

Wild, John. *Plato's Modern Enemies and the Theory of Natural Law.* Chicago: University of Chicago Press, 1953.

Xenophon. *Memorabilia Socratis dicta.* Trans. E. C. Marchant. Cambridge: Harvard University Press, 1938.

Zubiri, Xavier. "Socrates and Greek Wisdom," *The Thomist,* VII (1944), 40–45.

Chapter II

Alexander of Aphrodisias. *De fato imperatoris,* ed. Pierre Thillet. Paris: Presses Universitaires, 1963.

Ando, Takatura. *Aristotle's Theory of Practical Cognition.* The Hague: Nijhoff, 1965.

Aristotle. *Opera Omnia,* ed. I. Bekker. 4 vols. Berlin: Reimer, 1835–70.

———. *Works: The Oxford Translation,* ed. W. D. Ross and J. A. Smith. 12 vols. London: Oxford University Press, 1928–52.

———. *Ethica Nicomachea,* ed. I. Bywater. Oxford: Clarendon Press, 1890.

———. *Ethica Nicomachia,* ed. J. Burnet. London: Methuen, 1900. Trans, as *Nicomachean Ethics* by W. D. Ross (Vol. VIII of *Oxford Translation*). Also by J. A. K. Thomson. Baltimore: Penguin, 1955.

———. *Ethica Eudemía,* ed. F. Susemihl. Leipzig: Teubner, 1883. Trans, as *Eudemian Ethics* by J. Solomon (Vol. IX of *Oxford Translation*). Also by H. Rackham. Cambridge: Harvard University Press, 1952.

———. *Magna Moralia.* Greek text and trans., G. C. Armstrong. Cambridge: Harvard University Press, 1957.

Aubenque, Pierre. *La Prudence chez Aristote.* Paris: Presses Universitaires, 1963.

Commentaria Graeca in Aristotelem. 23 vols. Berlin: Reimer, 1891–1909. (The ethical commentaries are in Vols. XIX, XXII.)

During, I., and Owen, G. E. L. (eds.). *Aristotle and Plato.* Goteburg: Almqvist & Wiksell, 1960. (An important symposium.)

Galen. *On the Natural Faculties.* Ed. and trans., Arthur J. Brock. Cambridge: Harvard University Press, 1916.

Gauthier, R. A. *L'Ethique à Nicomaque.* Introduction, traduction et commentaire (avec J. Y. Jolif). 3 vols. Louvain-Paris: Nauwelaerts, 1958–59.

———. *La Morale d'Aristote*. Paris: Presses Universitaires, 1958.

Hamburger, M. *Morals and Law: the Growth of Aristotle's Legal Theory*. New Haven: Yale University Press, 1951.

Hatch, W. M. *The Moral Philosophy of Aristotle*. London: Murray, 1879.

Jaeger, Werner. "The Original Ethics," in *Aristotle: Fundamentals of the History of His Development*. Trans. Richard Robinson. Oxford: Clarendon Press, 1951; reprinted 1962.

Jaffa, H. V. *Thomism and Aristotelianism: a Study of the Commentary by Thomas Aquinas on the Nicomachean Ethics*. Chicago: University of Chicago Press, 1952.

Joachim, H. H. *Aristotle, the Nicomachean Ethics,* ed. D. A. Rees. Oxford: Clarendon Press, 1951; reprinted 1962.

Léonard, Jean. *Le Bonheur chez Aristote*. Bruxelles: Palais des Académies, 1948.

Luthardt, C. E. *Die Ethik des Aristoteles*. Leipzig: Meiner, 1876.

Mansion, Auguste. "Autour des Ethiques attribués à Aristote," *Revue Néoscolastique de Philosophie*, XXXIII (1931), 80–107, 216–36, 360–80.

Marshall, T. *Aristotle's Theory of Conduct*. London: Unwin, 1906.

May, W. E. "The Structure and Argument of the *Nicomachean Ethics," New Scholasticism*, XXXVI (1962), 1–28.

Monan, J. D. "Two Methodological Aspects of Moral Knowledge in the *Nicomachean Ethics*" in *Aristote et Problèmes de Méthode*. Louvain: Nauwelaerts, 1962.

Oates, W. J. *Aristotle and the Problem of Value.* Princeton, N.J.: Princeton University Press, 1963.

Prichard, H. A. "The Meaning of *agathon* in the Ethics of Aristotle," *Philosophy*, X, 37 (1935), 27–39.

Stewart, J. A. *Notes on the Nicomachean Ethics of Aristotle.* 2 vols. Oxford: Clarendon Press, 1892.

Theophrastus. *Characters.* Trans. J. M. Edmonds. Cambridge: Harvard University Press, 1929.

Vanier, Jean. *Le Bonheur principe et fin de la· morale aristotélicienne.* Paris: Desclée de Brouwer, 1965.

Veatch, H. B. *Rational Man; a Modern Interpretation of Aristotelian Ethics.* Bloomington: Indiana University Press, 1962.

Wittmann, Michael. *Die Ethik des Aristoteles.* Regensburg-München: Hueber, 1920.

Chapter III

Armstrong, A. H. (ed.). *The Cambridge History of Later Greek and Early Medieval Philosophy.* Cambridge: Heffer, 1966.

Arnim, J. von (ed.). *Stoicorum Veterum Fragmenta.* 3 vols. Leipzig: Teubner, 1914–21.

Arnold, E. V. *Roman Stoicism.* London: Cambridge University Press, 1911.

Arnou, René. *Le désir de Dieu dans la philosophic de Plotin.* Paris: Alcan, 1921.

Bevan, E. R. *Hellenistic Popular Philosophy*. London: Cambridge University Press, 1923.

Bonhoeffer, A. *Die Ethik der Stoiker Epiktet*. Stuttgart, 1894; reprinted Stuttgart: Fromman, 1965.

Bréhier, Emile. *The Hellenistic and Roman Age*. Trans. Wade Baskin. Chicago: University of Chicago Press, 1965.

Clark, Gordon H. *Selections from Hellenistic Philosophy*. New York: Appleton-Century-Crofts, 1940.

De Witt, Norman. *Epicurus and His Philosophy*. Minneapolis: University of Minnesota Press, 1954.

Dittrich, O. *Geschichte der Ethik*. Bde. 2 u. 3. Leipzig: Meiner, 1926.

Dodds, E. R. *The Greeks and the Irrational*. Berkeley: University of California Press, 1951.

Du Vair, Guillaume. *The Moral Philosophie of the Stoicks*, ed. R. Kirk. New Brunswick, N.J.: Rutgers University Press, 1951.

Edelstein, Ludwig. *The Meaning of Stoicism*. Cambridge: Heffer, 1966.

Fortin, E. L. *Christianisme et culture philosophique au cinquième siècle*. Paris: Etudes Augustiniennes, 1959.

Garofalo, Gaetano. *La morale della Grecia nell'età dell'ellenismo*. Roma: Ciranna, 1961.

Goodenough, E. R. *The Politics of Philo Judaeus*. New Haven: Yale University Press, 1938.

Hadas, Moses. *Essential Works of Stoicism*. New York: Bantam Books, 1961.

Katz, Joseph. *Plotinus' Search for the Good*. New York: Columbia University Press, 1950.

Kristeller, P. O. *Der Begriff der Seele in der Ethik des Plotin.* Heidelberg: Abhandlungen z. Philosophic, 1929.

Lewy, Hans. *Chaldean Oracles and Theurgy: Mysticism, Magic and Platonism in the Later Roman Empire.* Cairo: Institut Français d'Archéologie Orientale, 1956.

Lieshout, H. van. *La Théorie plotinienne de la vertu.* Paderborn: Schöningh, 1926.

Mancini, Guido. *L'Etica Stoica da Zenone a Crisippo.* Padova: Cedam, 1940.

Mead, G. R. S. *Thrice Greatest Hermes.* New York: Holt, 1906. Merlan, Philip. *From Platonism to Neoplatonism.* The Hague: Nijhoff, 1953.

More, Paul Elmer. *Hellenistic Philosophies.* Princeton, N.J.: Princeton University Press, 1923.

Oates, W. J. *The Stoic and Epicurean Philosophers: Epicurus, Epictetus, Lucretius, Marcus Aurelius.* New York: Random House, 1940.

Plotinus. *Opera,* ed. Paul Henry et H. R. Schwyzer. Paris: Desclée de Brouwer, 1951 (crit. ed. in course of publication).

———. *Ennéades.* 6 vols. Texte établit et traduit par Emile Bréhier. Paris: Les Belles Lettres, 1924–38.

———. *The Ethical Treatises.* Trans. Stephen MacKenna. London: Medici Society, 1926.

———. *The Essential Plotinus.* Trans. Elmer O'Brien. New York: Mentor, 1964.

Porphyry. *On Abstinence from Animal Food.* Trans. Thomas Taylor. Reprinted New York: Barnes & Noble, 1965.

Proclus. *Elements of Theology.* Revised text with trans, by E. R. Dodds. London: Oxford University Press, 1933.

Proosdij, B. A. van. *Seneca als Moralist.* 2 vols. Leiden: Brill, 1961.

Ritter, H., et Preller, L. *Historia Philosophiae Graecae.* Gotha: Perthes, 1913.

Rosan, L. J. *The Philosophy of Proclus: the Final Phase of Ancient Thought.* New York: Cosmas, 1949.

Shapiro, H., and Curley, E. M. *Hellenistic Philosophy: Selected Readings.* New York: Scribner's, 1965.

Tarn, W. W. *Hellenistic Civilization.* New York: Longmans, 1927.

Trouillard, Jean. *La purification Plotinienne.* Paris: Presses Universitaires, 1953.

Valente, Milton. *L'Ethique Stoicienne chez Cicéron.* Paris: Saint-Paul, 1956.

Wolfson, H. A. *Philo.* 2 vols. Cambridge: Harvard University Press, 1948.

Chapter IV

Alphandéry, P. *Les idées morales des hétérodoxes latins au debut du XIII' siècle.* Paris: Leroux, 1903.

Ambrose. *Some of the Principal Works.* Trans. H. de Romestin. Edinburgh: Clark, 1896.

Ancient Christian Writers, The Works of the Fathers in Translation, ed. J. Quasten and J. C. Plumpe. Westminster, Md.: Newman Press, 1946 ff.

Anselm. *Opera,* ed. F. S. Schmitt. 5 vols. Edinburgh: Nelson, 1938–51.

———. *Proslogium and Other Works.* Trans. S. N. Deane. Chicago: Open Court, 1903.

Augustine. *Opera Omnia,* in *Patrologia Latina,* Vols. 32–47. For more recent editions consult:

———. *Essential Augustine,* ed. V. J. Bourke. New York: Mentor, 1964, pp. 249–56.

———. *La Moral de San Agustin,* ed. G. Armas. Madrid: Difusora del Libro, 1954 (a complete selection of ethical texts in Latin).

———. *Basic Writings of St. Augustine,* 2 vols. ed. W. J. Oates. New York: Random House, 1948.

Bardy, Gustave. *The Christian Latin Literature of the First Six Centuries.* St. Louis: Herder, 1930.

———. *The Greek Literature of the Early Church.* St. Louis: Herder, 1929.

Bernard, St. *Select Treatises of St. Bernard.* Trans. W. W. Williams and B. R. V. Mills. Cambridge: Heffer, 1926.

———. *On the Love of God.* Trans. E. G. Gardner. London: Mowbray, 1915. Also in A. C. Pegis. *The Wisdom of Catholicism.* New York: Random House, 1949, pp. 230–68.

Bett, H. *Joachim of Flora.* London: Cambridge University Press, 1931.

———. *Johannes Scotus Erigena.* London: Cambridge University Press, 1925; reprinted, New York: Russell & Russell, 1964.

Bigg, Charles. *The Christian Platonists of Alexandria.* Oxford: Clarendon Press, 1886.

Boethius. *De consolatione philosophiae* and *Opuscula sacra,* ed. and trans. H. F. Stewart and E. K. Rand. Cambridge: Harvard University Press, 1918; reprinted 1946.

———. *Consolation of Philosophy.* Trans. J. J. Buchanan. New York: Ungar, 1957. Also trans. Richard Green. New York: Liberal Arts Press, 1964.

Bourke, V. J. *Will in Western Thought.* New York: Sheed & Ward, 1964.

Boyer, Charles. *Saint Augustin (Les Moralistes Chrétiens).* Paris: Gabalda, 1932.

Brandt, T. *Tertullians Ethik.* Gütersloh: Universitäts Dissertation, 1928.

Burch, G. B. *Early Medieval Philosophy.* New York: King's Crown Press, 1951.

Campbell, J. M. *The Greek Fathers.* New York: Longmans, Green, 1929.

Chadwick, Henry. *Early Christmn Thought and the Classical Tradition.* New York: Oxford University Press, 1966.

Clement of Alexandria. *Writings.* 2 vols. Trans. W. Wilson. Edinburgh: Clark, 1868–69. Cochrane, C. N. *Christianity and Classical Culture: A Study of Thought and Action from Augustus to Augustine.* London: Oxford University Press, 1944.

Corpus Christianorum. Series Graeca et Series Latina. The Hague: Nijhoff, 1953 ff.

Corpus Sciptorum Ecclesiasticorum Latinorum. Wien: Akademie der Wissenschaften, 1866 ff.

Delhaye, Philippe. "La place de l'éthique parmi les disciplines scientifiques au XIIme siècle," *Mélanges Arthur Janssen.* Louvain: Nauwelaerts, 1948, pp. 29–44.

―――. "L'Enseignement de la philosophic morale au XIIme siècle," *Mediaeval Studies,* XI (1949), 77–99.

―――. *Le problème de la conscience morale chez saint Bernard.* Namur: Editions Godenne, 1957.

Dempf, Alois. *Ethik des Mittelalters.* München-Berlin: Olden-bourg, 1927.

Dionysius, Pseudo-. *On the Divine Names, Mystical Theology.* Trans. C. E. Rolt. London: Society for the Promotion of Christian Knowledge, 1920.

―――. *The Celestial Hierarchy.* Trans, by the Shrine of Wisdom Society. London: Shrine of Wisdom Manual, 1935. Dittrich, O. *Geschichte der Ethik.* Bde. 2 u. 3. Leipzig: Meiner, 1926.

Dobler, E. *Nemesius von Emesa und die Psychologie des menschlichen Aktes.* Freiburg im Schweiz: Paulusdruckerei, 1950.

Enslin, M. S. *Ethics of Paul.* Nashville, Tenn.: Apex Books, 1963.

Fathers of the Church: a New Translation, ed. R. J. Deferrari. Washington, D.C.: Catholic University of America, 1947 ff.

Florilegium Morale Oxoniense, prima pars, ed. P. Delhaye. Lille: Giard, 1955. Secunda pars, ed. C. H. Talbot. *Id.,* 1956.

Forest, Aimé. *Le Mouvement doctrinal du IXe au XIVe siècle.* Paris: Bloud et Gay, 1951.

Gilson, Etienne. *History of Christian Philosophy in the Middle Ages.* New York: Random House, 1955.

Gregory, St. *Morals on the Book of Job.* 3 vols. Oxford, 1844–50.

Grou, S. J. *Morality Extracted from the Confessions.* Trans. P. Hudleston. London: Burns, Oates, 1934.

Harvey, J. F. *Moral Theology of the Confessions of St. Augustine.* Washington, D.C.: Catholic University Press, 1951.

Hausherr, I. *Philatie. De la tendresse pour soi à la charité selon saint Maxime le Confesseur.* Rome: Pontificium Institutum Orientalium Studiorum, 1952.

Heinig, H. *Die Ethik des Laktanz.* Leipzig, 1887.

Hunt, R. W. "English Learning in the Late Twelfth Century," *Transactions of the Royal Historical Society,* 4th series, XIX (1936), 19–41.

John Damascene. *De fide orthodoxa,* ed. E. M. Buytaert. St. Bonaventure, N.Y.: Franciscan Institute, 1955.

——— *Writings.* Trans. F. H. Chase, Jr. New York: Fathers of the Church, Inc. 1958.

Jolivet, Régis. *Le Problème du mal chez saint Augustin.* Paris: Beauchesne, 1936.

Koerner, Franz. *Vom Sein und Sollen des Menschen. Die existentialontologischen Grundlagen der Ethik in augustinischer Sicht.* Paris: Etudes Augustiniennes, 1963.

Labriolle, Pierre. *Histoire de la littérature latine chrétienne.* 2 vols. 3me éd. Paris: Les Belles Lettres, 1947.

Lactantius. *Works.* Trans. William Fletcher. Edinburgh: Clark, 1871.

———. *Institutes.* Trans. E. H. Blakeney. London: Society for the Promotion of Christian Knowledge, 1950.

Library of the Nicene and Post-Nicene Fathers, ed. P. Schaff *et al.* 34 vols. New York, 1886–87; reprinted, Grand Rapids, Mich.: Eerdmans, 1952–56.

Lottin, Odon. "Le Problème de la moralité intrinsèque, d'Abelard à saint Thomas d'Aquin," *Revue Thomiste,* XXXIX (1934), 477–515). Reprinted in *Psychologie et Morale.* Gembloux: Duculot, 1948. II, 421–465.

McKeon, R. P. *Selections from Medieval Philosophers.* 2 vols. New York: Scribner's, 1929.

Martini Episcopi Bracarensis. *Opera Omnia,* ed. C. W. Barlow. New Haven: Yale University Press, 1950.

Mausbach, Joseph. *Die Ethik des hl. Augustinus.* Freiburg im Breisgau: Herder, 1909; reprinted, 1929.

Nelson, N. E. *Cicero's De officiis in Christian Thought.* Ann Arbor: University of Michigan Press, 1933.

Nothdurft, K. D. *Studien zum Einfluss Senecas auf die Philosophie und Theologie des zwoelften Jahrhunderts.* Leiden: Brill, 1963.

Origen. *On First Principles.* Trans. G. W. Butterworth. London: Society for the Promotion of Christian Knowledge, 1936. Reprinted, New York: Harper Torchbooks, 1966.

———. *Contra Celsum.* Trans. H. Chadwick. London: Cambridge University Press, 1953.

Patch, H. R. *The Tradition of Boethius: A Study of His Importance in Medieval Culture.* New York: Oxford University Press, 1935.

Patrologia Latina. 221 vols. Paris: J. P. Migne éditeur, 1844–64. Series Graeca, 162 vols. Paris, 1857–66.

Peter Abelard. *Ethica,* ed. L. M. De Rijk. Assen: Van Gorcum, 1966.

———. *Abailard's Ethics.* Trans. J. R. McCallum. Oxford: Blackwell, 1935.

Pra, Mario dal. *Scoto Eriugena ed il neoplatonismo medievale.* Milano: Vita e Pensiero, 1941.

Puëch, Aimé. *Histoire de la littérature grecque chrétienne.* 3 vols. Paris: Les Belles Lettres, 1928–30.

Quasten, Johannes. *Patrology.* 4 vols. Westminster, Md.; Newman Press, 1950–66.

Rashdall, Hastings. *Conscience and Christ.* London: Duckworth, 1933·

Rohmer, Jean. *La finalité morale de saint Augustin à Duns Scot.* Paris: Vrin, 1939.

Rousselot, Pierre. *Pour l'histoire du problème de l'amour au moyen-âge.* (BGPM VI, 6.) Münster: Aschendorff, 1908.

Runciman, Steven. *The Medieval Manichee.* Cambridge, Eng.: University Press, 1947.

Schnackenburg, Rudolf. *The Moral Teaching of the New Testament.* New York: Herder & Herder, 1965.

Schiller, I. *Abelards Ethik im Vergleich zur Ethik seiner Zeit.* München: Universitäts Dissertation, 1906.

Schubert, Alois. *Augustins Lex-aeterna-Lehre.* Münster: Aschendorff, 1924.

Shapiro, Herman. *Medieval Philosophy.* New York: Random House, 1964.

Shortt, C. de L. *The Influence of Philosophy on the Mind of Tertullian*. London: Elliot Stock, 1933.

Siebert, Otto von. *Die Metaphysik und Ethik des Pseudo-Dionysius Areopagita*. Jena: Pohle, 1894.

Switalski, Bruno. *Neoplatonism and the Ethics of St. Augustine*. New York: Polish Institute of Arts and Sciences, 1946. Tertullian. *De anima,* ed. J. H. Waszink. Amsterdam: Swets, 1933.

———. *The Apology*. Trans. A. Souter. London: Cambridge University Press, 1917.

———. *Apologetical Works*. Trans. R. Arbesmann *et al.* New York: Fathers of the Church, Inc., 1950.

Thamin, R. *Saint Ambroise et la morale chrétienne au IVᵉ siècle*. Paris: Masson, 1895.

Thomas Aquinas. *In librum B. Dionysii de divinis nominibus Expositio*. Cura Fr. Ceslai Pera. Taurini: Marietti, 1950. Thouzellier, Christine (ed.). *Un traité cathare inédit du debut du XIIIᵉ siècle, d'après le 'Liber contra Manichaeos' de Durand de Huesca*. Louvain: Publications Universitaires, 1964. Ueberweg-Geyer. *Die patristische und scholastische Philosophie*. Aufl. 11. Berlin: Mittler, 1928.

Vacant, A., Mangenot, E., et Amann, E. (eds.). *Dictionnaire de Théologie Catholique*. Paris: Letouzey et Ané, 1903 ff. Vandenbroucke, F. *La morale monastique du XIᵉ au XVIᵉ siècle*. Louvain: Nauwelaerts, 1966.

Wulf, Maurice de. *History of Medieval Philosophy*. Vol. I. London: Longmans, 1935; reprinted, New York: Dover, 1952.

Chapter V

Afnan, S. M. *Avicenna: His Life and Works.* London: Allen and Unwin, 1958.

Al Ghazzali. *The Alchemy of Happiness.* Trans. C. Field, London: Wisdom of the East Series, 1910.

———. *The Inspired Treatise.* Trans. Margaret Smith. London: Journal Royal Asiatic Society, 1936.

———. *Deliverance from Error.* Trans. W. Montgomery Watt, in *The Faith and Practice of al-Ghazzali.* London: Allen and Unwin, 1953.

———. *O Disciple!* Trans. G. H. Scherer. Beirut: Catholic Press, 1951.

Arberry, A. J. *The Holy Koran, an Introduction with Selections.* London: Macmillan, 1953.

———. *The Koran Interpreted.* New York: Macmillan, 1964.

———. *The Romance of the Rubaiyat.* London: Macmillan, 1959.

Asin y Palacios, Miguel. *Algazel: Dogmatica, moral, ascetica.* Madrid-Saragossa, 1901.

Averroës (ibn Rushd). *On the Harmony of Religion and Philosophy.* Trans. G. F. Hourani. London: Luzac, 1961.

———. *Tahafut al-Tahafut: The Incoherence of the Incoherence.* Trans. Simon Van den Bergh. 2 vols. London: Oxford University Press, 1954.

———. *Commentary on Plato's Republic,* ed. and trans. E. I. J. Rosenthal. London: Cambridge University Press, 1956.

Bahya Ibn Pakuda. *Duties of the Heart.* Trans. Moses Hyamson. 5 vols. New York: Bloch, 1925–47.

Bar Hebraeus. *Book of the Dove,* with some chapters from his *Ethikon.* Trans. A. J. Wensinck. Leiden: De Goeje Fund, 1919.

Bauer, Hans. *Islamische Ethik.* Halle, 1916, 1917, 1922.

Beiträge zur Geschichte der Philosophie des Mittelalters, hrsg. von Clemens Baeumker *et al.* Münster: Aschendorff, 1891 ff. (About 40 vols. now published; abbreviated as BGPM.)

Boer, T. J. de. *History of Philosophy in Islam.* Trans. E. R. Jones. London: Luzac, 1903; reprinted, 1933.

Bokser, B. Z. *The Legacy of Maimonides.* New York: Philosophical Library, 1950.

Cohon, Samuel S. *Judaism: A Way of Life. Introduction to the Basic Ideas of Judaism.* New York: Schocken Books, 1958.

Corbin, Henry. *Avicenna and the Visionary Recital.* Trans. W. P. Trask. New York: Pantheon Books, 1960.

———. *Histoire de la philosophie islamique, I: Des origines jusqu'à la mort d'Averroës* (1198). Paris: Gallimard, 1964.

Dawani, Jalal. *Practical Philosophy of the Muhammadan People: Akhlaq-i Jalali.* Trans. W. F. Thompson. London: Oriental Translation Fund, 1839.

Donaldson, D. M. *Studies in Muslim Ethics.* London: Society for the Promotion of Christian Knowledge, 1953.

Duval, Rubens. *Anciennes littératures chrétiennes, II: La littérature syriaque.* 2me éd. Paris, 1900.

Efros, Israel I. *Ancient Jewish Philosophy: A Study in Metaphysics and Ethics.* Detroit: Wayne State University Press, 1964.

Gardet, Louis. *Mohammedanism.* Trans. William Burridge. New York: Hawthorn Books, 1961.

———. *Introduction à la· théologie musulmane,* avec G. Anawati. Paris: Vrin, 1948.

Goldman, Solomon. *The Ten Commandments.* Chicago: University of Chicago Press, 1962.

Guttmann, Julius. *Philosophies of Judaism.* Trans. D. W. Silverman. New York: Holt, Rinehart and Winston, 1964.

Hernandez, Cruz. *Historia· de la Filosofia Española: Filosofia Hispano-Musulmana.* 2 vols. Madrid: Difusora del Libro, 1957.

Hourani, G. F. "Averroes on Good and Evil," *Studia Islamica,* XVI (1962), 13–40.

Husik, Isaac. *A History of Medieval Jewish Philosophy.* Philadelphia: Jewish Publication Society, 1941.

Ibn Gabirol (Avicebron). *Fons Vitae,* ed. C. Baeumker. (BGPM I, 2–4.) Münster: Aschendorff, 1892–95.

———. *The Fountain of Life (Treatise Four).* Trans. H. E. Wedeck. New York: Philosophical Library, 1962.

Ibn Khaldun. *The Muqaddimah: An Introduction to History.* 3 vols. Trans. Franz Rosenthal. (Bollingen Series, 43.) New York: Pantheon Books, 1958.

Ibn Tufail. *Hayy the Son of Yaqzan.* Trans. G. N. Atiyeh. In Lerner and Mahdi (see below), pp. 134–62.

Joseph Albo. *Sefer ha-'ikkarim: Book of Principles,* ed. and trans. Isaac Husik. 5 vols. Philadelphia: Jewish Publication Society, 1946.

Kadushin, Max. *Worship and Ethics: A Study in Rabbinic Judaism.* Evanston, I11.: Northwestern University Press, 1964.

Lazarus, M. *The Ethics of Judaism.* 2 vols. Philadelphia: Jewish Publication Society, 1900.

Lerner, Ralph, and Mahdi, Muhsin (eds.). *Medieval Political Philosophy: A Sourcebook.* New York: Free Press, 1963.

Lewy, Hans, Altmann, A., and Heinemann, I. (eds.). *Three Jewish Philosophers.* Philadelphia: Jewish Publication Society, 1945; New York: Harper Torchbooks, 1965.

Maimonides, Moses. *The Guide of the Perplexed.* Trans. Shlomo Pines. Chicago: University of Chicago Press, 1963.

———. *The High Ways to Perfection.* Trans. S. Rosenblatt. New York: Columbia University Press, 1927.

———. *The Main Principles of the Creed and Ethics of the Jews.* Trans. H. H. Bernard. Cambridge, England, 1832.

———. *The Eight Chapters on Ethics,* ed. and trans. J. I. Gorfinkle. (Columbia University Oriental Studies, VII.) New York: Columbia University Press, 1912.

Minkin, J. S. *The World of Moses Maimonides, with Selections from His Writings.* New York: Yoseloff, 1957.

Munk, Salomon. *Mélanges de philosophie juive et arahe.* Paris: Franck, 1859.

Nasir ad-Din. *The Nasirean Ethics.* Trans. G. M. Wickens. London: Allen and Unwin, 1964.

O'Leary, De Lacy. *Arabic Thought and Its Place in History.* London: Routledge, 1957.

Patrick, Mary Mills. "The Ethics of the Koran," *Ethics,* XI (1901), 321–29.

Rescher, Nicholas. *Al-Farabi: An Annotated Bibliography.* Pittsburgh: University of Pittsburgh Press, 1962.

Roth, Leon. *The Guide for the Perplexed: Moses Maimonides.* London: Hutchinson's Library; New York: Longmans, 1950.

Saadia ben Josef. *The Book of Beliefs and Opinions.* Trans. S. Rosenblatt. New Haven: Yale University Press, 1948. Abbreviated version by A. Altmann, in *Three Jewish Philosophers,* pp. 9–191.

Sharif, M. M. (ed.). A *History of Muslim Philosophy.* 2 vols. Wiesbaden: Harrassowitz, 1963.

Snaith, N. H. *The Distinctive Ideas of the Old Testament.* New York: Schocken Books, 1944.

Tresmontant, Claude. *A Study of Hebrew Thought.* New York: Desclée, 1960.

Umaruddin, M. *The Ethical Philosophy of Al-Ghazzali.* Aligarh, India: Muslim University Press, 1962.

Ventura, M. *La philosophie de Saadia Gaon.* Paris: Vrin, 1934.

Weinburg, Julius. *A Short History of Medieval Philosophy.* Princeton, N.J.: Princeton University Press, 1964.

Wensinck, A. J. *The Muslim Creed.* London: Cambridge University Press, 1932.

Wickens, G. M. (ed.). *Avicenna: Scientist and Philosophers, a Millenary Symposium*. London: Luzac, 1952.

Wright, W. *A Short History of Syriac Literature*. London, 1894.

Chapter VI

Albert the Great. *Opera Omnia,* ed. A. Borgnet. 38 vols. Paris: Vivès, 1890–99.

———. *Summa de Bono,* ed. B. Geyer. Vol. XXVIII of the new critical ed. Köln-Münster: Albertus-Magnus Institut, 1951.

———. *Commentary in libros Ethicorum,* in *Opera Omnia,* ed. Borgnet, Vol. VII.

Alszeghy, Z. *Grundformen der Liebe. Die Theorie der Gottesliebe bei dem hl. Bonaventura.* Rome: Gregorianum, 1946.

Andreas Capellanus. *The Art of Courtly Love.* Trans. J. J. Parry. New York: Columbia University Press, 1941.

Bettoni, Efrem. *Duns Scotus: The Basic Principles of His Philosophy.* Trans. Bernardine Bonansea. Washington: Catholic University Press, 1961.

Binkowski, Johannes. *Die Wertlehre des Duns Scotus.* Berlin-Bonn: Dümmler, 1936.

Bizet, J. A. *Suso et le Minnesange, ou La Morale de l'amour courtoise.* Paris: Aubier, 1947.

Blakney, R. B. *Meister Eckhart: A Modern Translation.* New York: Harper, 1957.

Boethius of Dacia. *De summo bono sive de vita philosophi,* ed. by M. Grabmann. *In Mittelalterliches Geistesleben.* München: Hueber, 1936. Bde. 1, 200–4.

Bonaventure, Saint. *Opera Omnia,* ed. crit. 10 vols. Quaracchi: Collegio di San Bonaventura, 1882–1902.

———. *The Works of Bonaventure.* Trans. J. de Vinck. Paterson, N.J.: St. Anthony Guild Press, 1960 ff.

———. *Retracing the Arts to Theology.* Trans. Sister E. T. Healy. St. Bonaventure, N.Y.: Franciscan Institute, 1955.

Bonke, E. "Doctrina nominalistica de fundamento ordinis moralis apud G. de Ockham et Gabriel Biel," *Collectanea Franciscana,* CIV (1944), 57–83.

Bourke, V. J. *St. Thomas and the Greek Moralists.* Milwaukee: Marquette University Press, 1947.

———. *Pocket Aquinas.* New York: Washington Square Press, 1960.

———. *Ethics in Crisis.* Milwaukee. Bruce, 1966.

Brandl, L. *Die Sexualethik des hl. Albertus Magnus.* Regensburg: Pustet, 1955.

Davitt, Thomas. *The Nature of Law.* St. Louis: Herder, 1951.

Dittrich, O. *Geschichte der Ethik,* Bde. 3: *Mittelalter bis zur Kirchenreformation.* Leipzig: Meiner, 1926.

Emerson, E. H. "Reginald Pecock: Christian Rationalist," *Speculum,* XXI (1956), 235–42.

Etienne Tempier. "Condemnation of 219 Propositions." Trans. E. L. Fortin and P. D. O'Neill. In Lerner and Mahdi (see below), pp. 335–56.

Fairweather, E. R. *A Scholastic Miscellany: Anselm to Ockham.* (Library of Christian Classics, X.) Philadelphia: Westminster Press, 1956.

Feckes,K. *Die Rechtfertigungslehre des Gabriel Biel.* Münster: Aschendorff, 1925.

Feiler, W. *Die Moral des Albertus Magnus.* Leipzig: Universitäts Dissertation, 1891.

Francis of Assisi, Saint. *His Life and Writings.* Ed. by Leo Sherley-Price. Baltimore: Penguin, 1959.

Garvens, Anita. "Die Grundlagen der Ethik Wilhelms von Occam," *Franziskanische Studien,* XXI (1934), 243–73, 360–408.

Gauthier, R. A. "Trois commentaires 'averroistes' sur l'Ethíque à Nicomaque." *Archives d'histoire doctrinale et littéraire,* XVI (1947–48), 187–336.

Giles of Rome. *De differentia rhetoricae, ethicae et politicae,* ed. Gerardo Bruni, in *New Scholasticism,* VI (1932), 5–12.

———. *Errores Philosophorum,* ed. J. Koch, plus English trans. by J. O. Riedl. Milwaukee: Marquette University Press, 1944. Another version in Shapiro (see below), pp. 386–413.

Gilson, Etienne. *Dante the Philosopher.* Trans. David Moore. New York: Sheed & Ward, 1949.

———. *Saint Thomas d'Aquin (Les moralistes chrétiens).* Paris: Gabalda, 1931.

Henry of Ghent. *Summa Quaestionum ordinariorum.* 2 vols. Paris, 1520; reprinted St. Bonaventure, N.Y.: Franciscan Institute, 1953.

Hiller, Joseph A. *Albrecht von Eyb: Medieval Moralist.* Washington: Catholic University Press, 1939.

Hooker, Richard. *The Works,* ed. John Keble. 3 vols. Oxford: Clarendon, 1839; 6th ed., 1874.

———. *Of the Laws of Ecclesiastical Polity,* ed. Ernest Rhys. 2 vols. London: Dent, 1960; New York: Dutton, 1963.

Jarrett, Bede. *Saint Antonino and Medieval Economics.* St. Louis: Herder, 1914.

———. *Social Theories of the Middle Ages:* 1200–1500. London: Benn, 1926; reprinted, Westminster, Md.: Newman Press, 1942.

Johannes Eckhart, Meister. *Opera Latina.* Leipzig: Meiner, 1934 ff.

———. *Die deutschen und lateinischen Werke.* Stuttgart: Kohlhammer, 1936 ff.

John Duns Scotus. *Opera,* ed. Luke Wadding. 12 vols. Paris: Vivès, 1891–95.

———. *Opera Omnia.* Ed. crit., Carolo Balic. Vatican City: Commissio Scotistica, 1950 ff.

———. *Reason and Revelation, A Question from Duns Scotus.* Trans. N. Micklem. Edinburgh: Nelson, 1953.

———. *Philosophical Writings* (selections from the *Ordinatio*). Trans. Allan Wolter. Edinburgh: Nelson, 1962.

John Fortescue, Sir. *De laudibus legum Angliae,* ed. S. B. Chrimes. London: Cambridge University Press, 1942.

———. *The Works,* ed. Thomas Fortescue, Lord Clermont. London, 1869.

Klubertanz, G. P. *Habits and Virtues.* New York: Appleton Century-Crofts, 1965.

Kluxen, Wolfgang. *Philosophische Ethik bei Thomas von Aquin.* Mainz: Matthias-Grünewald, 1964.

Lacy, E. W. *Sir John Fortescue and the Law of Nature.* Urbana, Ill.: University of Illinois Dissertation, 1939.

Lagarde, Georges de. *La naissance de l'esprit läique au declin du moyen-âge.* 5 vols. Paris: Droz, 1942–63.

Lauer, A. *Die Moraltheologie Alberts des Grossen.* Freiburg im Breisgau: Herder, 1911.

Lehu, L. *La raison règle de la moralité d'après saint Thomas.* Paris: Gabalda, 1930.

Lerner, R., and Mahdi, M. *Medieval Political Philosophy.* New York: Free Press, 1963; see pp. 272–526.

L'Homme et son Destin, d'après les penseurs du moyen age. Louvain-Paris: Nauwelaerts, 1948.

Lottin, Odon. *Le droit naturel chez saint Thomas et ses prédécesseurs.* Bruges: Beyaert, 1931.

———. *Psychologie et Morale aux XIIe et XIIIe siècles.* 7 vols. Gembloux: Duculot, 1942–60.

———. *Etudes de morale.* Gembloux: Duculot, 1961.

McKeon, R. P. *Selections from Medieval Philosophers.* New York: Scribner's, 1929, Vol. II.

Maurer, A. A. *Medieval Philosophy.* New York: Random House, 1962.

Meinertz, Max, und Donders, Adolf. *Aus Ethik und Leben. Festschrift für Joseph Mausbach.* Münster: Aschendorff, 1931.

Miscellanea Moralia: In Honorem Eximii Domini Arthur Janssen. Louvain: Nauwelaerts, 1948.

Nardi, Bruno. *Sigieri di Brabante.* Roma: Edizioni Italiani, 1945. Noelkensmeyer, C. *Ethische Grundfragen bei Bonaventura.* Leipzig: Pustet, 1932.

Oakley, Francis. "Medieval Theories of Natural Law: William of Ockham and the Significance of the Voluntarist Tradition," *Natural Law Forum,* VI (1961), 65–83.

Oberman, H. A. *The Harvest of Medieval Theology: Gabriel Biel and Late Medieval Nominalism.* Cambridge: Harvard University Press, 1963.

Paré, G. *Le Roman de la Rose et la Scolastique Courtoise.* Paris: Vrin, 1941.

Pfister, A. *Die Wirtschaftsethik Antonins von Florenz.* Waldkirch: Universitäts Dissertation, 1949.

Pieper, Josef. *Die ontische Grundlage des Sittlichen nach Thomas von Aquin.* Münster: Aschendorff, 1929.

Powicke, F. M. *Robert Grosseteste and the Nicomachean Ethics.* London: Proceedings of the British Academy, 1930.

Prentice, Robert. *The Psychology of Love according to St. Bonaventure.* St. Bonaventure, N.Y.: Franciscan Institute, 1951.

Ramòn Lull. *Obres.* 17 vols. Palma de Mallorca, 1906–35.

———. Blanquerna. Trans. E. A. Peers. London: Jarrold, 1926.

Reade, W. H. V. *The Moral System of Dante's Inferno.* Oxford: Clarendon Press, 1909.

Reginald Pecock. *The Donet,* ed. E. V. Hitchcock. London: Oxford University Press, 1921.

———. *The Reule of Crysten Religioun,* ed. W. C. Greet. London: Oxford University Press, 1927.

Robert Grosseteste. *Summa in Ethica Nicomachea.* Lyons, 1542.

———. Die philosophischen Werke, ed. Ludwig Baur. (BGPM IX.) Münster: Aschendorff, 1912.

Roger Bacon. *Moralis Philosophiae,* ed. F. Delorme et E. Massa. Turino: In Aedibus Thesauri Mundi, 1953. Trans, as *Moral Philosophy* by R. P. McKeon, D. McCarthy, and E. L. Fortin, in Lerner and Mahdi (see above), pp. 355–90.

Rohmer, Jean. *La finalité morale chez les théologiens de saint Augustin à Duns Scot.* Paris: Vrin, 1939.

Sertillanges, A. D. *La philosophie morale de saint Thomas d'Aquin,* Paris: Aubier, 1946.

Siger de Brabant. *On the Necessity and Contingency of Causes.* Trans. J. P. Mullally. In Shapiro, *Medieval Philosophy,* pp. 415–38.

Stratenwerth, Günter. *Die Naturrechtslehre des J. D. Scotus.* Göttingen: Vandenhoeck und Ruprecht, 1951.

Suk, O. "The Connection of the Virtues according to Ockham," *Franciscan Studies,* X (1950), 9–32, 91–113.

Taylor, H. O. *Medieval Mind: A History of the Development of Thought and Emotion in the Middle Ages.* 5th ed. 2 vols. Cambridge: Harvard University Press, 1949.

Thomas Aquinas, Saint, *Opera Omnia.* 25 vols. Parma: Fiaccadori, 1852–73; editio Leonina, Rome: Commissio Leonina, 1882 ff. (17 vols. printed in 1966).

———. *Summa contra Gentiles.* Turin: Marietti, 1934. Trans, as *On the Truth of the Catholic Church,* by A. C. Pegis *et al.* New York: Doubleday, 1955–57.

———. *Commentary on the Nicomachean Ethics.* Trans. C. I. Litzinger. 2 vols. Chicago: Regnery, 1964.

———. *The Virtues.* Trans. J. P. Reid. Providence, R.I.: Providence College, 1951.

———. *Summa Theologiae.* 5 vols. Ottawa, Canada: Collège Dominicain, 1941–45. 60–volume Latin-English edition, ed. P. K. Meagher and Thomas Gilby. New York: McGraw-Hill, 1963 ff.

William Ockham. *Opera Plurima.* 4 vols. Lyons, 1494–96; reprinted, London, and Ridgewood, N.J.: Gregg Press, 1964.

———. *Opera Omnia.* Crit. ed., by E. M. Buytaert, E. A. Moody, *et al.* To be published from St. Bonaventure, N.Y.: Franciscan Institute.

———. *Philosophical Writings.* Trans. P. Boehner. Edinburgh: Nelson, 1957.

Wittmann, M. *Die Ethik des hl Thomas von Aquin.* München: Hueber, l933·

Chapter VII

Artz, F. B. *Renaissance Humanism, 1300–1500.* Kent, Ohio: Kent State University Press, 1966.

Baker, Herschel. *The Dignity of Man.* Cambridge: Harvard University Press, 1947. Reissued as *The Image of Man.* New York: Harper Torchbooks, 1961.

Baldwin, William. A *Treatise of Morall Philosophy.* London, 1597.

Bellarmine, Robert. *Opera Omnia.* 12 vols. Paris: Vivès, 1870–74.

———. *Ascent of the Mind to God.* Trans. J. Brodrick. London: Burns, Oates, 1928.

————. *De Laicis, or Treatise on Civil Government.* Trans. K. E. Murphy. New York: Fordham University Press, 1928.

Biéler, André. *L'Homme et la femme dans la morale calviniste,* Geneva: Editions Labor, 1963.

Boehme, Jakob. *Works,* ed. C. J. Barber. London: Watkins, 1909.

Boisset, Jean. *Sagesse et sainteté dans la pensée de Jean Calvin.* Paris: Ecole des Hautes Etudes, 1959.

Breen, Quirinus. *John Calvin: A Study in French Humanism.* Grand Rapids, Mich.: Zondervan, 1931.

Bruno, Giordano. *Dialoghi morali,* ed. G. Gentile. Bari: Laterza, 1908; Firenze: Sansoni, 1958.

————. *The Expulsion of the Triumphant Beast.* Trans. A. D. Imerti. New Brunswick, N.J.: Rutgers University Press, 1963.

————. *The Heroic Frenzies.* Trans. P. E. Memmo. Chapel Hill: University of North Carolina Press, 1963.

Bucer, Martin. *Opera Latina,* ed. F. Wendel. Paris: Presses Universitaires, 1954 ff.

————. *Deutsche Schriften,* ed. R. Stupperich. Gütersloh, 1960ff.

Calvin, John. *Institutes of the Christian Religion.* Trans. F. L. Battles. (Library of Christian Classics, 20–21.) Philadelphia: Westminster Press, 1960.

Campanella, Tommaso. *Civitas Solis.* Frankfurt, 1623. Trans, as *The City of the Sun* by T. W. Halliday, in Henry Morley, *Ideal Commonwealths.* London: Routledge, 1893.

Cassirer, Ernst. *The Individual and the Cosmos in Renaissance Philosophy.* Trans. Mario Domandi, New York: Harper, 1964. Cassirer, Ernst, Kristeller, Paul, and Randall, J. H. *The Renaissance Philosophy of Man.* Chicago: University of Chicago Press, 1948; reprinted 1955.

Charron, Pierre. *De la sagesse.* Paris, 1601. Trans, as *Of Wisdom* by Samson Lennard. London, 1670.

Collins, James. *The Lure of Wisdom.* Milwaukee: Marquette University Press, 1962.

Du Vair, Guillaume. *La philosophie morale des stoïques.* Paris: 1585. Englished as *The Moral Philosophy of the Stoicks* by Thomas James, ed. by Russell Kirk. New Brunswick, N.J.: Rutgers University Press, 1951.

Elyot, Thomas. *The Boke Named the Governour.* London, 1531; ed. F. Watson. New York: Dutton, 1907.

Farrell, Walter. *Natural Moral Law according to St. Thomas and Suarez.* Ditchling, Eng.: St. Dominic's Press, 1930.

Garin, Eugenio. *Italian Humanism, Philosophy and Civic Life in the Renaissance.* Trans. Peter Munz. New York: Harper & Row, 1966.

Gassendi, Pierre. *Opera Omnia.* 6 vols. Lyon, 1658.

Giacon, Carlo. *La seconda scolastica.* 3 vols. Milano: Fratelli Bocca, 1944–50.

Gragg, F. A. (ed.). *Latin Writings of the Italian Humanists.* New York: Scribner's, 1927.

Grimm, H. J. *The Reformation Era, 1500–1650,* rev. ed. New York: Macmillan, 1965.

Harkness, Georgia. *John Calvin: the Man and His Ethics.* New York: Holt, 1931.

Harrison, J. S. *Platonism in English Poetry of the Sixteenth and Seventeenth Centuries.* New York: Macmillan, 1903.

Herbert of Cherbury, Lord. *De veritate.* London, 1633. Trans, by M. H. Carré. Bristol: University of Bristol, 1937.

———. *De religione laici.* Trans. H. R. Hutcheson. New Haven: Yale University Press, 1944.

Kahler, Erich. *Man the Measure.* New York: Pantheon Books, 1943.

Keckermann, Bartholomaeus. *Systema ethicae.* Hanoviae, 1607. Koch, Karl. *Studium Pietatis: Martin Bucer als Ethiker.* Neukirchen: Neukirchener-Verlag, 1962.

Kristeller, Paul. *Renaissance Thought: the Classic, Scholastic and Humanist Strains.* New York: Harper & Row, 1961.

Lipse, Juste. *Tvvo Bookes of Constancie.* Trans. John Stradling, London, 1594. Ed. Russell Kirk. New Brunswick, N.J.: Rutgers University Press, 1939.

Litt, Theodore. *Ethik der Neuzeit.* München-Berlin: Oldenburg, 1926.

Luther, Martin. *Collected Works,* ed. Jaroslav Pelikan and H. T. Lehmann. St. Louis: Concordia, 1955 ff.

———. *Selections from His Writings,* ed. John Dillenberger. New York: Anchor Books, 1961.

Machiavelli, Niccolò. *The Prince and the Discourses.* Trans. L. Ricci and C. E. Detmold. New York: Random House, 1940.

MacIntyre, Alasdair. *Short History of Ethics.* New York: Macmillan, 1966. Chapter 10.

Mariana, Juan. *De rege et regis institutione.* Toledo, 1599. Trans. by G. A. Moore as *The King and the Education of the King.* Washington: Country Dollar Press, 1948.

Melanchthon, Philipp. *Scholia in Ethicam Aristotelis,* printed in *Aristotelis Opera.* 4 parts in 2 vols. Basel: J. Oporinus, 1542.

———. *Selected Writings.* Trans. C. L. Hill. Minneapolis: Augsburg, 1962.

Montaigne, Michel de. *Complete Works.* Trans. D. M. Frame. Palo Alto, Calif.: Stanford University Press, 1957.

More, Thomas. *Utopia.* Trans. Peter K. Marshall. New York: Washington Square Press, 1955.

Mullaney, T. V. *Suarez on Human Freedom.* Baltimore: Carroll Press, 1950.

Nardi, Bruno. *Studi sull'aristotelismo padovano dal secolo XIV al XVI.* Firenze: Sansoni, 1958.

Nicholas of Cusa, Cardinal. *Opera Omnia,* ed. E. Hoffmann and R. Klibansky. 5 vols. Leipzig: Meiner, 1932–41.

———. *Of Learned Ignorance.* Trans. Germain Heron. London: Routledge, 1954.

———. *The Vision of God.* Trans, by E. G. Salter. New York: Ungar, 1960.

———. *Unity and Reform. Selected Writings of Nicholas de Cusa,* ed. J. P. Dolan. Notre Dame, Ind.: Notre Dame University Press, 1962.

Pico della Mirandola, Giovanni. *Oration on the Dignity of Man.* Trans, by Robert Caponigri. Chicago: Regnery, 1956.

———. *The Rules of a Christian Lyfe.* Trans. Sir Thomas Elyot. London, 1534.

Pomponazzi, Pietro. *Libri Quinque De Fato, De Libero Arbitrio et De Praedestinatione,* ed. R. Lemay. Lucani: In Aedibus Thesauri Mundi, 1957.

———. *On the Immortality of the Soul.* Trans. W. Hay, in Cassirer *et al. The Renaissance Philosophy of Man,* pp. 280–381.

Popkin, R. H. *The History of Skepticism from Erasmus to Descartes.* Assen: Van Gorcum, 1960.

Rice, E. F. *The Renaissance Idea of Wisdom.* Cambridge: Harvard University Press, 1958.

Robinson, D. S. (ed.). *Anthology of Modern Philosophy.* New York: Crowell, 1931.

Ross, J. B., and McLaughlin, Mary M. (eds.)· *The Portable Renaissance Reader.* New York: Viking, 1953.

Santillana, Giorgio de (ed.). *The Age of Adventure. The Renaissance Philosophers.* New York: Mentor, 1956.

Saunders, J. L. *Justus Lipsius: The Philosophy of Renaissance Stoicism.* New York: Liberal Arts Press, 1955.

Smith, Gerard (ed.). *Jesuit Thinkers of the Renaissance.* Milwaukee: Marquette University Press, 1939.

Suárez, Francisco. *Opera Omnia,* ed. C. Berton. 28 vols. Paris: Vivès, 1856–78.

———. *Disputationes Metaphysicae* in *Opera Omnia,* Vols. XXV–XXVI. Reprinted, 2 vols. Hildesheim: Georg Olms, 1965.

———. *De Legibus* in *Opera Omnia,* Vol. V.

———. Selections from *On the Laws.* Trans, by G. L. Williams *et al.* In *The Classics of International Law,* ed. J. B. Scott. Oxford: Clarendon Press, 1944. Vol. II.

Trinkhaus, C. E. *Adversity's Noblemen: The Italian Humanists on Happiness.* New York: Columbia University Press, 1940.

Ueberweg, F., Frischeisen-Koehler, M., and Moog, Willy. *Die Philosophie der Neuzeit.* Berlin: Mittler, 1924.

Vanini, Lucilio. *Amphitheatrum aeternae providentiae.* Lugduni, 1615.

Vitoria, Francisco de. *On the Law of War.* Trans, by Ernest Nys. Washington: Carnegie Institution, 1917. Also in J. B. Scott, *The Spanish Origin of International Law,* Part I. Oxford: Clarendon Press, 1934.

———. *Commentarios a la Secunda Secundae de Santo Tomás,* ed. Beltran de Heredia. 2 vols. Salamanca: Biblioteca de teologos españoles, 1934.

Weigel, Erhard. *Analysis Aristotelica ex Euclide restituta.* Wittenberg, 1658.

Wilenius, Reijo. *The Social and Political Theory of Francis Suarez.* Helsinki: Philosophical Society of Finland, 1963.

Zanta, Léontine. *La Renaissance du stoicisme au XVIe siècle.* Paris: Champion, 1914.

Chapter VIII

Bacon, Francis. *Works,* ed. J. Spedding, R. L. Ellis, and D. Heath. 14 vols. London: Longmans, 1858–72.

———. *Advancement of Learning, and New Atlantis.* New York: Oxford University Press, 1938.

———. *Complete Essays,* ed. H. L. Finch. New York: Mentor, 1963.

———. *Selections,* ed. M. T. McClure. New York: Scribner's, 1928.

Balguy, John. *Foundation of Moral Goodness, Or an Inquiry into the Original of Our Ideas of Virtue, in Answer to Hutcheson's Inquiry.* London, 1728.

Bandini Luigi. *Shaftesbury, etica e religione, la· morale del sentimento.* Bari: Laterza, 1930.

Berkeley, Bishop George. *Works,* ed. A. A. Luce and T. E. Jessop. 9 vols. London: Nelson, 1948 ff.

———. A *Treatise concerning the Principles of Human Knowledge,* ed. A. C. Fraser. Oxford: Clarendon Press, 1901.

Blackstone, W. T. *Francis Hutcheson and Contemporary Ethical Theory.* Athens, Ga.: University of Georgia Press, 1965.

Bolingbroke, Henry St. John. *Philosophical Works.* 5 vols. London: Mallet, 1754.

Bonar, James. *The Moral Sense.* Oxford: Clarendon Press, 1930.

Bowie, John. *Hobbes and His Critics.* New York: Oxford University Press, 1952.

Broad, C. D. *Five Types of Ethical Theory.* New York: Harcourt, 1930.

Brogan, A. P. "John Locke and Utilitarianism," *Ethics,* LXIX (1959), 79–93.

Browne, Sir Thomas. *The Works,* ed. G. Keynes. 5 vols. London: Faber & Gwyer, 1928–31.

Butler, Joseph. *Works,* ed. S. Halifax. Oxford: Clarendon Press, 1874.

———. *Works,* ed. W. E. Gladstone. London: Oxford University Press, 1910.

———. *Fifteen Sermons,* ed. W. R. Matthews. London: Oxford University Press, 1949.

Campagnac, E. T. (ed.). *The Cambridge Platonists, Selections.* Oxford: Clarendon Press, 1901.

Carlsson, P. A. *Butler's Ethics.* The Hague: Mouton, 1964. Cassirer, Ernst. *The Platonic Renaissance in England.* Trans. J. P. Pettegrove. Austin, Tex.: University of Texas Press, 1953.

Clarke, John. *Examination of the Notion of Moral Good and Evil.* London, 1725.

———. *The Foundation of Morality in Theory and Practice.* York, 1730.

Clarke, Samuel. *Discourse concerning the Unchangeable Obligations of Natural Religion.* London, 1706.

Crowe, M. B. "Intellect and Will in John Locke's Conception of the Natural Law," *Atti del XII Congresso Internazionale di Filosofia,* XII (Firenze, 1960), 129–35.

Cudworth, Ralph. *The True Intellectual System of the Universe.* London, 1678.

———. *Treatise concerning Eternal and Immutable Morality.* London, 1731. Ed. J. Harrison. London, 1845.

Cumberland, Richard. *De legibus naturae disquisitio philosophica.* London: 1672. Trans. J. Maxwell, as *A*

Treatise of the Laws of Nature. London, 1727. Trans. J. Towers. Dublin, 1750.

De Pauley, W. C. *The Candle of the Lord: Studies in the Cambridge Platonists.* New York: Macmillan, 1937.

Duncan-Jones, A. *Butler's Moral Philosophy.* Baltimore: Penguin, 1952.

Garin, Eugenio. *L'Illuminismo inglese: I Moralisti.* Milano: Vallardi, 1941.

Gay, John. *Concerning the Fundamental Principle of Virtue or Morality,* dissertations prefixed to Edmund Law's translation of Archbishop King's *Essay on the Origin of Evil.* London, 1731.

Harris, W. G. *Teleology in the Philosophy of J. Butler and A. Tucker.* Philadelphia: University of Pennsylvania Press, 1942.

Hobbes, Thomas. *Opera Philosophica,* 5 vols. *English Works,* 11 vols. Ed. W. Molesworth. London: Bohn and Longmans, 1839–45.

———. *Leviathan,* ed. M. Oakeshott. Oxford: Blackwell, 1946.

Hutcheson, Francis. *Works.* 5 vols. Glasgow, 1772.

———. *Inquiry into the Original of Our Ideas of Beauty and Virtue.* London, 1725.

———. *Essay on the Nature and Conduct of the Passions* and *Illustrations upon the Moral Sense.* London, 1728.

———. A *System of Moral Philosophy,* ed. William Leechman. Glasgow, 1755.

Kames, Henry Home, Lord. *Essays on the Principles of Morality and Natural Religion.* London, 1751.

King, Archbishop William. *De origine mali.* Dublin, 1702–04.

King, Lord. *The Life of John Locke.* 2 vols. London, Colburn & Bentley, 1830. (Contains *inedita.)*

Lamprecht, S. P. *The Moral and Political Philosophy of John Locke.* New York: Columbia University Press, 1918. Reprinted, New York: Russell & Russell, 1964.

Leland, J. A *View of the Principal Deistical Writers.* 2 vols. London, 1837.

Le Rossignol, J. E. *The Ethical Philosophy of Samuel Clarke.* Leipzig, 1892.

Locke, John. *An Essay concerning Human Understanding,* ed. A. C. Fraser. 2 vols. Oxford: Clarendon Press, 1894.

———. *Essays on the Law of Nature (1660–1664),* ed. W. von Leyden. New York: Oxford University Press, 1954.

———. *Locke Selections,* ed. S. P. Lamprecht. New York: Scribner's, 1928.

Mackintosh, James. *On the Progress of Ethical Philosophy during the XVII and XVIII Centuries.* Edinburgh: Clarke, 1830; Philadelphia: Carey & Lea, 1832.

Macmillan, Michael. "Bacon's Moral Teaching," *Ethics,* XVII (1907), 55–70.

McPherson, T. "The Development of Bishop Butler's Ethics," *Philosophy,* XXIII (1948), 317–31.

Mandeville, Bernard de. *The Fable of the Bees, or Private Vices Publick Benefits.* 2 vols. London, 1714. Ed. F. B. Kaye. Oxford: Clarendon Press, 1924.

———. *An Enquiry into the Origin of Moral Virtue.* London, 1723.

Mintz, S. I. *The Hunting of Leviathan.* Cambridge, Eng.: University Press, 1962.

More, Henry. *Enchiridion Ethicum.* London, 1667; London: Facsimile Text Society, 1930.

———. *The Philosophical Writings of Henry More,* ed. Flora Mackinnon. New York: Oxford University Press, 1925.

Morgan, Thomas. *The Moral Philosopher.* London, 1738. Reprinted, Stuttgart, Fromman, 1965.

Moskowitz, H. *Die moralische Beurteilungsvermögen in der Ethik von Hobbes bis J. S. Mill.* Erlangen: Junge u. Sohn, 1906.

Norton, W. J. *Bishop Butler, Moralist and Divine.* New Brunswick, N.J.: Rutgers University Press, 1940.

Petzäll, A. *Ethics and Epistemology in John Locke's Essay concerning Human Understanding.* Göteborg: Wettergren & Kerber, 1937.

Polin, Raymond. *La Philosophie morale de John Locke.* Paris: Presses Universitaires, 1961.

Pope, Alexander. *The Poems of Alexander Pope,* ed. John Butt. New Haven: Yale University Press, 1966.

———. *An Essay on Man,* ed. Frank Brady. New York: Library of Liberal Arts, 1965.

Rand, Benjamin (ed.). *Classical Moralists.* Oxford: Clarendon Press, 1897.

Raphael, Daiches. "Bishop Butler's View of Conscience," *Philosophy,* XXIV (1949), 219–38.

Rogers, A. K. "The Ethics of Mandeville," *Ethics,* XXXVI (1926), 1–17.

Selby-Bigge, L. A. *British Moralists, Being Selections from Writers Principally of the Eighteenth Century.* Oxford: Clarendon Press, 1897. Reprinted, New York: Bobbs-Merrill, 1964.

Shaftesbury, Lord. *An Inquiry concerning Virtue.* London, 1699.

———. *The Moralists, or Philosophical Rhapsody.* London, 1709.

———. *Characteristics.* 3 vols. London, 1711. Ed. Stanley Grean. New York: Library of Liberal Arts, 1960.

Sidgwick, Henry. *The Methods of Ethics.* London: Macmillan, 1874; Chicago: University of Chicago Press, 1962.

Taylor, A. E. "The Ethical Doctrine of Hobbes," *Phüosophy,* XIII (1938), 406–24.

Tucker, Abraham. *The Light of Nature Pursued.* 3 vols. London, 1768. Ed. H. P. St. John Mildmay. 7 vols. London, 1805.

Tyrrell, Sir James. *A Brief Disquisition of the Law of Nature (with a Confutation of Hobbes).* London, 1692. 2nd ed., 1701.

Vigone, Lucia. *L'Etica del senso morale in Francis Hutcheson.* Milano: Marzorati, 1954.

Whewell, William. *Lectures on the History of Moral Philosophy in England.* London: Parker, 1852, 1868.

Willey, Basil. *The English Moralists.* New York: Norton, 1964.

Wollaston, William. *The Religion of Nature Delineated.* London, 1722.

Zani, L. *L'Etica di Lord Shaftesbury.* Milano: Marzorati, 1954.

Chapter IX

Attisani, A. *L'Utilitarismo di G. G. Rousseau.* Roma: Foro Italiano, 1930.

Battaglia, Felice. *Cristiano Thomasio, filosofo e giurista.* Roma: Foro Italiano, 1935.

Barckhausen, Henri. *Montesquieu, ses idées, son oeuvre.* Paris: Alcan, 1907.

Baumgardt, David. "The Ethics of Salomon Maimon," *Journal of the History of Ideas,* I (1963), 199–210.

Baumgarten, Alexander Gottlieb. *Initia philosophiae practicae primae.* Halle, 1760.

———. *Ethica philosophica.* Halle, 1740.

Bayet, Albert. *La Morale des Gaulois.* Paris: Alcan, 1930.

Beck, L. W. *A Commentary on Kant's Critique of Practical Reason.* Chicago: University of Chicago Press, 1960, 1964.

———. *Eighteenth-Century Philosophy.* New York: Free Press, 1966.

Becker, C. L. *The Heavenly City of the Eighteenth-Century Philosophers.* New Haven: Yale University Press, 1932.

Bidney, David. *The Psychology and Ethics of Spinoza.* New Haven: Yale University Press, 1940. 2nd ed., New York: Russell & Russell, 1962.

Cassirer, Emst. *The Philosophy of the Enlightenment.* Trans. F. Koelln and J. Pettegrove. Princeton, N.J.: Princeton University Press, 1951.

Chroust, A. H. "Hugo Grotius and the Scholastic Natural Law Tradition," *New Scholasticism,* XVII (1943), 101–33.

Cohen, Hermann. *Kants Begründung der Ethik.* Berlin: De Gruyter, 1910.

Delbos, Victor. *Le problème moral dans la philosophic de Spinoza.* Paris: Alcan, 1893.

———. *La philosophie pratique de Kant.* Paris: Alcan, 1905.

Descartes, René. *Oeuvres,* ed. Charles Adam et Paul Tannery. 11 vols. Paris: Cerf et Vrin, 1897–1909, 1913.

———. *Rules for the Direction of the Mind.* Trans. L. J. Lafleur. Indianapolis: Bobbs-Merrill, 1961.

———. *Discourse on Method.* Trans. Lafleur, *idem,* 1960.

———. *Principles of Philosophy.* Trans. J. Veitch, in *Descartes: Discourse on Method, etc.* New York: Dutton, 1924.

———. *Les passions de l'âme,* in *Oeuvres,* Vol. XI.

———. *Lettres sur la morale,* ed. J. Chevalier. Paris: Vrin, 1935, 1955.

———. *Philosophical Works.* Trans. E. S. Haldane and G. R. T. Ross. 2 vols. New York: Cambridge University Press, 1911. Duncan, A. R. C. *Practical Rule and Morality. A Study of Kant's Foundations for the Metaphysics of Ethics.* London-Edinburgh: Clarke, 1957.

Espinas, Alfred. *Descartes et la morale.* Paris: Bossard, 1925. *Ethica Cartesiana.* Halle, 1719.

Frankel, Charles. *The Faith of Reason: The Idea of Progress in the French Enlightenment.* New York: Columbia University Press, 1948.

Gerdil, Sigismond Cardinal. *Principes métaphysiques de la morale chrétienne,* printed in *Opere.* Rome: Poggioli, 1806–21, I, 1–119.

Geulincx, Arnold. *Opera Philosophica.* 3 vols. The Hague: Nijhoff, 1891–93. *Ethica,* in Vol. Ill of *Opera.*

Gregor, Mary J. *Laws of Freedom. A Study of Kant's Method of Applying the Categorical Imperative in the 'Metaphysik der Sitten.'* New York: Barnes & Noble; Oxford: Blackwell, 1963.

Grotius, Hugo. *De jure belli et pads.* Den Haag, 1625. Trans, by A. C. Campbell as *The Rights of War and Peace.* Pontefract, 1814. Also trans. F. W. Kelsey *et al.,* in *The Classics of International Law.* Oxford: Clarendon Press, 1925.

———. *Inleiding tot de Hollandsche Rechts-Geleerdheid.* S'Gravenhage, 1631. Trans, by R. W. Lee as *Introduction to Dutch Jurisprudence.* Oxford: Clarendon Press, 1926.

Hallett, H. F. *Benedict de Spinoza; the Elements of His Philosophy.* New York: Oxford University Press, 1957.

Hazard, Paul. *The European Mind: the Critical Years.* Trans. J. L. May. New Haven: Yale University Press, 1953.

Hendel, C. W. *Jean-Jacques Rousseau: Moraliste.* 2 vols. New York: Oxford University Press, 1934. Reprinted, New York: Liberal Arts Press, 1963.

Hodges, D. C. "Grotius on the Law of War," *The Modern Schoolman,* XXIV (1956), 36–44.

Joachim, H. H. *A Study of the Ethics of Spinoza.* Oxford: Clarendon Press, 1901.

Joesten, Clara. *Christian Wolffs Grundlegung der praktischen Philosophie.* Leipzig: Meiner, 1931.

Kant, Immanuel. *Gesammelte Schriften.* 23 vols. Berlin: Reimer u. De Gruyter, 1902–56.

———. *Philosophia practica universalis,* hrsg. Paul Menzer. Berlin, 1924. Trans, by Louis Infield as *Kant's Lectures on Ethics.* London: Methuen, 1931.

———. *Grundlegung zur Metaphysik der Sitten.* Riga, 1785. Trans. by L. W. Beck as *Foundations of the Metaphysic of Morals.* New York: Library of Liberal Arts, 1963.

———. *Kritik der praktischen Vernunft.* Riga, 1788. Trans, by L. W. Beck as *Critique of Practical Reason.* Chicago: University of Chicago Press, 1949.

———. *Metaphysik der Sitten.* 1797. Trans, by J. W. Semple as *The Metaphysics of Ethics.* Edinburgh, 1886. See also *The Metaphysical Principles of Virtue.* Trans. James Ellington. New York: Library of Liberal Arts, 1964. *Opus Postumum,* ed. Erich Adickes. Berlin: Reuter u. Reichard, 1920. *Kant Selections,* ed. T. M. Greene. New York: Scribner's, 1929.

Krieger, Leonard. *The Politics of Discretion. Pufendorf and the Acceptance of Natural Law.* Chicago: University of Chicago Press, 1965.

Kroner, Richard. *Kan"s Weltanschauung.* Chicago: University of Chicago Press, 1956.

Le Chevalier, L. *La morale de Leibniz.* Paris: Vrin, 1933.

Leibniz, Gottfried Wilhelm. *Sämtliche Schriften und Briefe.* Darmstadt: Reichl, 1926 ff.

———. *Leibniz: Textes inédits,* éd. par Gaston Grua. 2 vols. Paris: Presses Universitaires, 1948.

———. *Jurisprudence universelle,* éd. par G. Grua. Paris: Presses Universitaires, 1953.

———. *Philosophical Papers and Letters,* ed. L. E. Loemker. 2 vols. Chicago: University of Chicago Press, 1956.

McKeon, R. P. *The Philosophy of Spinoza.* New York: Longmans, 1928.

Maimon, Salomon. *Werke,* hrsg. Ernst Cassirer. 8 vols. Berlin: De Gruyter, 1936.

Marsak, L. M. (ed.). *French Philosophers from Descartes to Sartre.* New York: Meridian, 1961.

Mesnard, Pierre. *Essai sur la morale de Descartes.* Paris: Boivin, 1936.

Montesquieu, Charles Louis de Secondat. *Oeuvres complètes,* éd. par R. Caillois. 2 vols. Paris: La Pléiade, 1958.

———. *The Spirit of the Laws.* 2 vols. Trans. Thomas Nugent. New York: Hafner, 1949.

Paton, H. J. *The Categorical Imperative: A Study in Kant's Moral Philosophy.* Chicago: University of Chicago Press, 1948.

Popkin, R. H. (ed.). *Philosophy of the Sixteenth and Seventeenth Centuries.* New York: Free Press, 1965.

Pousa, Narciso. *Moral y Libertad en Descartes.* La Plata, Argentina: Instituto de Filosofía, 1960.

Pufendorf, Samuel. *Elementa Jurisprudence Universalis.* Leipzig, 1660. Trans, as *Elements of Universal Jurisprudence.* Oxford: Clarendon Press, 1931.

———. *De jure naturae et gentium.* 8 vols. Leipzig, 1672.

———. *Of the Law of Nature and of Nations.* Oxford, 1710. Also trans. C. H. and W. A. Oldfather. New York: Oxford University Press, 1934.

Reiche, Egon. *Rousseau und das Naturrecht.* Berlin: Junker, 1935.

Rodis-Lewis, G. *La morale de Descartes.* Paris: Presses Universitaires, 1957.

Ross, W. D. *Kant's Ethical Theory.* Oxford: Clarendon Press, 1954.

Rousseau, Jean Jacques. *Oeuvres complètes, éd.* par M. Raymond. 5 vols. Paris: La Pléiade, 1959.

———. *The Social Contract, etc.* Trans. G. D. H. Cole. New York: Dutton, 1926. Reprinted, New York: Hafner, 1947.

Schilpp, P. A. *Kant's Pre-Critical Ethics.* Evanston, Ill.: Northwestern University Press, 1938.

Spinoza, Baruch de. *Opera,* ed. J. van Vloten et J. P. N. Land. 4 vols. The Hague: Nijhofi, 1914.

———. *Short Treatise on God, Man and His Well-Being.* Trans. W. H. White. London: Black, 1910.

———. *Ethica ordine geometrico demonstrata.* Amsterdam, 1677. Trans, by W. H. White as *Ethics.* New York: Hafner, 1953.

———. *Chief Works.* Trans. R. H. M. Elwes. London: Bell, 1883.

Teale, A. E. *Kantian Ethics.* New York: Oxford University Press, 1951.

Terraillon, Eugène. *La morale de Geulincx dans ses rapports avec la philosophie de Descartes.* Paris: Alcan, 1912.

Thomasius, Christian. *Historia Juris Naturalis et Gentium.* Halle, 1719. Reprinted, Stuttgart: Frommann, 1965.

———. *Von der Kunst vernünfftig und Tugendhaft zu lieben: oder Einleitung zur Sittenlehre.* Halle, 1692. Reprinted, Hildesheim, Olms, 1965.

Welzel, Hans. *Die Naturrechtslehre Samuel Pufendorfs.* Berlin: De Gruyter, 1958.

Wolff, Christian L. B. *Vernünftige Gedanken von Gott, der Welt und der Seele.* Frankfurt-Leipzig, 1719. Excerpt from chap. 2 trans, as *Reasonable Thoughts on God, etc.,* in Beck, *Eighteenth-Century Philosophy,* pp. 215–22.

———. *Philosophia Practica Universalis.* 2 vols. Francofurti et Lipsiae, 1738–39.

———. *Philosophia Moralis, sive Ethica scientifica pertracta.* 5 vols. Magdeburg, 1750–53.

———. *A Preliminary Discourse on Philosophy in General.* Trans. R. J. Blackwell, New York: Library of Liberal Arts, 1963. Wolfson, H. E. *The Philosophy of Spinoza*. 2 vols. Cambridge: Harvard University Press, 1934; Cleveland: World, 1958.

Zac, Sylvain. *La morale de Spinoza*. Paris: Presses Universitaires, 1959.

An index covering both volumes of *History of Ethics* can be found at the end of Volume II.